Business and Macroeconomics

WITHDRAWN

Business and Macroeconomics is a concise introduction to macroeconomics, specifically designed to provide students (MBA and undergraduate business studies) and practitioners of business with an understanding of the workings of the national and international economic systems.

It examines key aspects of the economic environment which affect the business climate, such as inflation, business cycles, international trade and exchange rates, indicating how businesses both play a part in these processes and are affected by them. Thus, a main feature of the book is to show how an understanding of macroeconomics is relevant to modern decision-makers.

The approach adopted is 'hands-on', using a mixture of text examples and boxed illustrations, and topics are developed to highlight their relevance to firms. This new book is a companion volume to *Business and Microeconomics*, which focuses on the workings of the market system.

Christopher Pass is a Reader in Comparative Industrial Economics at the University of Bradford's Management Centre. **Bryan Lowes** is a Senior Lecturer in Managerial Economics and **Andrew Robinson** is a Lecturer in Financial Economics, also at Bradford.

D1401668

Ele**ts of Business Series**
S editor: David Weir
U ity *of Bradford Management Centre*

This important new series is designed to cover the core topics taught at MBA level with an approach suited to the modular teaching and shorter time frames that apply in the MBA sector. Based on current courses and teaching experience, these texts are tailor-made to the needs of today's MBA student.

Other titles in the series:

Business and Society
Edmund Marshall

Managing Accounting
Leslie Chadwick

Financial Accounting
Iain Ward-Campbell

Managing Human Resources
Christopher Molander and Jonathan Winterton

Business and Microeconomics
Christopher Pass and Bryan Lowes

Managerial Leadership
Peter Wright

Financial Management
Leslie Chadwick and Donald Kirby

Business and Macroeconomics

Christopher Pass, Bryan Lowes
and Andrew Robinson

London and New York

First published 1995
by Routledge
11 New Fetter Lane, London EC4P 4EE

Simultaneously published in the USA and Canada
by Routledge
29 West 35th Street, New York, NY 10001

Typeset in Garamond by Florencetype Ltd, Stoodleigh, Devon

Printed and bound in Great Britain by Biddles Ltd,
Guildford and King's Lynn

British Library Cataloguing in Publication Data
A catalogue record for this book is available from the
British Library

Library of Congress Cataloguing in Publication Data
A catalogue record for this book has been requested

ISBN 0-415-12399-2 (hbk)
ISBN 0-415-12400-X (pbk)

Contents

List of figures   viii
List of tables   xi
List of boxes   xiv
Preface   xvi

Acknowledgements   xvii

1 The macroeconomic environment of business: an overview   1

1.1   Why study macroeconomics?   1
1.2   The concepts of national income, gross national product
      (GNP) and gross domestic product (GDP)   4
1.3   The circular flow of national income model: an overview   6
1.4   The building blocks of national income analysis   9
1.5   The equilibrium level of national income   18
1.6   Short and medium-term fluctuations in national income:
      the business cycle   26
1.7   The role of money in the economy   28
1.8   Conclusion   34
      Questions   34

2 Macroeconomic objectives and the management of the economy   35

2.1   Macroeconomic objectives   36
2.2   Economic policy approaches   39
2.3   Constraints on macroeconomic policy   40
2.4   Demand management: an overview   42
2.5   Fiscal policy   47
2.6   Monetary policy   60
2.7   Supply-side policies   67
2.8   Conclusion   70
      Questions   70

3 Unemployment   71

   3.1   The labour force   72
   3.2   Trends in unemployment   77
   3.3   Causes of unemployment   81
   3.4   The labour market – a basic model   85
   3.5   Policies to remove unemployment   89
   3.6   Conclusion   90
   3.7   Implications for business   90
       Questions   92

4 Inflation   93

   4.1   Why governments seek to control inflation   93
   4.2   Trends in inflation   95
   4.3   Causes of inflation   96
   4.4   Inflation theory and policy   105
   4.5   Policies to control inflation   111
   4.6   Conclusion   114
   4.7   Implications for business   115
       Questions   117

5 Economic growth   118

   5.1   Measurement of economic growth   120
   5.2   Trends in economic growth   121
   5.3   Determinants of economic growth: an overview 124
   5.4   Demand and economic growth   135
   5.5   Policies to achieve higher economic growth 138
   5.6   Conclusion   141
   5.7   Implications for business   141
       Questions   142

6 Balance of payments   143

   6.1   The balance of payments   144
   6.2   Balance of payments adjustment: the current account 148
   6.3   External price adjustments   150
   6.4   Internal price and income adjustments   153
   6.5   Trade and foreign exchange restrictions   156
   6.6   Internal–external balance   158
   6.7   Conclusion   162
   6.8   Implications for business   162
       Questions   163

7 International trade: 1 Facts and theories   164

   7.1 Trends in international trade   165
   7.2 The nature and significance of comparative advantage   180
   7.3 Other explanations of trade flows   185
   7.4 Protectionism   189
   7.5 Conclusion   196
   7.6 Implications for business   196
        Questions   197

8 International trade: 2 Multilateral and regional trade policies 198

   8.1 Multilateral trade policy   199
   8.2 Regional trade integration   204
   8.3 Conclusion   219
   8.4 Implications for business   219
        Questions   220

9 International investment   221

   9.1 The growth of foreign direct investment   222
   9.2 FDI and multinational companies' global sourcing,
        production and marketing operations   227
   9.3 Macroeconomic effects of outward direct investment   232
   9.4 Macroeconomic effects of inward direct investment   234
   9.5 Conclusion   241
   9.6 Implications for business   241
        Questions   242

10 Exchange rates and international monetary relations   243

   10.1 Floating exchange rates   246
   10.2 Fixed exchange rate system   253
   10.3 International adjustment   258
   10.4 International money   262
   10.5 International indebtedness and financial aid   270
   10.6 Conclusion   276
   10.7 Implications for business   276
         Questions   279

   Bibliography   280
   Index   281

Figures

1.1	The business environment	2
1.2	Changes in GDP and return on capital in the UK	3
1.3	National income	5
1.4	Circular flow of national income model	8
1.5	Consumption schedule	11
1.6	Personal savings ratio	12
1.7	Investment schedule	15
1.8	Taxation schedule	16
1.9	Import schedule	17
1.10	Aggregate demand schedule	20
1.11	Aggregate supply schedule	20
1.12	Aggregate demand, aggregate supply and the equilibrium level of national income	21
1.13	Output (deflationary) and inflationary gaps	22
1.14	Change in the equilibrium level of national income due to a shift in the aggregate demand schedule	22
1.15	Multiplier effect of increased spending on national income	24
1.16	Multiplier	25
1.17	Business cycle	26
1.18	Money demand schedule	29
1.19	Money supply schedule	30
1.20	Equilibrium interest rate	32
1.21	Money supply and spending linkages	33
2.1	Phillips curve	37
2.2	Shifting the Phillips curve	39
2.3	Counter-cyclical demand management	44
2.4	Effect on companies of a government squeeze	46
2.5	Fiscal policy and aggregate demand	54
2.6	UK budget deficits and surpluses	56
2.7	Crowding out	59
2.8	Asset structure of a commercial bank	64

2.9	Interest rate	65
3.1	Employment flows	76
3.2	Demand-deficient unemployment	82
3.3	Labour market equilibrium with no market failure	85
3.4	Impact of market failure on the labour market	87
4.1	Causes of inflation	98
4.2	Demand-pull inflation	99
4.3	Cost-push inflation	103
4.4	Phillips curve	106
4.5	Unemployment and inflation trade-offs	106
4.6	Expectations-augmented Phillips curve	107
4.7	Monetarist analysis of unemployment and inflation	108
4.8	Removing demand-pull inflation	111
5.1	Causes of economic growth	125
5.2	Economic growth	127
6.1	Equilibrium rate of exchange between the pound sterling and the US dollar	150
6.2	Fall in US demand for UK goods	151
6.3	Devaluation	151
6.4	Deflation	156
6.5	Tariff	157
6.6	Exchange controls	158
6.7	Internal–external balance model	159
6.8	External balance	159
6.9	Internal balance	161
7.1	Production possibility frontiers	181
7.2	Production possibility frontiers and the gains from trade	184
7.3	Preference similarity	187
7.4	Effect of a tariff	192
7.5	Subsidy	194
8.1	Trade and the pro-welfare economic effects of the removal of a tariff	198
8.2	GATT rounds and the decline in industrial countries' tariffs	200
8.3	Trade creation	205
8.4	Trade creation and trade diversion	206
8.5	EU internal and external trade, 1958–91	217
10.1	International payments	247
10.2	The pound–dollar exchange rate	248
10.3	Floating exchange rates	249
10.4	Determinants of exchange rates	252

10.5   Support buying and selling   254
10.6   Devaluation and revaluation   255
10.7   Currency flows and reserve implications of a UK trade
       deficit with France   265

Tables

1.1   Components of gross domestic product, selected countries, 1990–2   10
1.2   UK national income, personal disposable income, consumption and saving, 1983-93   11
1.3   Multiplier process   23

2.1   Economic indicators, selected countries, 1976–93   43
2.2   UK government budget, 1992–3   51
2.3   Fiscal measures in Japan, 1992 and 1993   55
2.4   UK money supply definitions   62

3.1   Population and the labour force, selected industrial countries, 1992   72
3.2   Shares of main sectors in GDP and employment, 1975 and 1992   73
3.3   UK unemployment and vacancy rates, 1987–93   77
3.4   Labour market indicators, selected countries, 1989–93   78
3.5   Unemployment rates, industrial countries, 1976–93   79

4.1   Inflation rates, selected countries, 1976–93   96
4.2   Hourly earnings, productivity and unit labour costs in manufacturing, 1976–93   97

5.1   Real GDP, selected countries, 1976–93   122
5.2   Labour force, selected countries, 1977 and 1992   128
5.3   Labour productivity in manufacturing, 1967–93   128
5.4   Selected Ford plants in Europe, 1988   131
5.5   The skills gap: numbers qualifying in engineering and technology, 1985   132
5.6   Investment, saving and GDP growth rates, selected countries, 1985–93   133
5.7   Spending on research and development, selected countries, 1987–92   135

6.1   Balance of payments data, Japan, 1986–92   145
6.2   Components of balance of payments, selected countries,
       1992   147
6.3   UK merchandise trade, 1979–93   148
6.4   Trade dependence: selected countries, 1990–2   160

7.1   World merchandise trade and output, 1960–92   165
7.2   Shares in world trade, 1950–92   166
7.3   Leading exporters and importers in world merchandise
       trade, 1979 and 1992   168
7.4   Shares of intra- and inter-regional trade flows in each
       region's total exports, selected regions, 1992   170
7.5   Composition of world merchandise exports by product,
       1992   170
7.6   Main exports of selected developing countries, 1992   172
7.7   Changes in the product composition of exports and
       imports, selected countries, 1970 and 1990   174
7.8   Leading exporters and importers in world trade in
       commercial services, 1992   176
7.9   World trade in commercial services by main category, 1977
       and 1992   178
7.10   Physical output of wheat and bicycles from given
       factor inputs   181
7.11   Physical output of wheat and bicycles from given
       factor inputs, without specialisation   182
7.12   Physical output of wheat and bicycles from given
       factor inputs, with specialisation   182
7.13   Consumption of wheat and bicycles, after trade   183
7.14   Production and consumption possibilities with and
       without trade   184
7.15   Trade-weighted average tariff rates in developed economies,
       1992   193

8.1   Estimated average annual gains from the Uruguay round
       by the year 2002   202
8.2   EU and EFTA trade, 1993   215
8.3   Intra-union trade as a percentage of member states foreign
       trade, 1980, 1985 and 1993   216
8.4   Potential gains in economic welfare for the EU resulting
       from completion of the internal market   218

9.1   World outward and inward foreign direct investment flows:
       total and distribution, 1986–92   223
9.2   UK and Canadian stock of outward and inward direct
       investment by region, 1978 and 1992   225

9.3   Composition of stock of UK and Canadian outward and
       inward direct investment by industrial activity, 1992   227
9.4   Net FDI flows and current account position, selected
       countries, 1986–92   232
9.5   UK net earnings from foreign investment, 1987–93   233

10.1   Types of international monetary system   247
10.2   Effect of a depreciation on export and import prices   260
10.3   Components of international reserves and main
       individual country holders, 1992   264
10.4   Indicators of external debt for developing countries,
       1984-92   272
10.5   Net transfers, selected developing countries, 1980 and
       1991   273
10.6   Aggregate long-term net resource flows to developing
       countries, 1980, 1989, 1995   274
10.7   Tied aid, selected countries, 1991   276

Boxes

1.1   Gross national product: selected countries, total and per
      head   7
1.2   The marginal efficiency of capital/investment   14
1.3   Classical and Keynesian views of national income and
      output   19
1.4   The accelerator   26
1.5   Bank deposit or credit creation: the money multiplier   31

2.1   Economic trade-offs: inflation and unemployment   38
2.2   Macroeconomic forecasting   45
2.3   Money supply targeting in Germany   48
2.4   Recent developments in fiscal conditions in the UK, Japan
      and the USA   48
2.5   Types of tax   52
2.6   Banks' reserve-asset ratios   61
2.7   Interest rates   66
2.8   Recent monetary developments in the UK, Japan and the
      USA   68

3.1   Labour force data for Great Britain   74
3.2   Import penetration and unemployment   75
3.3   Unemployment in the UK, the USA and Japan   80
3.4   Wage rates, wage differentials and unemployment   83
3.5   Policies to deal with unemployment   91

4.1   Price indices and the measurement of inflation   94
4.2   National income and the price level   100
4.3   Non-inflationary wage increases   104
4.4   Inflation in the UK, Japan and the USA   112
4.5   Inflation, Brazilian style   116

5.1   Environmental issues   119
5.2   Real and money GNP   120
5.3   Distribution of income and wealth in the UK   123

5.4	Economic growth and productivity	129
5.5	Demand and output	136
6.1	Terms of trade	146
6.2	Exchange rates, inflation and international competition: an example	154
6.3	Depreciations/devaluations and trade performance	154
7.1	Leading exporters and importers of automotive and textile products, 1980 and 1992	171
7.2	Main exports of selected developed countries, 1992	172
7.3	Aspects of comparative advantage	178
7.4	Protectionism and the collapse of world trade	190
8.1	GATT rounds, 1947–93	201
8.2	Some regional alliances	208
8.3	European Union's tariff structure	210
8.4	The Lomé Convention	212
9.1	World portfolio investment, 1986–92	224
9.2	Foreign direct investment policies	226
9.3	Strategic reasons for FDI	229
9.4	Japanese car makers' investment in the UK	237
9.5	Transfer pricing and unitary taxation	239
9.6	'Poaching' inward investment?	240
10.1	The foreign exchange market	244
10.2	Exchange rate movements	250
10.3	Chronology of central rate changes within the ERM	257
10.4	IMF special funding facilities	269
10.5	Commodity prices and price support schemes	271
10.6	World Bank	275

Preface

A business operates in two main economic environments. One environment is the particular *markets* in which it sells its products. The firm's ability to meet and beat competitors in supplying products in these markets is fundamental to its corporate success. In addition, the firm's fortunes are also dependent on a broader, more remote *macroeconomic* environment: the domestic and international economies. Thus, for example, a booming domestic and international economy typically provides efficient and competitive firms with added opportunities for expanding their sales and profits; by contrast, a prolonged recession is likely to adversely affect the trading performance of even the strongest firms.

The objective of this book is to provide students and practitioners of business with an understanding of the various forces which shape the functioning of the domestic and international economies. The book examines such macroeconomic phenomena as the business cycle, unemployment and inflation, economic growth and international trade and investment, showing how businesses both play a part in these processes and are affected by them. Governments' role in regulating the economic system and the way domestic and international macroeconomic policy affects businesses is highlighted.

The book is primarily intended to cover the needs of MBA, DMS and undergraduate business students who have not studied economics before and who are seeking a relevant, straightforward and relatively non-technical introduction to macroeconomics.

Acknowledgements

We should like to thank Chris Barkby, Kathy Cousens and Pamela Anderson for their efficiency in typing drafts of the manuscript, and Rosemary Nixon, Sally Close, John Dust and Gabi Woolgar for their enthusiastic support of the work.

Christopher Pass, Bryan Lowes
and Andrew Robinson

Chapter 1

The macroeconomic environment of business: an overview

1.1 WHY STUDY MACROECONOMICS?

From a business perspective it is useful to think of the firm operating in two external environments – the immediate microeconomic or market environment for its products and the more general macroeconomic environment. The market environment comprises the factor markets where businesses buy or hire the resources they require, and the product markets where businesses sell their goods or services, usually in competition with other suppliers. (See Figure 1.1.) The broader macroeconomic environment within which businesses operate embraces political, economic, social and technical elements. (See Figure 1.1.)

These environments may be 'hostile' or 'friendly' at various times, but the firm as a bundle of internalised resources is in a position to react positively to minimise threats and maximise opportunities. For example, adversity in one product market can be hedged by product diversification, while adversity in one economy can be ameliorated by export sales or by foreign investment.

Macroeconomics is concerned with the functioning of the economy *overall*, in contrast to microeconomics, which is concerned with the provision of *individual* products. Macroeconomics investigates how the economy 'works' and seeks to identify strategic determinants of the levels of national income, output, employment and prices.

The business performance of private-enterprise firms is primarily affected by supply and demand conditions in the individual product markets in which they operate. However, their corporate prosperity is also affected by the prevailing economic 'climate' in so far as, for example, fluctuations in the level of spending in the economy will affect sales and profits. A booming domestic economy will provide firms with greater opportunities to sell their products and increase their profits; a prolonged recession characterised by low levels of demand may impose losses on firms and cause some firms to go bankrupt. Figure 1.2 shows annual percentage changes in real national output or gross domestic product for the UK and the percentage return on capital employed

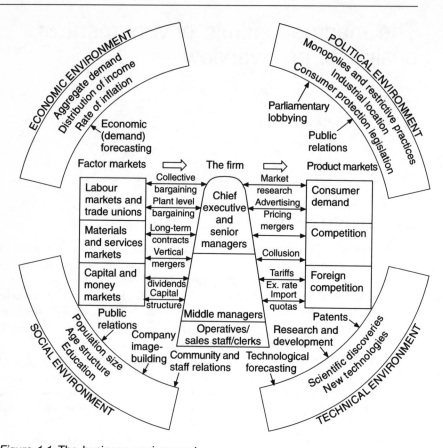

Figure 1.1 The business environment

earned by UK companies. Though the two variables do not coincide exactly it is clear that they move broadly in sympathy, with profitability rising as the economy expands and falling as the economy stagnates.

More specifically, many UK financial services groups, including the Prudential and Abbey National, acquired estate agencies in the late 1980s when UK house prices were booming, only to incur substantial losses on this activity when the housing market went into recession. Both groups have since sold their estate agency chains. The recession in the car industry in the early 1990s has likewise taken its toll. Ford, Vauxhall, Peugeot and Nissan have all cut back car production in the UK, while Nissan's parent company in Japan made a loss in 1992 and Toyota and Mazda reported sharply reduced profits.

Moreover, in the period since 1950 increasing emphasis on trade liberalisation through the GATT and the formation of regional trade blocs has

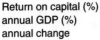

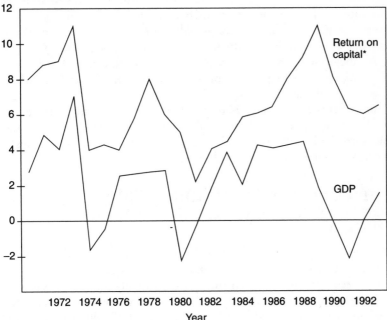

Figure 1.2 Changes in GDP and return on capital in the UK. *All UK companies (excluding oil companies)

Source: UK National Income Accounts, 1994; *Bank of England Quarterly*, 1994

resulted in a growing interdependency between countries and sharpened international competition. The removal of obstacles to international trade has provided greater export opportunities for progressive firms, and similar 'open door' initiatives in respect of international investment have facilitated the expansion of multinational companies. Changes in foreign currency values have a particular significance for businesses which rely extensively on international trade. Profits at Nintendo, the Japanese electronic games producer, for example, fell by 26 per cent in 1992–3 largely owing to the appreciation of the yen, which reduced export sales by 12 per cent and narrowed profit margins.

To aid our understanding of the functioning of businesses in the macro-economic environment, we must address two important issues. First, we need to quantify and measure the performance of the economy. Second, we need to gain some understanding of how the economy operates at the macroeconomic level.

These issues form the essence of this 'introductory' chapter. First, the concepts of national income, gross national product and gross domestic product are introduced, these being important aggregate measures of a country's economic prosperity. The issues which underpin the well-being and functioning of an economy are then examined. This is developed at two levels. At the first level a simplified exposition of how the whole economy operates is presented which centres on the *circular flow of income* model. At the second level the circular flow of income model is broken down into its component parts to provide a more detailed understanding of the workings of the economy.

The aim of this first chapter is to provide the reader with a firm grasp of how the economy works. It not only provides an introduction to the concepts surrounding the study of macroeconomics, but also provides a framework for understanding the subsequent chapters.

1.2 THE CONCEPTS OF NATIONAL INCOME, GROSS NATIONAL PRODUCT (GNP) AND GROSS DOMESTIC PRODUCT (GDP)

One of the most important measures of the performance of a country's economy is national income. National income is the total money income generated in an economy over a given time period (usually one year). National income is equal to the total money value of all final goods and services produced in an economy (gross domestic product, GDP) plus net property income from abroad (which adds up to gross national product, GNP) less capital consumption, as indicated in Figure 1.3. As Figure 1.3 reveals, national income can be derived from any of three basic sources: measures of output, income and expenditure. As we shall see, each requires various adjustments before a uniform measure of national income is obtained.

1.2.1 Output measure of national income

The domestic product/output of goods and services is produced by enterprises within the country (*value-added approach*). This total output does not include the value of imported goods and services. To avoid overstating the value of output by double-counting both the final output of goods and services and the output of intermediate components and services which are eventually absorbed in final output, only the value added at each stage of the production process is counted. The sum of all the value added by various sections of the economy (agriculture, manufacturing, etc.) is known as the *gross domestic product* (GDP). To arrive at the *gross national product* (GNP) it is necessary to add net property income from abroad (defined as net income in the form of interest, rent, profits and dividends accruing to a nation's citizens from their ownership of assets abroad).

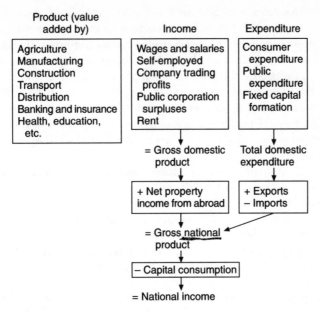

Figure 1.3 National income

1.2.2 Income measure of national income

The total income of residents of the country is derived from the current production of goods and services (*income approach*). Such incomes are called factor incomes because they accrue to factors of production, and they exclude transfer payments like sickness or unemployment benefits for which no goods or services are received in return. The sum of all these factor incomes (wages and salaries, incomes of the self-employed, etc.) should exactly match the gross domestic product, since each £1 worth of goods and services produced should simultaneously produce £1 of factor income for their producers. To get from gross domestic factor incomes (= gross domestic product) to gross national factor incomes (= gross national product) it is necessary to add net property income from abroad.

1.2.3 Expenditure measure of national income

The total domestic expenditure by residents of a country is on consumption and investment goods (*expenditure approach*). This includes expenditure on final goods and services (excluding expenditure on intermediate products), and includes goods which are unsold and added to stock (inventory investment). However, some domestic expenditure will be channelled to imported goods, while expenditure by non-residents on goods and services produced by domestic residents will add to the factor incomes of those residents. Thus, to get from total domestic expenditure to total national expenditure (= gross national product) it is necessary to deduct imports and add exports.

All three measures outlined above show the gross money value of goods and services produced – the gross national product. However, in the process of producing these goods and services the nation's capital stock will be subject to wear and tear, and so we must allow for the net money value of goods and services produced (allowing for the depreciation of the capital stock or capital consumption) – the net national product. This net national product is called national income.

In practice, data-collection problems mean that the three measures of national income give slightly different figures. Additionally, in order to highlight the difference between the money value and the real value of national income it is necessary to take account of the effects of inflation upon GNP by applying a broad-based price index called the GNP deflator.

National income data provide a useful indication of a country's economic prosperity and can be used to measure changes in a country's 'absolute' living standards. In this regard, however, a more appropriate measure of living standards is income per head (see Box 1.1), that is, a country's GNP divided by its population. Thus, although the USA had a higher absolute level of GNP in 1992 than Japan, its income per head was much lower. It will be noted that both Mozambique and Ethiopia had lower levels of income per head in 1992 compared with 1980, as population growth has continued to outstrip increases in output. However, even this measure is flawed as an indicator of typical living standards because, in practice, the distribution of income is not equal.

We now turn to issues surrounding the working of the economy which centre on the circular flow of national income.

1.3 THE CIRCULAR FLOW OF NATIONAL INCOME MODEL: AN OVERVIEW

The circular flow of national income model provides a simplified exposition of money and physical or real flows through the economy which serves as the basis of macroeconomic analysis. In Figure 1.4(a) the solid lines show how, in monetary terms, households purchase goods and services from businesses (consumption expenditure), using income received from supplying factor inputs to businesses. In physical terms (shown by the broken lines), businesses produce goods and services, using factor inputs supplied to them by households. Since the two offsetting flows are identical it is possible to simplify our analysis by concentrating upon the money flows shown by the solid lines.

The basic model can be developed to incorporate a number of 'injections' into, and 'withdrawals' from, the income flow. Injections into the

Box 1.1 Gross national product: selected countries, total and per head

	1980			1992		
	Population (millions)	GNP per head (US$)	Total (US$ millions)	Population (millions)	GNP per head (US$)	Total (US$ millions)
High income countries						
Switzerland	6.5	16,440	10,6860	6.9	36,080	248,952
Japan	116.8	9,890	1,155,152	124.5	28190	3,509,655
Germany*	60.9	13,590	827,631	80.6	23,030	1,856,218
USA	227.7	11,360	2,586,672	255.4	23,240	5,935,496
UK	55.9	7,920	442,728	57.8	17,790	1,028,262
Middle income countries						
Greece	9.6	4,380	42,048	10.3	7,290	75,087
Korea	38.2	1520	58,064	43.7	6,790	296,723
Mexico	69.8	2,090	145,882	85.0	3,470	294,950
Thailand	47.0	670	31,490	58.0	1,840	106,720
El Salvador	4.5	660	2,970	5.4	1,170	6,318
Low income countries						
Egypt	39.8	580	23,084	54.7	640	35,008
China	976.6	290	283,214	1,162.2	470	546,234
Rwanda	5.2	200	1,040	7.3	250	1,825
Mozambique	12.1	230	2,783	16.5	60	990
Ethiopia	31.1	140	4,354	54.8	110	6,028

*Germany 1992 includes East Germany.
Source: World Bank, *World Development Report*, 1994.

income flow in the form of increased investment, government expenditure and exports may to some extent be offset by counteracting withdrawals from the income flow such as increased levels of saving, taxation and imports. In Figure 1.4(b) not all the income received by households is spent – some is saved. Savings are a 'withdrawal' from the income flow. Increased levels of investment expenditure 'inject' funds into the income flow. Part of the income accruing to households is taxed by the government and the tax serves to reduce disposable income available for consumption expenditure. Taxation is a 'withdrawal' from the income flow. Government expenditure on products and factor inputs 'injects' funds into the income flow. Households spend some of their income on imported goods and services. Imports are a 'withdrawal' from the income flow. On the other hand, some

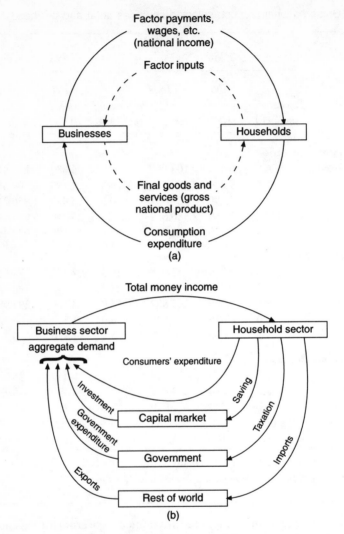

Figure 1.4 Circular flow of national income model

output is sold to overseas customers. Exports represent a demand for domestically produced goods and services and hence constitute an 'injection' into the income flow. All these factors can be viewed in terms of whether they lead to a net reduction in income circulating in the economy, that is, withdrawals, or whether they lead to an increase in income circulating around the economy, that is, injections.

1.4 THE BUILDING BLOCKS OF NATIONAL INCOME ANALYSIS

As we have seen, the economy, as represented by the circular flow of income, is made up of numerous variables which are of importance in their own right, especially if we are to build upon our existing understanding of how the economy works. Therefore before we look at the determination of the equilibrium level of national income it is necessary to look at some of the various variables introduced above (consumption, investment, saving, etc.) in a little more detail, indicating their determinants and their relation to national income. Table 1.1 provides information about the main components of gross domestic product for a number of countries.

1.4.1 Consumption expenditure

Consumption expenditure is spending by households on consumer goods and services (cars, food, haircuts, etc.) over a specified time period. Consumption expenditure is the largest component of aggregate demand in all major industrialised countries, for example, accounting for around 65 per cent of gross domestic product in the UK. It is also the most stable element of total demand, varying little from year to year. However, because of its very size even small percentage variations in consumption expenditure can create large variations in the demand for consumer goods and services. Table 1.2 shows recent trends in UK GDP, personal disposable income and consumer expenditure.

The main determinant of the level of consumption expenditure is the current level of national income or disposable income (that is, the amount of current income available to households after payment of personal income taxes and national insurance contributions). Income received in past periods (and 'stored' or 'saved' in the form of wealth or assets such as houses) and income anticipated in future years may also affect current consumption decisions. The 'consumption schedule' depicts the relationship between consumption expenditure and the level of national income or disposable income. At very low levels of disposable income households consume more than their current income (dissavings), drawing on past savings or selling assets to maintain consumption at some desired minimum level. At higher levels of disposable income they consume only a part of their current income and save the rest. Figure 1.5 shows a simple *consumption schedule* which takes the linear form $C = a + bY$, where C is consumption, Y is disposable income and a is the minimum level of consumption expenditure at zero disposable income (autonomous consumption). Thereafter consumption expenditure increases as income increases (induced consumption) and b is the proportion of each extra pound of disposable income which is spent. Thus b, representing the slope of the consumption function, is equal

Table 1.1 Components of gross domestic product, selected countries, 1990-2 (%)

Country	Private consumption expenditure	Government consumption expenditure	Investment expenditure	Exports of goods and services	Imports of goods and services
Developed					
Australia	62	19	19	18	−18
Belgium	63	15	19	69	−66
Canada	61	22	19	26	−28
Denmark	52	25	15	37	−29
France	60	19	20	23	−22
Germany	54	18	21	33	−26
Greece	71	20	20	23	−34
Italy	63	18	19	18	−18
Japan	57	9	31	10	−9
Netherlands	60	14	20	52	−46
New Zealand	61	15	19	31	−28
Norway	52	22	18	43	−45
Sweden	55	28	14	33	−30
Switzerland	58	15	23	36	−32
UK	65	22	15	23	−25
USA	67	18	16	11	−12
Developing					
Brazil	65	14	19	10	−6
Cameroon	66	10	26	15	−17
Chile	64	10	24	32	−30
Equador	68	7	21	31	−27
Egypt	73	10	20	29	−32
Ghana	84	13	12	16	−25
Hungary	56	26	21	36	−39
Indonesia	53	10	35	29	−37
Iraq	56	33	8	27	−24
Israel	61	28	25	31	−45
Jamaica	68	13	27	45	−53
Kenya	72	16	17	27	−32
Korea (South)	53	11	35	31	−31
Kuwait	40	38	36	35	−49
Malaysia	49	12	33	80	−74
Mexico	71	8	22	16	−17
Pakistan	73	13	18	17	−21
Poland	64	19	18	21	−22
Taiwan	56	17	24	44	−41
Thailand	60	9	37	37	−43

Source: Europa World Yearbook, 1994.

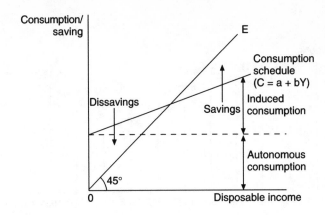

Figure 1.5 Consumption schedule

to the *marginal propensity to consume*(MPC). The marginal propensity to consume is the fraction of any change in national income or disposable income which is spent on consumption:

$$\text{MPC} = \frac{\text{change in consumption}}{\text{change in income}} = b$$

The 45° line OE shows what consumption expenditure would have been had it exactly matched disposable income. The difference between OE and the consumption schedule indicates the extent of dissavings or savings at various income levels.

Table 1.2 UK national income, personal disposable income, consumption and saving, 1983-93

	Gross domestic product (£bn)	Total personal disposable income (£bn)	Consumers expenditure (£bn)	Consumption ratio (%)	Savings ratio (%)
1983	304.4	205.5	185.6	90.3	9.7
1984	325.8	223.6	198.8	88.9	11.1
1985	357.3	243.5	217.5	89.3	10.7
1986	384.8	264.5	241.6	91.2	8.8
1987	423.4	285.4	265.3	92.9	7.1
1988	471.4	317.7	299.4	94.2	5.8
1989	515.9	352.9	327.4	92.7	7.3
1990	551.1	380.1	347.5	91.4	8.6
1991	575.3	406.1	365.1	89.9	10.1
1992	597.1	436.2	382.4	87.7	12.3
1993	630.0	458.2	405.9	88.6	11.4

Source: UK national income accounts, 1994.

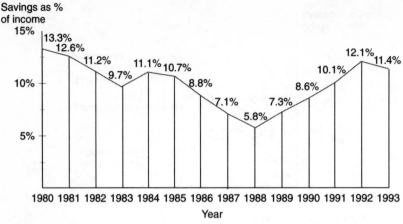

Figure 1.6 Personal savings ratio

1.4.2 Saving

Saving is income that is not spent on current consumption. The level of personal savings by households depends largely upon the amount of their disposable income and their spending decisions, though it may also be influenced by the amount of their outstanding debt; interest rates (the reward for saving); and the age structure of the population (in so far as older adults tend to save more of their income). Savings can tend to be somewhat volatile over time, as indicated by Figure 1.6, which shows the personal savings ratio as a percentage of income in the UK.

The fraction of any national income or disposable income that is not spent on current consumption is known as the *marginal propensity to save* (MPS). Hence:

$$\text{MPS} = \frac{\text{change in saving}}{\text{change in income}}$$

If all income (Y) is either consumed (C) or saved (S) then:

$$Y = C + S$$

so that anything not consumed must be saved, and anything not saved must be consumed. Consequently:

$$\text{MPC} = 1 - \text{MPS}$$

and

$$\text{MPS} = 1 - \text{MPC}$$

As the 'mirror image' of consumption, the level of saving (and dissaving) is determined primarily by the level of income.

In the simple circular flow model, all saving is undertaken by households; in the extended model, saving is also undertaken by businesses (retained profits) and by the government (budget surplus). Thus the level of saving is also influenced by companies' dividend and profit retention policies and by governments' demand management policies (see Chapter 2).

In real terms, saving is important in that it 'finances' physical investment. Saving (forgoing current consumption) releases resources which can be devoted to increasing the country's capital stock and hence its capacity to produce a greater quantity of goods and services in the future.

1.4.3 Investment expenditure

In national income analysis investment expenditure relates specifically to spending by private sector businesses (and nationalised industries) on the purchase of productive assets such as plant, offices, machinery and equipment (fixed investment) and stocks (inventory investment), that is, *physical* or *real* investment. The term 'investment' excludes 'portfolio' or financial investment (which merely transfers the ownership of *existing* assets from one person or institution to another); it also excludes investment in dwellings by households and in the provision of social products such as roads, hospitals and schools by governments. The former is included as part of consumption expenditure and the latter as part of government expenditure (see below). Investment expenditure is a moderately large component of aggregate demand in all major industrialised countries, for example, accounting for around 15 per cent of gross domestic product in the UK. It is also one of the more volatile components of demand, tending to vary considerably from year to year.

Fixed investment can be split up into gross and net investment. Gross investment is the total amount of investment that is undertaken in an economy over a specified time period. Net investment is gross investment less replacement investment or capital consumption, that is, investment which is necessary to replace that part of the economy's existing capital stock which is used up or depreciated in producing this year's output.

The amount of fixed investment undertaken is dependent on a number of factors other than capital consumption considerations. In national income analysis, the *marginal efficiency of capital/investment and the interest rate* are important determinants of the level of investment (see Box 1.2). The marginal efficiency of capital/investment itself is dependent upon business confidence and expectations about future demand levels and therefore plant utilisation. The volatility of business expectations in the short run means that planned levels of fixed investment can vary significantly over time, leading to changes in the demand for capital goods, thus serving to exacerbate fluctuations in the level of economic activity (see Section 1.5). Similar considerations apply to inventory investment, with stock levels being

Box 1.2 The marginal efficiency of capital/investment

The marginal efficiency of capital/investment is the rate of return – (profits) expected on an extra pound's worth of investment. The marginal efficiency of investment decreases as the amount of investment increases, as shown in Figure (a). This is because initial investments are concentrated on the 'best' opportunities and yield high rates of return; later investments are less productive and secure progressively lower returns.

The amount of investment undertaken depends not only on expected returns but also on the cost of capital, that is, the interest rate. Investment will be profitable up to the point where the marginal efficiency of investment is equal to the cost of capital. In Figure (a) at an interest rate of 20 per cent only OX amount of investment is worthwhile. A fall in the interest rate to 15 per cent increases the amount of profitable investment to OY.

It will be readily apparent from Figure (a) that there is a link between the monetary side of the economy and the real economy: a fall in interest rates will stimulate more investment, which in turn will result in a higher level of national income (see Section 1.6).

If expectations change and investors expect to receive better returns from each investment because, for example, of technological progress, then at any given rate of interest (such as 20 per cent) more investment will be undertaken than before; that is, the marginal efficiency of investment schedule will shift to the right, as shown in Figure (b), and investment will have increased from OX to OZ.

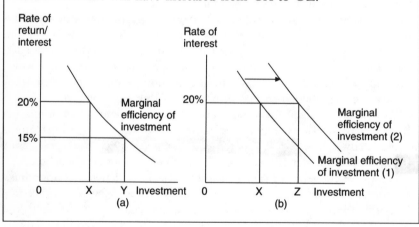

increased or decreased over time according to changing business expectations. Figure 1.7 depicts the *investment schedule*, which shows the relationship between investment and the level of national income. In the short and
medium term the investment schedule would tend to have a positive slope
and a positive intercept with the vertical axis as indicated by the solid line
in Figure 1.7 in so far as some investment (autonomous investment) will
take place even when national income is zero.

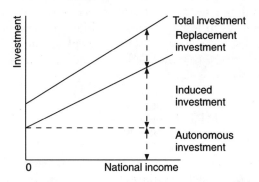

Figure 1.7 Investment schedule

As shown in Figure 1.7 the investment schedule is made up of a number
of elements:

1 *Autonomous* investment, which is related to non-income factors such as
   technological changes and cost-cutting, will be undertaken irrespective
   of the level of income.
2 *Replacement* investment, which is required to maintain the economy's
   existing capital stock and which tends to vary in line with changes in
   levels of national income in so far as a greater amount (in absolute terms)
   of replacement investment is required to maintain the economy's existing
   capital stock as national income and output rise:

	£	£
National income	1,000	2,000
Capital stock	100	200
Replacement investment	10	20

3 *Induced* investment, which takes place as rising demand puts pressure on
   existing capacity and raises profitability, thereby encouraging businesses
   to invest more. Thus the more rapid the *rate of growth* of national income,
   the higher the *level* of induced investment. (See Box 1.4.)

1.4.4 Taxation

Taxation represents government receipts from the imposition of various taxes on persons' and businesses' income, on spending on domestic and imported products, on wealth and capital gains, and on properties. Figure 1.8 depicts the *taxation schedule* which shows the relationship between taxation receipts and the level of national income. Under progressive taxation systems the schedule has a positive slope, with taxation receipts increasing as the level of income rises. Likewise, receipts from expenditure taxes will be greater as the level of spending rises. Other factors affecting the level of taxation are governments' policies in respect of the provision of social products (roads, schools, etc.) and social security (against unemployment, sickness, etc.).

The *marginal propensity to tax* (MPT) is the fraction of any change in national income which is taken in taxation:

$$MPT = \frac{change\ in\ tax}{change\ in\ income}$$

Where governments operate progressive taxation systems, with higher rates of tax charged on larger incomes, the marginal propensity to tax will increase at higher income levels, causing the taxation schedule to curve upwards, increasing its slope at higher income levels.

1.4.5 Government expenditure

Government expenditure is spending by the public authorities (central government and local authorities) on the provision of social goods and services (health, education, defence, roads, etc.), marketed goods and services (coal, postal services, etc) and transfer payments (unemployment benefit, state pensions, etc.). In the circular flow of income model, transfer payments are excluded from government spending because they are not made in return for productive services (that is, they do not add to total output)

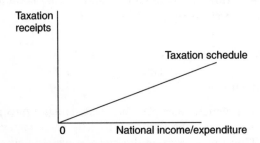

Figure 1.8 Taxation schedule

but merely transfer taxation receipts from one household to another. Government purchases of goods and services are a moderately large component of aggregate demand in all major industrialised countries accounting, for example, for around 18 per cent of gross domestic product in the UK.

Government expenditure is financed by taxation and by borrowing. The level of government spending is determined by both political and economic considerations. Politically, if the state assumes greater responsibility for the provision of goods and services, thus altering the 'balance' of the mixed economy as between the 'public' and 'private' sectors, then this will increase the importance of government spending relative to the other components of aggregate demand. The government's role as a 'regulator' of the economic system will also have a bearing on the amount of spending it undertakes; for example, it may deliberately seek to increase total spending in the economy by running a budget deficit (see Chapter 2).

1.4.6 Imports

Imports represent spending by domestic households and businesses on goods and services supplied by foreign businesses. Imports can often represent an important element in relatively 'open' economies like Japan, Germany and the UK which need to import large quantities of raw materials. For example, imports are equal to around 25 per cent of gross domestic product in the UK.

Figure 1.9 depicts the import schedule, which shows the relationship between national income and spending on imports. As incomes rise consumers will tend to buy more of all goods and services, leading to an increase in imported final goods and services and an increase in imported raw materials.

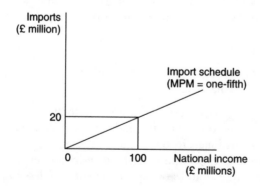

Figure 1.9 Import schedule

The slope of the import schedule measures the *marginal propensity to import* (MPM), that is, the fraction of any change in national income which is spent on imports:

$$MPM = \frac{\text{change in imports}}{\text{change in income}}$$

1.4.7 Exports

Exports represent spending by overseas households and businesses on domestically produced goods and services and, hence, constitute an injection in the circular flow of national income model. Exports are often an important element of total demand, especially in relatively open economies where exports (and imports) represent a significant proportion of national output. For example, UK exports are equal to around 23 per cent of gross domestic product.

Exports are shown as independent of a country's *own* level of national income, being determined primarily by the price and non-price competitiveness of the country's goods and services in international trade and by income levels in importing countries.

1.5 THE EQUILIBRIUM LEVEL OF NATIONAL INCOME

While the circular flow of national income model provides a basic overview of income, spending and product flows in the economy it is, by its very nature, a never-ending process which is in a continuous state of change. However, for analytical purposes it is useful on occasion to stop the 'movie film' and obtain a 'snapshot' view of the balance between the current level of total spending (aggregate demand) in the economy and the ability of the economy to produce goods and services (aggregate supply). (See Box 1.3.) This is achieved by using the aggregate demand and aggregate supply framework to discuss the determination of the equilibrium national income.

1.5.1 Aggregate demand, aggregate supply and the determination of the equilibrium level of national income

Aggregate demand or aggregate expenditure is the total amount of expenditure (in nominal terms) on domestic goods and services. As noted from the circular flow of national income model above, aggregate demand comprises consumption expenditure (C), investment expenditure (I), government expenditure (G) and net exports (exports, X less imports, M):

$$\text{aggregate demand} = C + I + G + (X - M)$$

Box 1.3 Classical and Keynesian views of national income and output

Modern national income analysis is based extensively on the work of the British economist John Maynard Keynes, in particular his seminal book *The General Theory of Employment, Interest and Money* (1936). Keynes gave economics a new direction and an explanation of the phenomenon of mass unemployment so prevalent in the 1930s. Prior to Keynes, classical economics had maintained that in a market economy the economic system would spontaneously tend to produce full employment of resources because the market mechanism would ensure correspondence between total supply and demand. Consequently the classicists were confident that business depressions would cure themselves, with interest rates falling under the pressure of accumulating savings, so encouraging businesspeople to borrow and invest more, and with wage rates falling, so reducing production costs and encouraging businesspeople to employ more workers.

By contrast Keynes argued that there is no assurance that savings will accumulate during a depression and reduce interest rates, since savings depend on income and with high unemployment incomes are low.

Furthermore, he argued that investment depends primarily on business confidence, which would be low during a depression so that investment would be unlikely to rise even if interest rates fell. Finally, he argued that the wage rate would be unlikely to fall much during a depression, given its 'stickiness', and even if it did fall, that would merely exacerbate the depression by reducing consumption.

Keynes saw the root cause of a depression as reduced aggregate demand – a low level of consumption and investment spending. Thus, in order for the economy to recover, a higher level of demand is required which, in the absence of an (unlikely) automatic stimulus to demand, Keynes argued, will require intervention by the government to boost spending by, for example, cutting income taxes and increasing its own expenditure.

Figure 1.10 presents the aggregate demand schedule, which shows the total amount of spending on domestic goods and services at various levels of national income.

Aggregate supply is the total amount of domestic goods and services supplied by businesses. The aggregate supply schedule depicts the total amount of domestic goods and services supplied by businesses at various levels of total expenditure. As shown in Figure 1.11, the aggregate supply

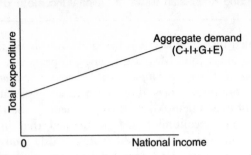

Figure 1.10 Aggregate demand schedule

schedule is generally drawn as a 45° line because businesses will offer any *particular* level of national output only if they expect total spending (aggregate demand) to be just sufficient to buy all that output.

Thus, as indicated in Figure 1.11, £100 million of expenditure calls forth £100 million of aggregate supply, £200 million of expenditure calls forth £200 million of aggregate supply, and so on. However, this process cannot continue indefinitely, for once the economy's resources are fully employed in supplying products then additional expenditure cannot be met from additional domestic resources because the potential output ceiling of the economy has been reached (potential GNP). Consequently, beyond the full-resource utilisation level of national income, Y_F, the aggregate supply schedule becomes vertical. (Over the longer term, aggregate supply can increase as a result of an expansion in the resources – labour, capital, etc. – available to the economy; see Chapter 5.)

The *equilibrium level of national income* is that level of national income at which total spending and the supply of goods and services in the economy

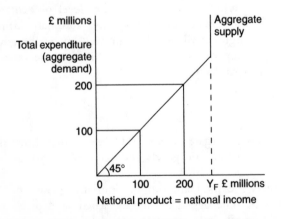

Figure 1.11 Aggregate supply schedule

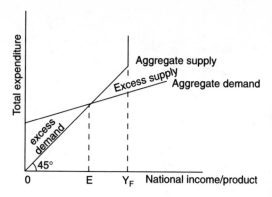

Figure 1.12 Aggregate demand, aggregate supply and the equilibrium level of national income

are synchronised. This occurs at the intersection of the aggregate demand (AD) schedule with the aggregate supply (AS) schedule, as shown by output E in Figure 1.12. Income levels *above* income level E are not sustainable because total spending is insufficient to buy up all the output being produced. Businesses find themselves with unplanned stocks on their hands and thus cut back production. Conversely, at income levels *below* output E aggregate demand exceeds aggregate supply. Businesses find that they can sell all their current output and are encouraged to expand production.

1.5.2 National income, output, employment and prices: a simple overview

As noted in section 1.5.1 the economy's ability to produce goods and services in the short run is constrained by the limited availability of resources. Once all resources are fully employed, the aggregate supply schedule becomes vertical. An important point to emphasise is that (left unregulated) it is unlikely that the equilibrium level of national income will coincide exactly with the full employment/non-inflationary level of national income. Figure 1.13 presents, by way of illustration, three possibilities. In the case of aggregate demand (AD_1) there is a shortfall in total spending relative to the supply capacity of the economy. The intersection of AD_1 with the aggregate supply schedule results in an actual output of OE.

This output (OE) is less than the potential (that is, full employment) output level (OY_F), leaving an 'output gap' equal to EY_F.

By contrast, in the case of aggregate demand (AD_2), the level of total spending is greater than the supply capacity of the economy. Once the full employment level of output (OY_F) has been reached it is impossible to

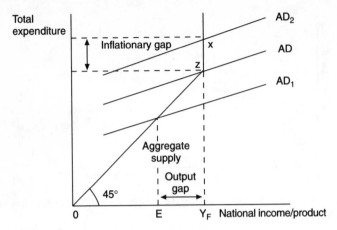

Figure 1.13 Output (deflationary) and inflationary gaps

supply more goods and services, and the existence of 'excess demand' will serve to increase prices, creating an 'inflationary gap' equal to XZ. In the case of aggregate demand (AD), the level of spending is such as to bring about both full employment and price stability. (This is, of course, a simplified view of employment and inflation, since factors other than the level of spending will affect them – see Chapters 3 and 4.)

1.5.3 The 'multiplier' and shifts in the equilibrium level of national income

The equilibrium level of national income will change if there is a shift in the aggregate demand schedule. This will come about if there is a change

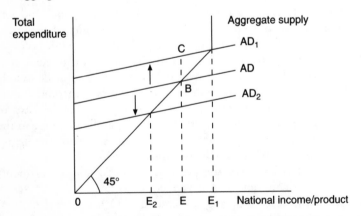

Figure 1.14 Change in the equilibrium level of national income due to a shift in the aggregate demand schedule

in any of the components of aggregate demand: an increase/decrease in consumption, an increase/decrease in government spending, an increase/decrease in investment, or an increase/decrease in net exports. For example, if as shown in Figure 1.14 aggregate demand increases from AD to AD_1 this results in an increase in the equilibrium level of national income from OE to OE_1. By contrast, if aggregate demand falls from AD to AD_2, the equilibrium level of national income will fall from OE to OE_2.

One key factor which can be observed by inspection of Figure 1.14 is that a given change in aggregate demand such as BC results in a change in the equilibrium level of national income such as EE_1 which is greater than the initial change in aggregate demand or injections. This phenomenon is known as the *multiplier* effect.

The multiplier is defined as the ratio of an induced change in the equilibrium level of national income to an initial change in the level of spending. Two important features of the multiplier need to be noted: (1) it is a cumulative process rather than an instantaneous effect, and as such is best viewed in terms of a series of successive 'rounds' of additions to income; (2) the value of the multiplier depends on the fraction of extra income that is spent on consumption (the marginal propensity to consume, MPC) at each successive round.

For simplicity, let us assume that all income is either consumed or 'withdrawn' as savings. (That is, the MPC and the marginal propensity to save (MPS) together = 1.) The value of the multiplier (K) is then given by the formula:

$$K = \frac{1}{1 - MPC} \quad \text{or} \quad \frac{1}{MPS}$$

The larger an increase in consumption from an increment of income, the larger is the multiplier. Thus, if MPC is 0.9 and MPS is 0.1, the multiplier value is 10; if MPC is 0.75 and MPS is 0.25, the multiplier value is only 4.

The multiplier effect is illustrated in Table 1.3 and Figure 1.15. With a

Table 1.3 Multiplier process

Round	Change in national income £ million	Change in consumption (MPC = 0.75)	Change in savings (MPS = 0.25)
1 Initial increase in spending	500	375	125
2	375	281	94
3	281	211	70
4	211	158	53
5	158	119	39
All later rounds	475	356	119
	2,000	1,500	500

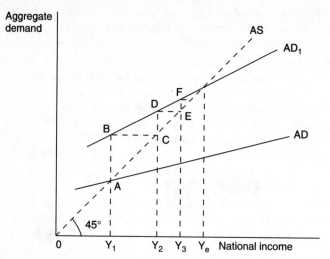

Figure 1.15 Multiplier effect of increased spending on national income

multiplier value of 4, an initial £500 million of extra spending results in a £2 billion increase in national income, as Table 1.3 shows. In each round a proportion of the additional income created is saved and so leaks from the circular flow, failing to get passed on as additional consumption expenditure in the next round. When the cumulative total of these savings leakages is equal to the initial increase in spending the multiplier process ceases and the economy reaches a new equilibrium.

Figure 1.15 demonstrates the multiplier effect in graphical form. Starting with a national income level OY_1, if aggregate demand increases from AD to AD_1, then the initial injection of extra spending AB would serve to increase output and income by Y_1Y_2. This additional income would induce yet more spending (CD) which would in turn increase output and income by Y_2Y_3. This additional income would induce yet more spending (EF) which would in turn increase output and income yet further, and so on. The process ends when the new equilibrium level of income Y_e is reached.

In addition, of course, to the savings 'withdrawal' from the income flow there are also taxation and import withdrawals which further reduce the value of the multiplier. Thus the more sophisticated multiplier is given by the formula:

$$K = \frac{1}{MPS + MPT + MPM}$$

where MPT is the marginal propensity to tax and MPM is the marginal propensity to import. Figure 1.16 depicts the manner in which this more

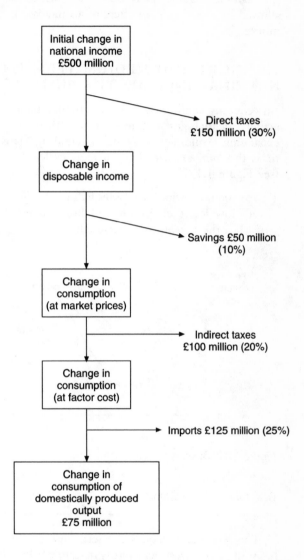

Figure 1.16 Multiplier

sophisticated multiplier is likely to work through. It is noticeable from the sample figures presented that with the additional withdrawals allowed for the multiplier effect of an increase in the demand will be more modest.

1.6 SHORT AND MEDIUM-TERM FLUCTUATIONS IN NATIONAL INCOME: THE BUSINESS CYCLE

An economy is often characterised by fluctuations in the level of economic activity (actual gross national product), with periods of declining and expanding economic conditions alternating. This phenomenon is referred to as the *business cycle*. The business cycle is characterised by four phases (see Figure 1.17):

1 *Depression*, a period of rapidly falling aggregate demand accompanied by very low levels of output and heavy unemployment which eventually reaches the bottom of the trough.

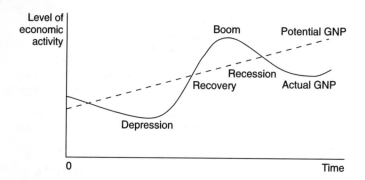

Figure 1.17 Business cycle

Box 1.4 The accelerator

The accelerator depicts the relationship between the amount of net or induced investment (gross investment less replacement investment) and the rate of change of national income. A rapid rise in income and consumption spending will put pressure on existing capacity and encourage businesses not only to invest to replace existing capital as it wears out but also to invest in new plant and equipment to meet the increase in demand.

By way of simple illustration, let us suppose a business meets the existing demand for its product utilising ten machines, one of which is replaced each year. If demand increases by 20 per cent, it must invest in two new machines to accommodate that demand, in addition to the one replacement machine.

Investment is thus, in part, a function of changes in the level of income: I depends upon Y. A rise in induced investment, in turn, serves to reinforce the multiplier effect in increasing national income.

The combined effect of accelerator and multiplier forces working through an investment cycle has been offered as an explanation of changes in the *level* of economic activity associated with the business cycle. Because the *level* of investment depends upon the *rate of change* of GNP, when GNP is rising rapidly investment will be at a high level as producers seek to add to their capacity (time t in the figure). This high level of investment will add to aggregate demand and help to maintain a high level of GNP. However, as the rate of growth of GNP slows down from time t onward, businesspeople will no longer need to add as rapidly to capacity, and investment will decline towards replacement investment levels. This lower level of investment will reduce aggregate demand and contribute towards the eventual fall in GNP. Once GNP has persisted at a low level for some time, machines will gradually wear out and businesspeople will need to replace some of these machines if they are to maintain sufficient production capacity to meet even the lower level of aggregate demand experienced. This increase in the level of investment at time t_1 will increase aggregate demand and stimulate the growth of GNP.

Like fixed investment, investment in stock is also to some extent a function of the rate of change of income so that inventory investment is subject to similar accelerator effects.

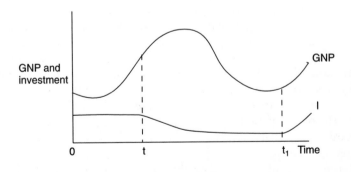

2 *Recovery*, an upturn in aggregate demand accompanied by rising output and a reduction in unemployment.

3 *Boom*: aggregate demand reaches and then exceeds sustainable output levels (potential gross national product) as the peak of the cycle is reached. Full employment is attained and the emergence of excess demand causes the general price level to increase.

4 *Recession*: the boom comes to an end, and is followed by recession. Aggregate demand falls, bringing with it, initially, modest falls in output and employment, but then, as demand continues to contract, the onset of depression.

What causes the economy to fluctuate in this way? One prominent factor is the volatility of fixed investment and inventory investment expenditures (the investment cycle), which are themselves a function of businesspeople's expectations about future demand. At the top of the business cycle income begins to level off and investment in new supply capacity finally 'catches up' with demand (see Box 1.4). This causes a reduction in induced investment and, via contracting multiplier effects, leads to a fall in national income which reduces investment even further. At the bottom of the depression investment may rise – for example, owing to the introduction of new technologies or through the revival of replacement investment. In that case the increase in investment spending will, via expansionary multiplier effects, lead to an increase in national income and a greater volume of induced investment.

Finally in our discussion of the workings of the economy and the determination of equilibrium national income we introduce the monetary side of the economy.

1.7 THE ROLE OF MONEY IN THE ECONOMY

In modern economies economic transactions are conducted using *money* as a medium of exchange (notes and coins, bank deposits, etc.). Individual goods and services, and other physical assets, are 'priced' in terms of money and are exchanged using money as a common denominator, rather than one type of goods, etc., being exchanged directly for another (as in barter). The use of money as a means of payment enables an economy to produce more because it facilitates specialisation in production and reduces the time spent by sellers and buyers in arranging exchanges. Other important functions of money are its use as a store of value or purchasing power (money can be held over a period of time and used to finance future payments), a standard of deferred payment (money is used as an agreed measure of future receipts and payments in contracts), and as a unit of account (money is used to measure and record the value of goods or services – for example, gross national product – over time).

1.7.1 The demand for, and the supply of money and the interest rate

1.7.1.1 The money demand schedule

In national income analysis money is demanded for three purposes: the *transaction* demand for money (that is, money held on a day-to-day basis to finance current expenditure on goods and services); the *precautionary* demand for money (that is, money held to cover for unforeseen contingencies); and the *speculative* demand for money (that is, money held to purchase bonds or other financial securities in anticipation of a rise in interest rates or a fall in bond prices).

The quantity of money demanded, or liquidity preference, Q_d, depends upon the interest rate (i) and the level of national income (Y): Q_d depends upon (i, Y). The relationship can be portrayed in terms of the money demand schedule which shows the relationship between the quantity of money demanded at various interest rates, with a given level of national income.

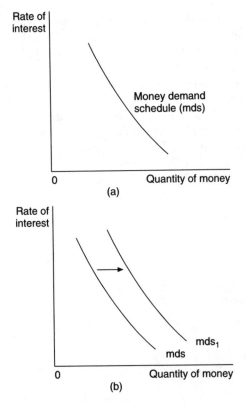

Figure 1.18 Money demand schedule: (a) constant national income, (b) effect of an increase in national income

If the rate of interest falls, that increases the speculative demand for money. The rate of interest varies inversely with the price of bonds: for example, if the nominal return on a bond is £10 and the price of the bond is £100, then the effective interest rate is 10 per cent; if the price of the bond falls to £50, the effective interest rate increases to 20 per cent. Consequently the lower the rate of interest the higher will be the price of bonds. The higher the price of bonds the less likely it is that bond prices will continue to rise and the greater the chances that they will fall. Thus, as shown in Figure 1.18(a), the lower the rate of interest the greater is the inducement to hold cash for speculative purposes.

An increase in national income increases the transaction demand for money and may increase the precautionary demand for money, shifting the money demand schedule outwards to the right, from mds to mds₁ in Figure 1.18 (b).

1.7.1.2 The money supply schedule

In national income analysis the money supply schedule depicts the amount of money supplied and the interest rate. In some analyses the money supply is drawn as a vertical straight line; that is, the money supply is exogenously determined, being put into the economic system 'from outside' by the government (for example, government-issued notes and coins which form part of 'narrow' M0 money – see Chapter 2). However, a significant part of the 'wider' money supply (M3 money) is endogenously determined – for example, bank deposits are 'created' by the banking system (see Box 1.5) and these are highly interest rate-sensitive. Thus, as a general proposition, the higher the rate of interest (the higher the return on loanable funds) the greater the quantity of money supplied, as shown in Figure 1.19.

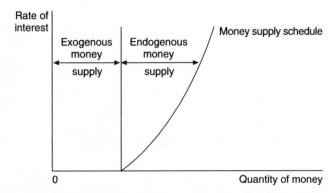

Figure 1.19 Money supply schedule

Box 1.5 *Bank deposit or credit creation: the money multiplier*

Bank deposit creation is the process whereby the commercial banking system is able to create new bank deposits and hence increase the money supply. Commercial banks accept deposits of currency from the general public. Some of this money is retained by the banks to meet day-to-day withdrawals (the reserve assets). The remainder of the money is used to make loans or is invested. When a bank on-lends it creates additional deposits in favour of borrowers. The amount of new deposits the banking system as a whole can create depends on the magnitude of the reserve–asset ratio. In the example set out in the figure the banks are assumed to operate with a 40 per cent reserve–asset ratio: Bank 1 receives initial deposits of £100 million from the general public. It keeps £40 million for liquidity purposes and on-lends £60 million. This £60 million when spent is redeposited with Bank 2; Bank 2 keeps £24 million as part of its reserve assets and on-lends £36 million; and so on. Thus, as a result of an initial deposit of £100 million, the banking system has been able to 'create' an additional £150 million of new deposits.

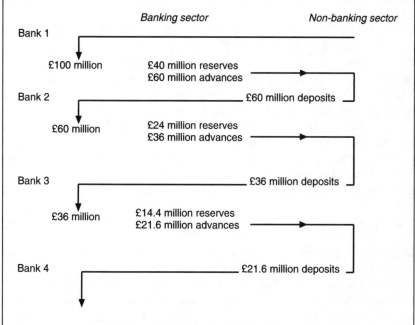

Outcome: as a result of the original deposit of £100 million a further £150 million of deposits are created (£60 million + £36 million + £21.6 million, etc.).

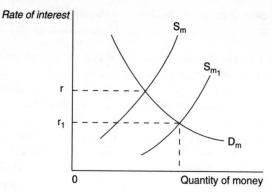

Figure 1.20 Equilibrium interest rate

1.7.1.3 The interest rate

Interest is defined in economic analysis as a charge made for borrowing money in the form of a loan. The *interest rate* is the particular amount of interest which a household or business borrower is required to pay to a lender for borrowing a particular sum of money to finance spending on consumption and investment.

The level of interest rates is determined by the supply of and demand for finance in the money market. The cheaper the cost of borrowing money the more money will be demanded by households and businesses. The higher the rate of interest the greater the supply of loanable funds. The 'equilibrium' rate of interest is determined by the intersection of the demand for (D_m) and supply of (S_m), loanable funds – interest rate O_r in Figure 1.20. In theory, the monetary authorities can control the rate of interest by changes in the money supply. If the money supply is increased from S_m to S_{m1}, the effect will be to lower the equilibrium rate of interest from O_r to O_{r1} and through the rate of interest the level of total spending (aggregate demand) in the economy. (See Figure 1.21.)

1.7.2 Linkages between the real and money sides of the economy

Money is used to finance spending on real goods and services. The 'link' between the money aggregates and the real aggregates in the economy can be viewed in two ways. The Keynesian position is that the link is indirect, as depicted in Figure 1.21. In brief, an increase in the money supply (from OM to OM$_1$ in Figure 1.21(a) brings about a fall in the rate of interest (from Or to Or$_1$), which results in an increase in planned investment from OI to OI$_1$ (Figure 1.21 (b)). The rise in investment, in turn, increases

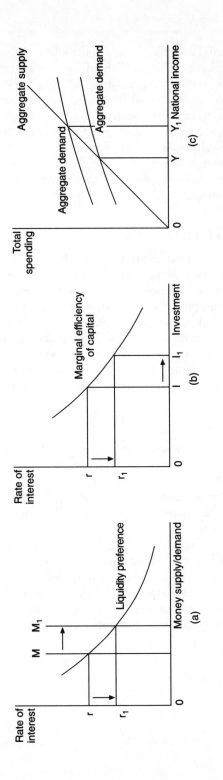

Figure 1.21 Money supply and spending linkages

aggregate demand and, via the multiplier effect, raises national income from OY to OY_1 (Figure 1.21(c)). The fall in interest rates can also be shown to increase consumption expenditure. (The lower cost of borrowing encourages people to use more loan finance to buy cars, televisions, etc.)

By contrast, monetarists contend that the link is much more direct. In brief, an increase in the money supply feeds directly into an increase in demand for final goods and services, and not just for investment goods. This proposition is based on the assumption that when households and businesses have more money than they need to hold they will spend the excess on goods and services.

1.8 CONCLUSION

This chapter has aimed at bringing together the basic theoretical tools that underpin the study of macroeconomics. It stresses that an economy as depicted by the circular flow of income is made up of many macroeconomic variables (consumption, investment, savings, government expenditure, taxation, exports and imports being just a few) which provide the building blocks for understanding the workings of the economy. The high degree of interdependence between many of these variables not only makes understanding the functioning of the economy more difficult, but makes the role of the policy-maker much more complex. This is the issue we turn to next.

QUESTIONS

1 Explain the nature and significance of the following components of national income: (a) consumption expenditure, (b) investment expenditure and (c) government expenditure.
2 Explain what is meant by the concept 'equilibrium level of national income'. What factors might cause a shift in the equilibrium level of national income?
3 What is the 'multiplier' and how does the multiplier explain changes in the equilibrium level of national income?
4 Describe and comment on the main phases of the 'business cycle'. What causes economic activity to fluctuate in this way?
5 Compare and contrast the Keynesian and monetarist views on the linkages between changes in the money supply and the level of spending in the economy.

Chapter 2

Macroeconomic objectives and the management of the economy

Macroeconomic policy is primarily concerned with attempting to intervene and change the functioning of the economy in order to improve its performance. As such it implicitly assumes that the economy, left to regulate itself, will not settle at the optimum outcome. Recognition that it is possible, at least in principle, to improve the macroeconomic performance of the economy is only the beginning of macroeconomic policy. It then becomes necessary to specify the objectives/targets of policy more precisely and to determine their order of priority in the event of possible conflict.

However, even if it is possible to decide upon one's policy objectives and rank them in order of importance, the policy-maker is then faced with the need to specify which policy instruments, among a multitude of possibilities, are desirable to achieve those policy objectives. While in some cases genuine alternative policy instruments may exist, it is more likely that the choice of policy instruments will in part reflect differences in the way the policy-maker views the functioning of the economy. In essence this may revolve around the divergent theoretical stances (e.g. Keynesian versus monetarist) which policy-makers adhere to.

To summarise, macroeconomic policy involves three initial steps:

1 The determination of the policy objectives, and, given some conflict between objectives, their ranking in order of importance.
2 The formulation of policies (instruments) which are consistent with attaining the aforementioned objectives. This stance should be underpinned by a relevant and formal theoretical structure.
3 Some elementary cost–benefit calculations of policy effectiveness to ensure that the net benefits outweigh the costs involved.

2.1 MACROECONOMIC OBJECTIVES

2.1.1 Objectives

Although considerable differences of opinion exist with regard to the relative ranking of policy objectives there exists a remarkable consensus upon what broadly constitute the main macroeconomic objectives.

1 *Full employment.* Unemployment is to be avoided because it results in output 'lost' to the economy; resources are left idle and the country's actual GNP is below its potential GNP. In addition, unemployment reduces the incomes of former workers, increases poverty and leads to demoralisation among the unemployed.
2 *Price stability.* Inflation is regarded as a major source of concern because it confers few benefits but imposes major costs on society. For example, people on fixed incomes suffer a fall in their standard of living; debtors gain at the expense of creditors as the real value of debts or loans falls; and the country's exports become uncompetitive in international trade.
3 *Balance of payments.* The balance of payments objective is identified as the desire for long-run equality between international payments and receipts. It arises from the awareness that there are costs associated with an imbalance between payments and receipts. The nature of the costs involved, however, will depend upon whether the exchange rate regime is fixed or flexible (see Chapter 6).
4 *Economic growth.* Increased real income per head permits the increased consumption of all goods and hence an increase in economic welfare. Second, with natural increases in the labour force combined with a tendency for economic activity to become increasingly capital-intensive, economic growth becomes a necessary prerequisite for the maintenance of full employment and for the elimination of the social tensions which accompany unemployment. There are also costs involved in uncontrolled growth: congestion, depletion of natural resources, problems of urbanisation, pollution and ecological damage.

2.1.2 Interdependences

Whilst we represent the above four objectives as being independent, in reality the objectives tend to be interdependent and in some cases incompatible. This then requires governments to prioritise their objectives, focusing on one or two objectives at a time. The 'Phillips curve' is often used to illustrate the policy dilemma facing governments. In brief, the Phillips curve (based on empirical work by the British economist A. W. Phillips) depicts the relationship between the level of unemployment and the rate of change of money wages and, by inference, the rate of change of prices (that is, inflation). In Figure 2.1 point X is the 'non-accelerating

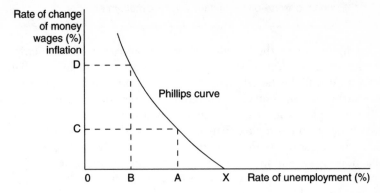

Figure 2.1 Phillips curve

inflation rate of unemployment' (NAIRU), which is the level of unemployment that is consistent with stable prices. A fall in unemployment (from A to B) due to an increase in aggregate demand brings about an acceleration in the rate of increase of money wages (from C to D), reflecting employers' greater willingness to grant wage increases as the demand for their products expands. By contrast, a fall in demand and rising unemployment lead to a slowing down in the rate of increase of money wages. The 'curve' thus suggests that there is a 'trade-off' between unemployment and demand-pull inflation – should the government seek to stimulate the economy to remove unemployment, excess demand will be created which will stoke up inflationary pressures; the 'price' of achieving full employment is thus a higher rate of inflation. By the same token, pursuit of price stability requires a higher level of unemployment (see Box 2.1).

The Phillips curve relationship has received much empirical support. However, it is rejected by many economists as simplistic, reflecting not some immutable 'given' state of the economy but rather the use of insufficiently sensitive control instruments. They argue that to use only conventional fiscal and monetary measures to tackle both unemployment and inflation is unduly limiting. What is required is a broader range of instruments which can be used in *combination* to achieve multiple objectives. To illustrate this point in the specific context of the Phillips curve it could be suggested that *supply-side* measures to improve the *flexibility* of labour markets should be used to bring down the underlying (NAIRU) rate of unemployment, while simultaneously conventional fiscal measures should be used to curb inflationary tendencies – that is, policy should be directed to shifting the Phillips curve inwards towards the origin, as shown in Figure 2.2.

Assuming that it is possible to define adequately the policy objectives and their order of priority in the event of conflict, the next step is to decide how the government will achieve them. Basically the government has at its

Box 2.1 Economic trade-offs: inflation and unemployment

The figure shows the so-called 'sacrifice ratio', the extra unemployment which is created when governments attempt to bring inflation down. It will be noted that there are marked differences between countries in this respect. This raises the question why, for example, the unemployment cost of reducing inflation in the UK and Spain has been so much higher than in Sweden and the USA. The answer, studies suggest, is that Sweden has a highly centralised wage bargaining system in which employers and unions determine what wage increases the country 'can afford' without prejudicing employment. In the USA 10 million new jobs have been created in the low-pay, non-unionised service sector. Spain and the UK (despite various trade union reforms to make the labour market more 'flexible') are characterised by relatively powerful plant-level unions and unco-ordinated, decentralised wage rounds which make it difficult for employers to reduce their wage settlements below the 'going rate'. Unfortunately, in the UK's case, wage rates have continued to rise (above the underlying rate of productivity growth, and despite recession) and this has led – to use Chancellor Lawson's famous phrase – to labour 'pricing itself out of jobs'.

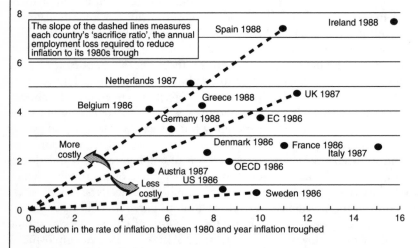

Unemployment cost of reducing inflation, 1980–8: annual average increase in the unemployment rate. The increase in the unemployment rate over the disinflation period is computed as the average of the annual deviations of the actual unemployment rate from that observed in 1980, when the annual inflation rate peaked

Source: OECD estimates, *Financial Times,* 23 March 1992

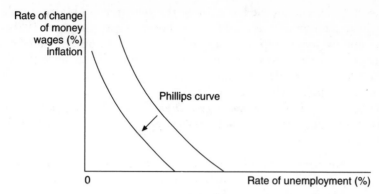

Figure 2.2 Shifting the Phillips curve

disposal a number of devices called policy instruments, such as government expenditure, taxation levels, and interest rates, which it directly controls and so can fix their value at whatever level it believes is necessary to maximise its objectives. The next section outlines these various policy instruments.

2.2 ECONOMIC POLICY APPROACHES

There are various ways in which policy instruments can influence macro-economic objectives. Three broad approaches to economic policy may be identified:

1 *Direct controls*, using policy instruments which operate directly on the goal variable. For example, an incomes policy restricting wage settlements to no more than the rate of inflation sends a direct message to all employers and employees about future wage bargaining and thus directly affects public expectations about the future rate of inflation.
2 '*Keynesian*'. Keynesian policy uses less direct, intermediate, policy instruments to affect markets. Keynesian policy approaches normally involve two stages: the government uses a policy instrument to influence the goods market, which in turn influences the goal variable. For example, if the goal is to lower inflation, a government may adopt a policy instrument (increased taxation) which will lower the level of demand in the goods market and thus affect the goal variable, lower demand-pull inflation.

    Fiscal policy is the best known form of Keynesian policy, and is defined to encompass any change in the level, composition or timing of government expenditure or any change in the burden, structure or frequency of tax payments. Given that the level of government expenditure and tax receipts determines the basic size of the government's budget surplus or deficit, the size of the public sector borrowing requirement (PSBR) is commonly looked upon as an indicator of the government's fiscal stance. Such a view, however, must be carefully qualified, since the size of the PSBR will vary in response to changing income levels quite independently of policy changes (see later).

3 *Financial policy (including monetary policy).* Financial policy is the most indirect of the three economic policy approaches. Financial policy involves three stages:

(a) The monetary authorities (usually the central bank) change one of their potential monetary instruments in order to create a particular disturbance in the financial system.
(b) This disturbance in the financial system will lead to a change in either the price of money (interest rates) or the quantity of money (the size of the money supply) in financial markets. This variable is called the intermediate target.
(c) The effect of a change either in the price or the quantity of money in the financial markets is to influence the real sector, that is, the goods market or the labour market. In this way the government will hope to achieve its final target, or goal variable.

Take the example of inflation again. To use financial policy to curb inflation, the monetary authorities may increase the value of deposits that banks need to deposit with the central bank. The effect of this is that commercial banks have fewer liquid reserves and are less able to lend money to prospective customers; thus the overall quantity of money in the economy will decline (the intermediate target). The repercussions of these changes in the financial markets will then be reflected in the goods market. Less money in the economy leads to fewer consumer and capital goods being bought and thus to lower demand. In turn lower demand counters the threat of demand-pull inflation.

2.3 CONSTRAINTS ON MACROECONOMIC POLICY

Both the objectives and the instruments of macroeconomic policy have been outlined. To complete our 'model' of macroeconomic policy we need to consider the major constraints which might inhibit policy formation.

1 *International agreements.* Agreements or commitments to such bodies as the International Monetary Fund (IMF), the General Agreement on Tariffs and Trade (GATT) and the European Union (EU) will circumscribe the ability of governments to alter tariffs, quotas and taxes, and may also imply a commitment to particular money supply targets.

2 *Non-macroeconomic objectives.* Other objectives of policy may conflict with the attainment of macroeconomic goals. For example, the belief in the desirability of a *laissez-faire* economy and the maintenance of a non-interventionist stance may inhibit the adoption of some macroeconomic measures.

3 *Legislative sanction.* Virtually any macroeconomic policy with a sizeable impact will require legislative approval. The force of this constraint, and the extent to which it influences the modification of policy proposals, is determined by the relevant political institutions and systems of government in any particular country. For example, in the UK the government's annual proposed changes in tax rates and government expenditure are presented by the Chancellor of the Exchequer to the House of Commons but must then be scrutinised by various sub-committees of the House of Commons before being passed by the House of Commons and the House of Lords as the Finance Act for that year.

4 *Uncertainty.* Perhaps the single most important constraint stems from the existence of uncertainty as to the outcome of any given policy measure. Imperfect information may dissuade the policy-maker from adopting certain policies which seemed optimal, because of the risk of the policy proving to be wrong. Instead the policy-maker may adopt alternative, more cautious policies which minimise the risk of an unacceptable outcome.

The case for macroeconomic policy has been established – at least in principle – and the problems facing the individuals charged with the decision-making process have been examined. The next issue to address is how to evaluate the success or otherwise of the macroeconomic policies followed by the government. Obviously the leading indicator is going to be the economic performance of a country.

It is difficult to be categoric about economic performances since the measurement of performance tends to be subjective and complicated when multiple goals are being pursued and constrained by 'external' forces. For example, what is deemed to be an 'acceptable' rate of inflation by the incumbent government of a country may not be considered to be so by opposition parties in that country, nor by other countries' governments. Then there is the matter of trade-offs. For some countries 'success' may be measured in terms of a low inflation rate even though it may be associated with high rates of unemployment, while for other countries a low unemployment rate may be the priority even if it means sacrificing other objectives. For example, the UK pursued an economic strategy through the 1980s and early 1990s aimed at bringing inflation down to 0–2 per cent. The restrictions this involved in checking the growth of demand adversely affected employment, the number of persons unemployed rising from under 2 million at the start of the 1980s to over 3 million in 1992. Studies of the inflation/unemployment trade-off have indicated that a reduction of 2 per cent in the UK inflation rate has required unemployment to rise by 1 per cent (see Box 2.1). Thus 'success' is a relative phenomenon rather than an absolute one and needs to be looked at 'in the round'.

Moreover, 'success' is bounded by the practicalities of the situation and the inability to exercise full control over economic events, which are often unpredictable. For example, oil-importing countries' anti-inflationary policies were totally blown off course by the quadrupling of oil prices by the OPEC countries in 1973 and a further rise in 1979. The oil exporting countries were able to 'transfer' world income to themselves via the oil price increase. This raises the issue that the 'success' of one country or group of countries may be at the expense of others. Japan, for example, has a $70 billion trade surplus, mainly with the USA and the European Union bloc. Since international trade is a multilateral process, ideally there should be a mutual responsibility to ensure that the gains from trade are shared around rather than pre-empted by one country. The same kind of argument applies to the responsibility of the richer developed countries to help developing countries by allowing market access to the developing countries' exports and by providing economic aid packages to assist those countries' development programmes.

Finally, it is to be noted that a country's performance can vary over time both generally and in respect of specific elements. Table 2.1 presents comparative performance data for a number of industrial countries. Readers are invited to draw their own inferences from the data. In the last analysis it might be suggested that the growth in *income per head* is perhaps the best measure of success, since it relates to an improvement in the average economic standard of living of the populace. (See also Box 1.1.) Even this measure, however, is flawed to some extent because, in practice, the *distribution* of income can be very unequal in some countries and non-monetary elements of lifestyle quality differ as between different people.

2.4 DEMAND MANAGEMENT: AN OVERVIEW

In this section we focus on the role of demand management in stabilising the performance of the economy. We then proceed to explain in more detail the two major components of demand management (fiscal and monetary policy), how they operate and different views about their effectiveness.

2.4.1 Counter-cyclical demand management

Demand management has traditionally been used to moderate or eliminate fluctuations in the level of economic activity associated with the business cycle. The general objective of demand management is to 'fine-tune' aggregate demand so that it is neither deficient relative to potential gross national

Table 2.1 Economic indicators, selected countries, 1976-93

Country	1976–85	1986	1987	1988	1989	1990	1991	1992	1993
Real GDP (% change)									
USA	2.9	2.9	3.1	3.9	2.5	1.2	–0.7	2.6	3.0
Japan	4.2	2.6	4.1	6.2	4.7	4.8	4.3	1.1	0.1
Germany	2.2	2.3	1.5	3.7	3.6	5.7	1.0	2.1	–1.2
UK	1.9	4.3	4.8	5.0	2.2	0.4	–2.2	–0.6	1.9
Unemployment (% rate)									
USA	7.5	7.0	6.2	5.5	5.3	5.5	6.7	7.4	6.8
Japan	2.3	2.8	2.8	2.5	2.3	2.1	2.1	2.2	2.5
Germany	5.2	7.6	7.6	7.6	6.8	6.2	6.7	7.7	8.9
UK	7.1	11.1	10.0	8.0	6.3	5.8	8.1	9.8	10.3
Inflation (% change)									
USA	7.2	1.9	3.7	4.1	4.8	5.4	4.2	3.0	3.0
Japan	4.7	0.9	0.1	0.7	2.3	2.8	3.3	1.7	1.3
Germany	4.0	–0.1	0.2	1.3	2.8	2.7	4.5	4.9	4.7
UK	10.5	3.6	4.1	4.6	5.9	8.1	6.8	4.7	3.0
Current account (US$ billion)									
USA		–150	–167	–127	–102	–92	–8	–66	–109
Japan		86	87	80	57	36	73	118	131
Germany		40	46	51	58	47	–20	–25	–22
UK		–1	–8	–30	–37	–33	–14	–18	–16

Source: IMF, *World Economic Outlook*, 1994

product (thereby avoiding a loss of output and unemployment) nor over-full (thereby avoiding inflation).

An unregulated economy will tend to go through periods of depression and boom, as indicated by the continuous line in Figure 2.3. Governments generally try to smooth out such fluctuations by stimulating aggregate demand when the economy is depressed and reducing aggregate demand when the economy is overheating. Ideally, the government would wish to manage aggregate demand so that it grows exactly in line with the underlying growth of potential GNP, the dashed line in Figure 2.3, exactly offsetting the amplitude of troughs and peaks of the business cycle.

However, two main problems exist: (1) the establishment of the correct timing of such an injection or withdrawal; (2) the establishment of the correct magnitude of an injection or withdrawal into the economy (to counter depressions and booms). With perfect timing and magnitude the economy would follow the trend line of potential GNP.

A number of stages are involved in applying a stabilisation policy as shown in the figure. For example, at time period 0 the onset of a recession/depression would be reflected in a downturn in economic activity, though delays in the collection of economic statistics mean that it is often time period 1 before data become available about unemployment rates, etc. Once sufficient data are to hand, the authorities are able to diagnose the nature

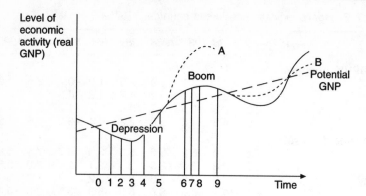

Figure 2.3 Counter-cyclical demand management; time period 0 recession begins, 1 statistics available, 2 diagnose problem, 3 plan intervention, 4 intervention, 5 measures begin to affect economy, 6 forecast of recession, 7 plan intervention, 8 intervene, 9 government measures begin to affect the economy

of the problem (time period 2) and plan appropriate intervention such as tax cuts or increases in government expenditure (time period 3). At time period 4 the agreed measures are then implemented, though it may take some time before the measures have an effect on consumption, investment, imports, etc. If the timing of these activities is incorrect, then the authorities may find that they have stimulated the economy at a time when it was already beginning to recover from recession/depression, so that their actions have served to exacerbate the original fluctuation (dotted line A in Figure 2.3). The authorities could also exacerbate the fluctuation (dotted line A) if they get the magnitude wrong by injecting too much purchasing power into the economy, creating excess demand.

If the authorities can get the timing and magnitude correct, then they should be able to counterbalance the effects of recession/depression and follow the path indicated as dotted line B in Figure 2.3. Reducing the intensity of the recession in this way requires the authorities to forecast accurately the onset of recession some time ahead, perhaps while the economy is still buoyant (time period 6). On the basis of these forecasts the authorities can then plan their intervention to stimulate the economy (time period 7) and activate the measures (time period 8), so that the measures begin to take effect and stimulate the economy as economic activity levels fall (time period 9). Box 2.2 outlines the essentials of macroeconomic forecasting.

Much government action is inaccurate in timing and magnitude owing to the institutional and behavioural complexities of the economy. Where the government has not been successful in adequately eradicating such peaks and troughs in the business cycle, it is frequently accused of having stop–go policies, that is, of stimulating a recovering economy which then 'overheats', and subsequently withdrawing too much at the wrong time, 'braking' too

Box 2.2 Macroeconomic forecasting

Macroeconomic forecasting is the process of making predictions about future general economic conditions as a basis for decision-making by government. Various forecasting methods can be used to estimate future economic conditions:

1 Survey techniques involving the use of interviews or mailed questionnaires can be used to monitor and predict changes in business or consumer confidence about economic prospects. Since expectations affect businesspeople's investment plans and consumer spending plans such data can be very useful.
2 Extrapolation methods can be used to predict future economic trends from past economic data. These methods implicitly assume that the historical relationships which have held in the past will continue to hold in the future, without examining causal relationships between the variables involved. Techniques such as moving averages can be used to analyse and extrapolate time series of economic variables like consumer spending, though they are generally unable to predict sharp upturns or downturns in the economic variables.
3 Barometric forecasts can be used to predict the future value of economic variables from the present values of particular statistical indicators which have a consistent relationship with those economic variables. Such leading indicators as business capital investment plans and new house-building starts can be used as a barometer for forecasting values like economic activity levels or consumption expenditure and they can be useful for predicting sharp changes in those values.
4 Econometric methods can be used to predict future values of an economic variable by examining other variables which are causally related to it. Econometric models link variables in the form of equations which can be estimated statistically and then used as a basis for forecasting. Judgement has to be exercised in identifying the independent variables which causally affect the dependent variable to be forecast. For example, in order to predict future consumer expenditure (C) we would formulate an equation linking it to disposable income (Y):

$$C = a + bY$$

then use past data to estimate the regression coefficients a and b, for example:

$$C = 200 + 0.8Y$$

Econometric models may consist of just one equation like this, but often in complex economic situations the independent variables in one equation are themselves influenced by other variables, so that many equations may be necessary to represent all the causal relationships involved. For example, the macroeconomic forecasting model used by the British Treasury to predict future economic activity levels has over 600 equations.

No forecasting method will generate completely accurate predictions, so when making any forecast we must allow for a *margin of error* in that forecast, recognising that there is a range of possible future outcomes centred around the forecast value. Forecasters need to exercise judgement in predicting future economic conditions, both in choosing which forecasting methods to use and in combining information from different forecasts.

hard. In these cases, far from stabilising the economy, intervention can be highly destabilising.

Figure 2.4 traces the typical sequence of effects upon companies of counter-cyclical demand policies, specifically a government squeeze on aggregate demand through higher taxes and a tight monetary policy. The initial effect is often to curtail consumption spending, leading to a build-up of unsold stock by businesses and consequent pressure upon company liquidity and profitability. As businesses respond to lower demand by cutting back on output (and employment), stocks begin to return to normal levels. As companies operate their plant below capacity they will curtail their investment plans. The effects upon business performance will also affect

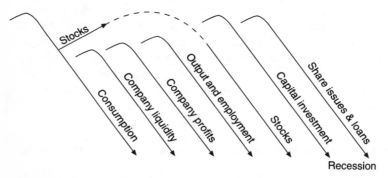

Figure 2.4 Effect on companies of a government squeeze: 1 higher taxes, 2 tight money

financial markets, leading to a decline in new share issues and loans and falling share prices. The combined effect of all these changes is to move the economy towards a lower level of economic activity and towards a recession. Though all the economic variables described above move broadly downward in response to a government squeeze they do not always move in this particular sequence. Sometimes a government squeeze has an immediate effect upon business confidence, leading to a rapid and immediate decline in capital investment.

2.4.2 Medium-term demand management

Because of the problems associated with short-term demand management some economists, most notably those of the monetarist school, have advocated a longer time frame in the application of macro policies. Specifically, monetarists recommend that the broad aim of macro policy should be to strike a 'balance' between the growth of *money aggregates* (particularly the money supply) and the growth of *real aggregates* (particularly real potential gross national product) over the longer term. The objective is broadly to balance purchasing power (aggregate demand) and the underlying capacity of the economy to produce goods and services over time. This approach was taken up in the UK in the 1980s in the form of the 'Medium Term Financial Strategy' (MTFS). The MTFS set out a target range for the growth of the money supply and target values for the public sector borrowing requirement (see next section) expressed as a percentage of gross domestic product. The first UK MTFS was introduced in 1980, covered a period of five years ahead, and was extended at annual intervals to provide a set of rolling plans for the economy. Similarly, medium-term targeting of the money supply is a key feature of economic policy in Germany (see Box 2.3).

Controlling the economy on a medium-term basis can be just as problematic as short-term intervention. In the case of the UK, the MTFS was frequently blown off course by 'technical' problems associated with controlling the money supply and the depth of the recession, which caused public sector borrowing limits to be exceeded. For some countries, the exposure of the domestic economy to *international* influences is a further major factor affecting the 'controllability' of the situation by the domestic authorities.

2.5 FISCAL POLICY

Fiscal policy was widely used by governments of the industrialised countries throughout the 1950s, 1960s and 1970s, though it received less emphasis in the 1980s. However, there is growing realisation that an active fiscal policy has some role to play in regulating the macroeconomic environment, especially in conjunction with monetary policy. (See Box 2.4.)

Box 2.3 Money supply targeting in Germany

Control of the money supply plays a key role in the application of German economic policy. The Bundesbank uses 'rolling' targets for the growth in the broad money supply measure M3 (notes and coin in circulation and bank deposits – see Table 2.4). A target band for M3 growth was set at 3.5–5.5 per cent for 1991 to 1993 but revised upwards to 4.5–6.5 per cent in January 1993 when the early target was exceeded owing to an acceleration of private bank lending and a strong increase in public sector borrowing from the banks. This surge in money supply growth made the Bundesbank (which, unlike the Bank of England, makes its own decisions independently of the governing political party) reluctant to reduce interest rates, a major factor in the European Monetary System's 'French franc crisis' of July 1993 (see Chapter 10).

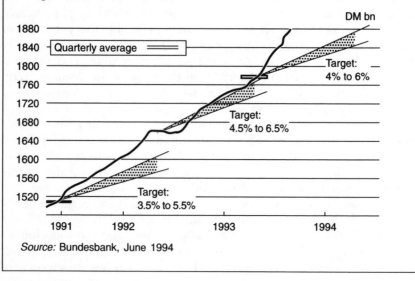

Source: Bundesbank, June 1994

Box 2.4 Recent developments in fiscal conditions in the UK, Japan and the USA

UK

The deepening recession of the early 1990s led to a massive increase in the size of the public sector borrowing requirement (PSBR) as a result of reduced taxation receipts and increased spending on unemployment benefit, etc. The PSBR totalled £37 billion in 1992–3 and £48 billion in 1993-4. (See Figure 2.6). In 1991 the standard rate of value added tax (VAT) was increased from 15 per cent to 17.5 per cent, while in 1992 the government introduced public spending ceilings on non-cyclical expenditure. Some stimulus was given to private investment to boost the economy – corporation tax was reduced from 35 per cent to 33 per cent in 1991 and there was an increase in capital allowances for investment from 25 per cent to 40 per cent in 1992. In March 1993 8 per cent VAT was introduced on domestic fuel and most excise taxes were increased by 5 per cent while the November 1993 budget imposed a freeze on public sector running costs until 1997, national insurance contributions were increased from 9 per cent to 10 per cent and it was announced that VAT on domestic fuel was to be raised in 1994–5 (since abandoned).

Overall, UK fiscal policy has been aimed primarily at restoring budget balance over the medium term, leaving monetary policies to stimulate economic recovery.

Japan
See p.54 and Table 2.3.

USA
In 1990 the Budget Reconciliation Act was passed, which was intended to bring about a massive reduction in the federal budget deficit through limitations on public spending programmes. Several tax increases were imposed in 1991: excise duties were increased and a luxury goods tax was introduced. In the event the budget deficit increased in 1991 and 1992 as recession took its toll. Budget deficit reduction has continued to remain a priority, with major cuts on the spending side (in particular, public health care programmes and defence) and tax rises in 1993 on high-income earners. In 1993 the Clinton administration drew up a programme of spending restrictions aimed at reducing the budget deficit to some $206 billion in 1997 (around 2.7 per cent of GDP).

Fiscal balances of central government (percentage of GDP)

Country	1986	1987	1988	1989	1990	1991	1992	1993
UK	–2.4	–1.3	1.1	1.2	–0.8	–2.0	–6.9	–9.2
Japan	–3.2	–2.2	–1.3	–1.2	–0.5	–0.2	–1.6	–2.6
USA	–3.4	–2.5	–2.0	–1.5	–2.9	–3.6	–4.6	–3.5

Source: IMF, World Economic Outlook, 1994.

The re-emergence of an active fiscal policy is in part recognition of the major impact fiscal policy can have on aggregate demand and output. For example, central and local government together buy about one-quarter of the total output of goods and services in the UK, while total taxes amount to more than one-third of GNP. On the other hand fiscal policy requires strict management of the government's finances. In particular deficits are frequent, and most governments are normally indebted to the private sector and to foreigners. By 1990 the UK national debt was well above £100 billion, or about £2,000 per person. As we shall see below, this concern has often implied that fiscal policy should purely be tailored towards balancing the budget over the business cycle.

In the following section we explore the major aspects of fiscal policy. First, we analyse both the possibilities and the difficulties of using fiscal policy for stabilisation. Second, we note the significance of the government's budget deficit, especially the size of the deficit and how much we should worry about it. Finally, we look at the issue of national debt, which builds up when the budget is in deficit. Notably we are concerned with how the national debt should be serviced and its implications for the money supply and inflation.

A useful starting point in introducing fiscal policy as a demand management instrument is to look at the government's budget.

2.5.1 The government's budgetary position

The government's budgetary position not only identifies the broad options open to the government in applying fiscal policy but also places it in the context of the government's wider economic and social obligations in a (mixed) economy. The government is itself a major user of economic resources and a supplier of both non-marketed goods and services (for example defence, health and education) and marketed goods and services (for example, in some countries, gas, electricity, railways, etc.). The provision of such goods and services requires the government to adopt longer-term planning commitments which go beyond the traditional short-term preoccupation with 'fine-tuning' the economy as part of demand management. Thus the application of fiscal policy may be constrained to a greater or lesser degree by the role of the government as an economic actor in its own right, often competing with the private sector for the use of limited economic resources (see Section 2.5.6).

By way of illustration Table 2.2 gives details of the UK government's budget position for 1992–3, showing the main sources of revenue and the main expenditure categories. The chief sources of current revenue are taxation, principally income and expenditure taxes, and national insurance contributions. The main current outgoings of government expenditure are the provision of goods and services (principally wage payments to health, education

Table 2.2 UK government budget, 1992–3 (£ million)

Current receipts		225,738
of which:		
Taxes on income	(73,070)	
Taxes on expenditure	(91,361)	
National Insurance	(38,503)	
Current expenditure		257,390
of which:		
Spending on provision of goods and services	(138,224)	
Transfer payments	(71,910)	
Debt interest	(18,446)	
Capital receipts (taxes on capital, etc.)		2,627
Capital expenditure		19,639
of which:		
Capital formation	(11,070)	
Overall budget deficit		–48,664

Source: UK national income accounts, 1994.

and other public sector employees) and transfer payments (old age pensions, unemployment benefit, sick pay, etc.). Capital receipts accrue mainly from taxes on capital, while a substantial proportion of capital expenditure represents fixed capital formation (investment by central government, local authorities and nationalised industries in plant and equipment).

2.5.2 Effect of fiscal policy

In general, the government may use fiscal policy by varying the level of its expenditure and/or its tax revenue to influence the behaviour of the economy. More formally fiscal policy may be defined as any measure that alters the level, timing or composition of government spending, and/or the level, timing or structure of tax payments.

2.5.2.1 Government expenditure

The government can use changes in its own expenditure to affect spending levels; for example, a cut in current purchases of products or in capital investment by the government serves to reduce total spending in the economy.

Changes in government expenditure have a direct effect on aggregate demand and therefore on output and employment. In general, an increase in government expenditure leads to an increase in equilibrium output equal to the increase in government expenditure times the multiplier. However, it is not easy to manipulate government expenditure in such a way as to fine-tune the economy. One reason is that it is difficult to bring about changes in spending quickly. Many government expenditure programmes take a long time to plan and complete. Variations in government expenditure are undertaken in the context of a much longer time horizon than that envisaged for short-run stabilisation policies.

2.5.2.2 Net taxes

The fiscal authorities (for example the Treasury in the UK) can employ a number of taxation measures to control aggregate demand or spending: direct taxes on individuals (income tax) and companies (corporation tax) can be increased if spending needs to be reduced, for example, to control inflation. Alternatively, spending can be reduced by increasing indirect taxes: an increase in value-added taxes on products in general, or an increase in excise duties on particular products such as petrol and cigarettes will, by increasing their price, lead to a reduction in purchasing power. (See Box 2.5.)

Boxes 2.5 *Types of tax*

Direct taxes

Direct taxes are taxes which are levied on the income and wealth received by households and businesses. The main forms of direct taxes in the UK are:

1 *Income tax.* A tax levied on the income (wages, rent, dividends) received by individuals. Income tax is usually applied on a progressive scale, that is, the higher the individual's income the greater the amount of tax paid. In the UK, for example, there are currently three income tax bands, income up to £3,000 being taxed at 20 per cent, the next £20,700 of income being taxed at 25 per cent and any income above £23,700 being taxed at 40 per cent. The income tax rate is important to households in so far as it determines the size of their *disposable income*, and hence their ability to purchase products.

2 *Corporation tax.* A tax levied on the profits earned by businesses. The standard rate of corporation tax in the UK is currently 33 per cent. The level of corporation tax is important to businesses in so far as it determines the amount of after-tax profit which is available to pay out in dividends to shareholders or to *reinvest* in the business (ie. profits are an important means of financing investment in plant and equipment).

3 *National insurance contributions.* Payments made by businesses and

their employees, on a (currently) two-thirds and one-third basis, respectively, up to a specified maximum limit. As with income tax, national insurance contributions affect the size of individuals' disposable income.

4 *Wealth tax.* A tax levied on an individual's private assets when those assets are transferred to the person's beneficiaries. In the UK *inheritance* tax is the current means of taxing wealth.

Indirect taxes
Indirect or 'spending' taxes are taxes which are levied on goods and services (that is, incorporated into the product's final price). The main forms of indirect taxes are:

1 *Value-added tax (or sales tax).* A tax levied on the value added to a product (that is, the difference between the selling price of the product and the cost of inputs in producing it). Value-added tax (VAT) rates may be applied uniformly at a single rate on all products, or applied on a discretionary basis, with VAT being levied at different rates on different groups of products.

2 *Excise duty.* A tax levied on a *particular* product, usually one (such as tobacco, drink) for which demand is highly price-inelastic.

Direct taxes are *progressive* in so far as the amount paid, as noted above, will vary according to the income of the taxpayer, while indirect taxes are *regressive* in so far as the same amount is paid by each consumer irrespective of whether they are rich or poor.

Unlike government expenditure, tax rates (both direct and indirect) can be varied fairly quickly and have therefore been the main instrument of fiscal short-run stabilisation policies. A reduction in tax rates (on income) will increase people's disposable income and thus lead to an increase consumer spending. This increase will be followed by further rounds of spending, leading to a multiplier effect on output and employment. For the UK it is generally believed that the income tax multiplier is approximately 1.5, implying that an initial increase in after-tax income of £1 will eventually generate £1.50 of additional demand.

Overall, indirect tax changes have the advantage over direct taxes that they affect consumer spending quickly. It is also argued that indirect taxes do not affect the incentive to work, since they leave the workers more disposable income which they can choose to save or spend. However, indirect taxes are regressive and bear more heavily on the poor. On the other hand direct taxes are more equitable (progressive) but often provide a disincentive to work, especially if the tax rate as a proportion of gross income is high.

As the above discussion emphasises, a decrease in government spending and an increase in taxes (a withdrawal from the circular flow of national income) reduce aggregate demand and through the multiplier process serve to reduce inflationary pressures when the economy is 'overheating'. By contrast, an increase in government spending and/or a decrease in taxes (an injection into the circular flow of national income) stimulates aggregate demand and via the multiplier effect creates additional jobs to counteract unemployment. Figure 2.5 shows the effect of an increase in government expenditure and/or cuts in taxes in raising aggregate demand from AD to AD_1 and national income from OY to OY_1. It also shows the effect of a decrease in government expenditure and/or increases in taxes, lowering aggregate demand from AD to AD_2 and national income from OY to OY_2.

Recent fiscal initiatives in Japan provide a useful illustration of these demand management techniques. Japan has resorted to an orthodox Keynesian 'pump priming' programme to revitalise its flagging economy. In August 1992 a ¥10,700 billion stimulus was applied (see Table 2.3). consisting of increases in public investment and loans to private industry. A further package was introduced in April 1993 worth ¥13,050 billion, again consisting of increased public investment and private sector loans. The continuing weakness of the economy in 1994, however, led the authorities to apply yet another fiscal stimulus: income tax cuts totalling ¥5,500 billion were implemented in 1994, to be followed by further cuts of ¥5,500 billion in each of the years 1995 and 1996.

2.5.3 Combined effects of adjusting government expenditure and taxation

A natural assumption stemming from the above discussion is that an equivalent increase in government expenditure and tax revenue would leave aggregate demand and equilibrium output unchanged. Yet if we compare the relative multiplier effects of an increase in government expenditure with

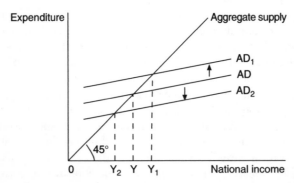

Figure 2.5 Fiscal policy and aggregate demand

Table 2.3 Fiscal measures in Japan, 1992 and 1993 (¥ billion)

Measure	April 1993 measures	August 1992 measures
Increase in public investment		
Public works	4,170	4,450
Investment in education and social welfare	1,150	550
Investment by local government	3,500	2,800
Housing loans	1,800	800
	10,620	8,600
Lending by government-affiliated financial institutions		
Measures for small and medium-sized firms	1,910	1,200
Promotion of private equipment investment	520	900
	2,430	2,100
Total	13,050	10,700
Multiplier effect as % of GNP	2.6	2.4

Source: Ministry of Finance.

the multiplier effects of an increase in taxation (which exactly matches the increase in government expenditure) aggregate demand will actually increase.

Take, for example, a situation in which a £100 million increase in government expenditure is financed by a £100 million increase in tax revenue (taxes are increased). While government expenditure will in the first instance increase national income by the entire £100 million, in the latter case some part of consumers' reduced disposable income (because of higher taxes) will be matched by reduced saving, so that not all the £100 million will be removed from the circular flow of income in the first round of income changes. This notion helps explain the concept of the *balanced budget multiplier*, the idea that, because the multiplier effect of a change in government expenditure is greater than that of an equal change in tax, a balanced budget will have an expansionary effect on output and employment.

Therefore in discussing the impact of a particular budget programme it is important to take into account that changes in taxation and spending have different multiplier effects on the level of economic activity.

2.5.4 Measuring the stance of fiscal policy

As we have seen, governments attempt to influence aggregate demand and thus stabilise the level of economic activity by budget manipulation (adjusting government expenditure and taxation). This raises two questions. (1) What is meant by the government budget? (2) What implication does the size of the budget have for the stance of fiscal policy? Obviously, in planning policy some measure is needed to indicate the direction and impact of a particular budget programme in the economy.

2.5.4.1 The government budget

The budget balance equals total tax revenue minus total government spending. When the budget balance is in deficit (revenue is less than expenditure) fiscal policy is considered to be expansionary and the level of aggregate demand will increase. A budget surplus (revenue more than expenditure) is considered restrictive, and will result in a reduction in the level of aggregate demand. The state of the budget surplus or deficit is thus determined by three things: the tax rate, the level of government spending, and the level of income.

However, caution must be exercised in interpreting the actual budget balance (see Figure 2.6) as an indicator of the direction of policy, notably because its size can change for reasons that have nothing to do with fiscal policy. The budget balance depends not only upon the size of the government's fundamental spending and taxation plans (its underlying fiscal stance) but also on the level of economic activity and the rate of inflation.

Fluctuations in economic activity lead to movements in the budget balance. The budget deficit tends to increase in a recession as total tax revenues fall and social security payments rise in response to lower incomes and higher unemployment. By contrast, the budget deficit tends to fall during a boom as tax revenues rise and social security payments fall in response to higher incomes and lower unemployment. (These tendencies are often referred to as automatic, built-in, stabilisers because they act to

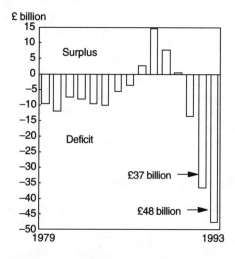

Figure 2.6 UK budget deficits and surpluses

dampen the severity of economic fluctuations.) In order to remove the impact of cyclical fluctuations in economic activity levels upon the budget balance, it is necessary to calculate the cyclically adjusted or full employment budget balance.

2.5.4.2 Full employment budget balance

The full employment budget balance equals the difference between total tax revenue at the full employment level of national income and total government expenditure at the full employment level of national income. By removing from the budget balance figure the effect of cyclical variations, the full employment budget balance measures what the tax receipts and expenditure would be if the economy were at full employment. In doing so it attempts to separate out the influence of the economy on the budget. A budget deficit at full employment indicates an expansionary policy, and vice versa. Planned fiscal changes will be reflected in a change in the full employment budget balance.

2.5.4.3 Inflation-adjusting the government deficit

A second reason why the actual government budget deficit is a poor measure of underlying fiscal stance concerns the distinction between nominal and real (inflation-adjusted) interest rates. Measures of the budget deficit treat the whole of the nominal interest paid by the government on the national debt as an item of government expenditure. In fact, in a world with significant inflation, in which nominal and real interest rates may diverge considerably, it would make more sense to count only the real interest rate times the outstanding government debt as an item of expense to the deficit. When the effects of the high inflation rates of the 1970s were allowed for, what originally seemed to be large fiscal deficits in many countries turned out instead to be fiscal surpluses. The public sector had been adding to its nominal stock of debt at a lower rate than that at which inflation had been eroding the value of past borrowing.

Thus, to gauge the underlying fiscal stance, it is inappropriate to look at the actual or simple government deficit; instead we must look at figures which have been adjusted to counteract the effect of cyclical factors within the economy and the effect of inflation.

2.5.5 The national debt and the budget deficit

In many countries the golden age of active fiscal policy to 'fine-tune' the level of aggregate demand was the 1950s and 1960s. Output and employment levels were held close to their full employment levels in the UK and elsewhere. The question that needs to be posed is: why since the mid-1970s have governments in the UK and elsewhere been reluctant to adopt expansionary fiscal policies which might have offset the reductions in other sources of aggregate demand and prevented the rise in unemployment? The answer to this question may lie in the effect of budget deficits upon the national debt, and it is to this issue we now turn.

Budget deficits usually require the government to finance the imbalance between spending and revenue by borrowing the money it needs to bridge the 'gap'. It could, of course, resort to directly printing and minting more money ('M0 type' money – see next section), but most governments tend to prefer the more indirect route of borrowing (although this itself can serve to increase the money supply – see below).

However, evidence suggests that concern about the size of the debt problem in the UK and elsewhere may be overstated. In the first instance, the vast majority of the UK debt (85 per cent) is owed to UK citizens who hold government bonds. It is a debt we owe ourselves as a nation. Interest payments on the debt financed by taxation merely represent transfers between one section of the community (the taxpayer) to another (the receiver of the interest). There is also a transfer between generations, since borrowings are repaid by the government at a later date. These payments need not impose any burden on society, since any 'undesirable' allocation of wealth implied by the transfers could be altered by taxation.

Externally held debt represents a different situation. Payments of interest and repayment of the debt on maturity represent transfers not between domestic residents but between residents and non-residents. There is therefore a loss of real resources to the residents of a country. However, consideration of the use to which these borrowed resources have been applied may lessen the impact, especially if some of the money which the public sector has borrowed in the past has been used to finance physical investment or investment in human capital, which will raise future tax revenue and help pay off the debt. Approximately 15 per cent of UK debt is externally held, of which only 4 per cent takes the form of external foreign currency debt.

Why then should we worry about the scale of the public debt at all? Two concerns about public debt remain. (1) If the debt becomes large relative to GNP, high tax rates may be required to meet the interest payments. High tax rates may have disincentive effects. (2) If the government is unwilling or unable to raise taxes beyond a certain point, a sufficiently large debt may lead to large deficits which the government can finance only by borrowing or printing money. Since borrowing merely compounds the problem, the incentive to print more money may prove irresistible. This, apart from causing inflation, will have implications for the control of monetary policy.

There is therefore some truth in the widely held view that the national debt represents a burden on the present and future inhabitants of a country. Nevertheless the extent of the burden seems quite small.

2.5.6 Budget deficits and crowding out

Where government spending exceeds taxes so that the government runs a budget deficit there is a possibility that the government will 'crowd out' private sector economic activity. If the government expands its own spending this will directly pre-empt resources which might have been employed in the private sector of the economy, leading to direct crowding out (see Figure 2.7). Again, if the government runs a budget deficit it will need to finance its resulting *public sector borrowing requirement.* This funding requires the government to borrow more by issuing more long-term government securities, medium-term government bonds or short-term government securities like Treasury bills. In order to persuade the public, financial institutions and overseas lenders to buy these government securities and bonds, the government must generally offer higher interest rates on these securities and bonds. The effect of extra government borrowing is therefore to push up interest rates in financial markets. In turn, higher interest rates make it more expensive for businesses to borrow money to finance investment projects and more expensive for consumers to borrow money to finance consumption. Budget deficits can therefore lead to financial crowding out of the private sector (see Figure 2.7).

The extent to which budget deficits crowd out the private sector depends upon the extent to which the government and the private sector are

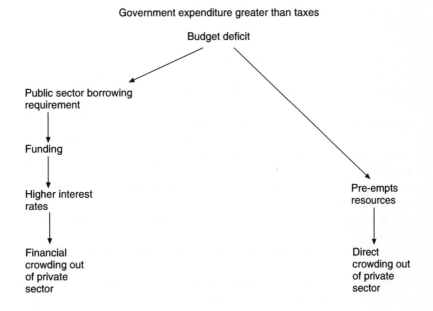

Figure 2.7 Crowding out

competing for resources. When there is widespread unemployment increased government spending can be resourced by drawing upon unemployed resources rather than taking them from the private sector, so that real crowding out generally occurs only when the economy is at or near full employment. Again when domestic or overseas financial markets can easily fund extra government borrowing the impact of the public sector borrowing requirement upon market interest rates may be quite small.

2.6 MONETARY POLICY

Monetary or fiscal policies are rarely carried out in isolation, and to gain an overall understanding of macroeconomic policy we must look at the use of these policies in tandem. During the 1980s macroeconomic policy in many industrialised countries was influenced by monetarist ideas. These generally involved fiscal policy taking a secondary role to monetary policy. However, the monetarist experiment attempted by many governments in the 1980s has been increasingly modified to the extent that now macroeconomic policy once again stresses the need for a balance between monetary and fiscal policy.

Monetary policy involves controlling the quantity of money in existence, or its rate of growth, by controlling either the supply of money or the demand for money. In general, a reduction in the money supply produces a 'multiplied' contraction in national income. Similar results would occur if the government operated a restrictive monetary policy by either increasing interest rates or imposing direct controls to restrict the quantity of credit available to finance expenditure. Conversely, opposite effects would be achieved if the government pursued an expansionary monetary policy by (1) increasing the money supply, (2) reducing interest rates or (3) removing any controls which impeded the flow of credit.

As we saw in Section 1.7, money is demanded primarily to finance the purchase of goods, services and financial assets. The supply of money in modern economies is determined both by the government and by the banking system. Money created by the government consists of government-issued notes (for example, Bank of England £5, £10, £20, £50 notes) and coins (for example, Treasury-minted 5p, 10p, 20p, 50p and £1 coins). In monetary analysis notes and coins constitute the *exogenous* component of the money supply, being put into the economic system 'from outside' by the government.

However, a significant part of the 'wider' supply is determined *endogenously* within the economic system – for example, bank deposits are 'created' by the banking system and these are highly interest rate-sensitive. Thus, as a general proposition, the higher the rate of interest (the higher the return on loanable funds), the greater the quantity of money supplied. (See Figure 1.19.) Because of the crucial position of bank deposits in the wider money

Box 2.6 Banks' reserve–asset ratios

The reserve–asset ratio or liquidity ratio is the proportion of a commercial bank's total assets which it keeps in the form of liquid assets to meet day-to-day currency withdrawals by its customers and other financial commitments. In the UK assets held as part of a bank's reserve–asset ratio include: till money (notes and coin) and balances with the Bank of England which together comprise the *cash reserve ratio*; call money (short-term deposits with the discount market); and near-mature bills of exchange (three-month bills issued by companies to raise credit) and Treasury bills (three-month bills issued by the government as a means of borrowing).

The ratio of liquid assets to total assets held can be dictated by reasons of commercial prudence to maintain customers' confidence in the banks' ability to repay their deposits on demand. This is a matter of individual discretion. In some countries, however, the monetary authorities prescribe *mandatory* and uniform minimum reserve–asset ratios for the banking sector in order to improve the effectiveness of monetary policy.

supply it is important to understand how the commercial banking system can create new bank deposits, and through a *money multiplier* process, affect the size of the money supply. Briefly, commercial banks accept deposits of currency from the general public. A proportion of this money is retained by the banks to meet day-to-day withdrawals (their reserve–asset ratio, see Box 2.6). The remainder of the money is used to grant loans or is invested. When a bank on-lends it creates additional deposits in favour of borrowers. The amount of new deposits the banking system as a whole can create depends on the magnitude of the reserve–asset ratio.

In summary, the money supply is dependent on:

1 The total value of cash in existence.
2 The proportion of cash held by the banks.
3 The ratio of cash to deposits desired by the banks.
4 The demand for loans. Unless people are willing and able to borrow money banks cannot lend, even if they have sufficient reserves to do so.

2.6.1 Measuring the money stock

An essential element of monetary policy is the measurement of the money stock. Its importance derives from the fact that governments need to control the quantity of money in existence in order to achieve their macroeconomic policy objectives. However, the monetary authorities have a problem, because, given the number of possible definitions of the money supply, it is difficult for them to decide which is the most appropriate money supply category to target for control purposes. Moreover, having targeted a particular definition, they face the added difficulty of actually controlling it because of the potential for asset-switching from one category of money to another (see below).

Table 2.4 indicates how the money supply can be specified in a variety of ways, and the total value of money in circulation depends on which definition of the money supply is adopted. 'Narrow' definitions of the money supply include only assets characterised by ready liquidity (that is, assets which can be used *directly* to finance a transaction – for example, notes and coin). 'Broad' definitions include other assets which are less liquid but are nonetheless important in underpinning spending (for example, many building society deposits have first to be withdrawn and 'converted' into notes and coin before they can be spent).

The main point is that money aggregates behave differently. The broader aggregates are more stable, but it is the narrower aggregates which respond more sensitively to changing external pressures. The choice of money aggregate and the information it imparts are therefore crucial if the instruments of monetary policy are to be correctly applied.

2.6.2 How to control the money supply

If governments are to influence investment spending and consumer spending they need to control the money supply. Three broad approaches to monetary control can be identified:

1 By price, that is, changes in interest rates.
2 By quantity control, that is, some form of rationing.
3 By direct controls, for example credit controls.

These policies are elaborated below.

Table 2.4 UK money supply definitions (£ billion), June 1994

'Narrow' money	(money held predominantly for spending)	
M0	Bank notes and coin in circulation plus banks' till money and operational balances at the Bank of England	21
M1	M0 plus UK private sector sight bank deposits	165
'Broad' money	(money held for spending and/or as a store of value)	
M3	M1 plus UK private sector time bank deposits and UK public sector sterling deposits	380
M4	M3 plus net building society deposits	557

Source: Bank of England Quarterly Bulletin, August 1994.

The monetary authorities (in the UK principally the Bank of England) can employ a number of measures to regulate the money supply, in particular that part of it which is used to underpin the provision of credit, including open market operations in government bonds and Treasury bills, special deposits and directives.

Open market operations are targeted at the liquidity base of the banking system and involve the sale or purchase of government bonds and Treasury bills, which alters the amount of cash and near cash assets held by the commercial banks and thus their capacity to advance loans and overdrafts to customers. For example, if the authorities wish to reduce the money supply they can sell government bonds or bills to the general public. Buyers pay for these bonds by running down their bank deposits, thereby withdrawing cash from the commercial banks. This forces the banks in turn to reduce the volume of their lending in order to remain within their reserve–assets ratio limits. For example, if commercial banks operate with a reserve–asset ratio of 20 per cent, then by selling £100 million of government bonds to the general public the monetary authorities can force the banks to contract their total lending by £500 million in order to compensate for the loss of £100 million of liquid assets and so maintain their reserve–assets ratio.

Figure 2.8 shows the asset structure of a typical commercial bank. The bank is torn between the conflicting goals of earning profits and maintaining liquidity. The former goal will encourage the bank to lend as much of its funds as possible to customers in order to make profits from the interest charges on the advances. On the other hand, the need to maintain the confidence of depositors that their deposits will be quickly repaid when necessary forces the bank to retain a proportion of its assets in liquid form, either as cash or as short-term loans or investments in bills which can be quickly converted into cash. Given this asset structure, government open market operations which reduce the bank's liquid or reserve assets (the light shaded area) will have a multiplier effect upon its total lending (the dark shaded area).

Other control measures are available. A *special deposit* call by the authorities requires the banks to place a specified portion of their liquid assets on deposit with the Bank of England. That portion is then 'frozen', that is, it cannot be used by the banks for advancing loans and overdrafts to customers, again reducing the money supply. A *directive* is a request by the Bank of England to the banks to keep their total lending below a specified global ceiling or to reduce their lending for particular purposes (for example, car purchases).

The authorities can also operate *instalment credit* controls on lending by finance houses to limit spending. They can, for example, discourage potential borrowers from using instalment facilities by increasing the down-payment required and by reducing the maximum period of the loan; the

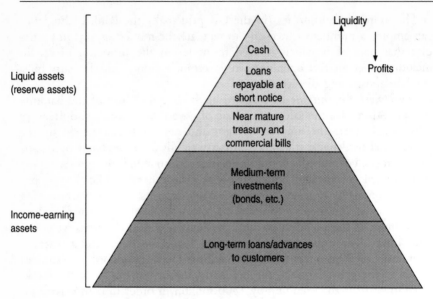

Figure 2.8 Asset structure of a commercial bank

former stipulation requires the borrower to find more ready cash, while the latter increases the effective interest charge payable.

The authorities may seek to influence interest rates on a broader basis than particular categories of borrowing. (See Box 2.7.) The level of interest rates is determined by the forces of supply and demand for finance in the money markets. The cheaper the cost of borrowing money, the more money will be demanded by households and businesses. The higher the rate of interest, the greater the supply of loanable funds. The 'equilibrium' rate of interest is determined by the intersection of the demand for (D_m) and supply of (S_m) loanable funds – interest rate OR in Figure 2.9. In theory, the monetary authorities can control the rate of interest by changes in the money supply. For example, by increasing the supply of money relative to the demand for it, the authorities can lower the cost of borrowing. If the money supply is increased from S_m to S_{m1} the effect will be to lower the equilibrium rate of interest from OR to OR_1.

Lower interest rates will encourage households and businesses to borrow more, thus increasing the total level of spending in the economy (see Figure 1.19). However, there is some controversy about the interest sensitivity of the demand for money and supply of money schedules. Keynesians argue that saving is largely a function of the level of income rather than of the rate of interest, so that the supply of loanable funds is relatively interest-inelastic. Keynesians also argue that investment plans are primarily determined by businesspeople's expectations about future levels of economic

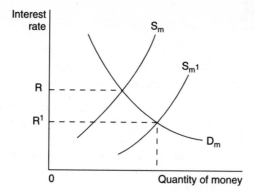

Figure 2.9 Interest rate

activity, with the cost of capital being of secondary importance, so that the demand for loanable funds is also relatively interest-inelastic. This means that even quite large changes in interest rates are unlikely to have much effect upon the amounts of money demanded and supplied, and thus upon levels of consumer and investment spending. By contrast, monetarists argue that both the supply of and the demand for loanable funds are relatively interest-elastic so that only small changes in interest rates can have a large effect on consumer and investment spending. Although the issue remains controversial, empirical evidence tends to support the Keynesian view that interest rates have only a limited effect on investment.

2.6.3 Monetary policy in practice

In practice, the application of monetary policy is fraught with difficulties. As noted above, one problem is that there is no single reliable definition of the money supply, so that any attempt to target a particular specification of the money supply tends to be undermined by asset-switching from other categories. To illustrate briefly: if the authorities target M3 (mainly currency plus bank deposits) for control purposes and use the various instruments noted above to reduce the level of bank deposits, this may not be sufficient in itself to reduce spending. Spenders may simply switch to M4-type money, running down their building society deposits to finance current purchases instead of using bank deposits. The complexity of applying monetary policy has been compounded by the development by financial institutions of new financial products and processes for the transmission of money and the lending and borrowing of funds – for example, direct debit systems, credit cards, etc. These developments have augmented the traditional means of transmitting money (cash, cheques) and may have served to increase the velocity of circulation of money. They have also increased

Box 2.7 Interest rates

Although for expository purposes it is conventional to refer to 'the' interest rate, in practice there are a number of interest rates. In the UK, for example, various interest rates are of significance:

1 *The interbank clearing interest rate.* The interest rate at which the commercial banks lend short-term sterling funds to one another.
2 *The bill-discounting interest rate.* The interest rate at which the Bank of England is prepared to lend money to discount houses (institutions which 'discount' bills of exchange and Treasury bills) in its capacity as 'lender of last resort'.
3 *Base rate.* The 'floor' interest rate which is used by the commercial banks and other financial institutions as the basis for charging interest on loans and overdrafts to their personal and business customers.

In Germany the key interest rates are the discount rate and the Lombard rate. The discount rate is the 'floor' rate at which the Bundesbank finances the banking system. The Lombard rate represents the Bundesbank's 'ceiling' to German money market rates.

As part of the application of monetary policy central banks typically 'announce' a change in key interest rates which will then have knock-on effects down the whole interest rate structure. For example, on 2 June 1993 the Bundesbank announced an immediate cut in the Lombard rate from 8.5 per cent to 8.25 per cent and a reduction in the discount rate from 7.25 per cent to 6.75 per cent.

the availability of credit and by creating new 'near money' assets have served to extend the liquidity base of the economy.

In addition, the 'openness' of national economies to inflows and outflows of foreign currencies makes it difficult for a government to operate domestic monetary policy without having to consider the international implications of its policy. For example, a country pursuing a policy of contracting domestic credit, leading to higher interest rates, will tend to attract inflows of foreign currencies which serve to increase the exchange rate value of its currency. These problems have been particularly noticeable in the UK, a country which was in the forefront of the monetarist experiment.

For most of the period since 1945, UK monetary policy has been used as a short-term stabilisation technique, and has largely taken second place to fiscal policy. However, with the upsurge in monetarist ideas, control of the money supply on a longer-term basis has taken centre-stage in the application of economic policy. In the 1980s the UK government, as part of its medium-term financial strategy, set 'target bands' for the growth of, initially, sterling M3 and later M0. In recent years formal targeting of the money supply has been abandoned, although the authorities have continued to 'monitor' M0, together with M4, as 'indicators' of general monetary conditions in the economy. (See Box 2.8.)

The 'decline' of the monetarist experiment in part reflected the aforementioned problems of measuring and controlling the money supply, especially in an environment of financial deregulation. However, part of its failure also lay in the fact that monetary policy failed to achieve its objectives. In the UK an expansionary policy was adopted in 1971–3 and 1985–8. On both occasions the results were inflationary. Excessive money balances concentrated growth in the purchase of certain assets, in particular foreign assets (factories, shares and property), and consumer durables (causing balance of payments problems), shares and financial assets (stock market boom) and houses (house price boom) during the 1980s. Conversely, attempts to use monetary policy as a deflationary measure in 1973, 1979–80 and 1988–9 were largely unsuccessful.

2.7 SUPPLY-SIDE POLICIES

The various fiscal and monetary policies outlined above are used as policy instruments by governments to regulate levels of aggregate demand in the economy in order to help them achieve their macroeconomic objectives. These demand management policy instruments are essentially geared to short and medium-term policies for stabilising economic activity levels and avoiding the fluctuations in output associated with business cycles.

However, such short-term demand-side policies must be viewed in relation to the longer-term changes in the supply capacity of the economy.

The potential output of the economy (as affected by supply-side factors) constrains the extent to which output can respond to changes in demand. For example, slow growth in a country's potential output can mean that even at fairly modest rates of growth of demand the economy experiences inflationary pressures and rising imports. Furthermore, some short-term demand management policies can have an effect upon potential output. For example, the use of monetary policy instruments to affect interest rates and investment spending will also affect potential output, since not only is investment an element of short-term aggregate demand but also investment levels are an important determinant of the supply capacity of the economy over the longer term. Thus governments must take account of the impact of their demand management policy instruments upon supply capacity, and, more positively, must develop appropriate supply-side policies to expand the productive capacity of the economy.

An economy's capacity for supplying goods and services depends upon the efficiency of its companies and employees and the flexibility of markets

Box 2.8 Recent monetary developments in the UK, Japan and USA

UK

Since 1979 the general goal of monetary policy has been to reduce inflation. Interest rates were kept high and repeated (largely unsuccessful) attempts were made to reduce the rate of growth of broad money (M3). The UK's entry into the European Exchange Rate Mechanism (ERM) in October 1990 at £1=DM2.95 (considered by many economists to be unrealistically high) was also seen as anti-inflationary, 'forcing' UK firms to keep prices down. In the 1990s concern at deepening recession led to an easing of monetary conditions to stimulate a 'gentle' non-inflationary expansion of demand. Between February and September 1991 interest rates were cut in seven half-percentage point steps from 14 per cent to 10.5 per cent, and in May 1992 they were cut further to 10 per cent. However, sterling was coming under increasing speculative pressure within the ERM. On 16 September 1991 this reached crisis proportions. In an attempt to hold the pound's parity, interest rates were first raised to 12 per cent and then to 15 per cent, but even this failed to eliminate selling pressure on the pound and the UK left the ERM. Interest rates were then restored to 10 per cent and cut to 9 per cent later in the month. (This incident serves to illustrate the conflict which sometimes arises between the 'internal' and 'external' uses of monetary policy.) Interest rates were lowered again in October 1992 (by 1 per cent) and in November 1992 (by 1 per cent). From 1992, with a continuing fall in inflation, interest rates were progressively reduced to 5.25 per cent in early 1994. Interest rates were increased to 5.75 per cent in September 1994 on fears of increased inflation.

Japan

Unlike the UK, Japan experienced relatively low inflation rates in the 1980s. The aim of monetary policy has been to create conditions conducive to achieving non-inflationary sustainable growth. Broad money growth (see below) has been much lower than in the UK but higher than in the USA. Concern at monetary expansion led to a progressive increase in 1989 and 1990 of the official discount rate (ODR): 3.25 per cent (May 1989), 3.75 per cent (October 1989), 4.25 per cent (December 1989), 5.25 per cent (March 1990) and 6.0 per cent (August 1990). Since 1991 the easing of inflationary pressures (with the economy still running at near full employment) has been reflected in a gradual but cautious easing of monetary conditions. In July 1991 the ODR was reduced to 5.5 per cent, then to 5 per cent (November 1991), 4.5 per cent (December 1991), 3.75

per cent (April 1992) and 3.25 per cent (July 1992). In February 1993 the ODR was cut to 2.5 per cent and further reduced in September 1993 to 1.75 per cent.

USA

The aim of monetary policy in recent years has been to keep inflation in check while providing some scope for stimulating the economy. With the inflation rate at relatively modest levels and the economy in recession, interest rates have been reduced. The Federal Reserve Board reduced its discount rate in stages from 8.25 per cent in October 1990 to 3 per cent in July 1992, holding it at this level through the first half of 1994.

Money supply aggregates: annual percentage change

Country	1984	1985	1986	1987	1988	1989	1990	1991	1992	1993
Narrow money										
UK	5.5	4.6	4.0	4.8	6.8	5.7	5.2	2.3	2.3	4.8
Japan	6.9	3.0	10.4	4.8	8.6	2.4	4.5	9.5	2.9	7.0
USA	6.0	12.3	16.8	3.5	4.9	0.9	4.0	8.7	14.3	10.5
Broad money										
UK	13.6	13.0	16.1	15.9	17.3	19.0	12.0	5.7	3.5	4.9
Japan	7.8	8.7	9.2	10.8	10.2	12.0	7.4	2.3	-0.2	2.2
USA	8.6	8.2	9.4	3.5	5.5	5.1	3.5	3.0	1.9	1.3

Source: IMF, *World Economic Outlook*, 1994.

in responding to demand changes. Governments can adopt a number of supply-side policies to improve efficiency and flexibility, and the main measures are listed below.

2.7.1 Labour efficiency

1 To improve the supply of required skills, education and training policies may be developed.
2 To encourage labour mobility, regional policy assistance, private rented accommodation and portable pensions may be developed.
3 To improve the flexibility of labour markets, government may act to reduce the power of trade unions and reduce social security benefits.

2.7.2 Company efficiency

1 To encourage industrial efficiency, the government can opt for privatisation and reduce its control of industry (deregulation).
2 To improve the efficiency of capital markets, the government can encourage more competition in the financial sector (stock exchange, building societies).
3 To provide incentives to work harder and take risks, governments may lower tax rates.
4 To promote an enterprise culture the government can promote wider share ownership, and improve help for the self-employed.

These measures can help to increase economic growth rates and reduce unemployment. Supply side policies are elaborated later in Chapters 3 and 5.

2.8 CONCLUSION

By the end of the 1980s it had become clear in many countries that policy was beginning to move away from strict monetarism. Governments were moving instead towards a more balanced mix of monetary and fiscal measures backed by facilitative supply-side policies, which it was hoped would be more successful in tackling the economic problems of a recessionary world economy. Notably, although the control of inflation was still of paramount importance, concern was being expressed at the growing levels of unemployment in the industrialised economies of the Western world. The dual topics of unemployment and inflation are discussed in the next two chapters.

QUESTIONS

1 Comment on the nature and significance of the four major macroeconomic objectives pursued by governments. What choices and problems can arise in achieving these objectives?
2 Evaluate the main monetary measures which governments can use to regulate spending in the economy and comment on their effectiveness.
3 Put forward the case for and against the use of an active fiscal policy.
4 Indicate the nature of 'supply-side' policies and how they may affect the workings of the economy.
5 What is meant by the term 'public sector borrowing requirement' (PSBR)? What causes the PSBR to change over time?
6 Compare and contrast Keynesian and 'supply-side' views of how the economy functions and examine the differing policy prescriptions deriving from each.

Chapter 3

Unemployment

During the last twenty years developed market economies in general, and the UK in particular, have experienced a dramatic increase in recorded unemployment. In the UK case, recorded unemployment has reached levels which have not been experienced since the inter-war period. For many years it has been widely accepted that there are economic and social grounds for positive intervention in the labour market to reduce unemployment. The number of people available for work is an important element in an economy's capacity to produce goods and services. Ideally, all those people available for work should be in productive employment; if they are not and are unemployed then the economy's resources are not being used to their maximum capacity and the economy will not have achieved the full employment level of national output. (Not only that, but some of the income created by those in work will need to be 'transferred' to unemployed people via the payment of unemployment and social security benefits.) Recent debate about unemployment has been characterised by a marked paucity of policy prescription with respect to what can or should be done. The control of inflation has superseded unemployment as the prime objective of economic policy in many advanced industrial countries, to the extent that it is now believed that only through controlling inflation will the problems of unemployment ever be solved. The nature and causes of unemployment have provided much controversy among economist,s making it difficult to analyse the causes of unemployment and to formulate appropriate policy responses. The aim of this chapter is to clarify some of these issues and offer insights into how the level of unemployment might be reduced.

The chapter is split into three broad sections. In the first section the principal features of unemployment in the leading industrialised countries are examined in an attempt to build up a general picture of unemployment. This specifically involves an examination of the measurement and definition of unemployment, the changing pattern of unemployment over time and differences in unemployment patterns between countries.

The second section provides an outline of the main features of economic models of unemployment. Specifically, it focuses upon both equilibrium (classical) and disequilibrium (Keynesian) wage theories. These theories concentrate on examining the microeconomic foundations (through supply and demand interactions) of the macroeconomic problem of unemployment. This approach enables us to focus on the type of choices made by (1) firms which demand labour and (2) people who supply labour. The third section discusses the implications of the analysis for unemployment policies.

3.1 THE LABOUR FORCE

The labour force or working population is the total number of workers available for employment in a country. The labour force comprises those persons currently working as employees, the self-employed and people currently unemployed. Table 3.1 gives details of the labour force in a number of industrial countries. The size of the labour force depends upon a country's total population and the proportion of that population offering themselves for work – the *activity rate* or *participation rate*. For example, in 1992 the UK's total population was 57.6 million and its labour force numbered some 28 million, giving an overall 'activity rate' of almost 50 per cent (or 78 per cent of the age 16–64 population).

The activity rate in any country is affected by the age and gender distribution of the population, in particular the number of very young and very old citizens. Activity rates are also influenced by social customs and government policies affecting, for example, the school leaving age and the proportion of young people remaining in further and higher education beyond that age; the 'official' retirement age and the proportion of older people retiring early or working beyond the retirement age. Opportunities for part-time work and job-sharing can also influence, in particular, female activity rates. In addition, government policies can also affect activity rates in so far as, for example, high marginal tax rates or generous social security payments may serve to deter some people from offering themselves for employment.

Table 3.1 Population and the labour force, selected industrial countries, 1992

Country	Total labour force (millions)	Total population (millions)	Activity rate* (%)
UK	28.8	57.6	49.9
Germany	31.3	63.9	49.1
Japan	63.6	123.6	51.4
USA	128.6	255.1	50.4

* Proportion of the population making up the labour force.

Source: International Labour Office, 1994.

Depending upon the purpose, a more detailed analysis of the structure of the labour force may be required, based, for example, on age distribution, gender distribution, industrial activity distribution and regional distribution (see Box 3.1).

A notable trend in high income developed countries has been for the industrial sector (goods) to grow more slowly than the services sector, a process referred to as 'deindustrialisation'. As a result the relative shares of these sectors in gross domestic product (GDP) and total employment have undergone a significant change, as shown in Table 3.2. For the UK the share of industry in GDP fell from 40 per cent in 1975 to 36 per cent in 1992 and the share of industry in employment fell from 38 per cent in 1975 to 26 per cent in 1992. Over the same period services increased their share of GDP from 58 per cent in 1975 to 62 per cent of GDP in 1992 and their share of employment from 57 per cent in 1975 to 71 per cent in 1992.

Changes in sector shares may simply reflect changes in the pattern of final demand for goods and services over time, and as such may be regarded as a 'natural' development associated with a maturing economy, with additional income being spent on services rather than goods. Deindustrialisation, however, may be aggravated by supply-side deficiencies (high costs, lack of investment) which put an economy at a disadvantage in international trade, leading to the displacement of domestic output by imports and increased unemployment (see Box 3.2).

Table 3.2 Shares of main sectors in GDP and employment, 1975 and 1992 (%)

| Country | Agriculture and mining | | | | Industry* | | | |
| | 1975 | | 1992 | | 1975 | | 1992 | |
	GDP	Employment	GDP	Employment	GDP	Employment	GDP	Employment
UK	2	4	2	3	40	38	36	26
US	3	5	2	3	35	30	29	26
Japan	5	12	3	7	41	35	41	33
Germany	3	8	2	4	49	43	39	36

| Country | Manufacturing | | | | Services | | | |
| | 1975 | | 1992 | | 1975 | | 1992 | |
	GDP	Employment	GDP	Employment	GDP	Employment	GDP	Employment
UK	32	31	20	19	58	57	62	71
US	25	24	17	18	62	65	69	71
Japan	30	26	29	23	54	53	56	60
Germany	39	36	31	29	48	44	59	60

* The figures for industry include manufacturing.

Sources: World Bank and International Labour Office, 1994.

Box 3.1 Labour force data for Great Britain,* March 1994 (000)

Total available labour force
Employees in employment:
   Male 10,799 (including 1,140 part-time)
   Female 10,600 (including 4,887 part-time)

Total	21,399
Self-employed	3,230
HM forces	254
Work-related government training programmes	342
Total work force in employment	25,225
Unemployed	2,777
Total labour force	28,002

Distribution of employees in employment by industrial activity

Primary sector	369
Manufacturing sector	4,241
Construction	780
Service sector	16,009
Total	21,399

Distribution of employees in employment by region

Greater London	3,229
South East	3,907
East Anglia	796
South West	1,708
West Midlands	1,964
East Midlands	1,539
Yorkshire and Humberside	1,855
North West	2,371
North	1,060
Wales	968
Scotland	2,002
Total	21,399

* UK excluding Northern Ireland.

Employment (and unemployment) levels tend to vary over time as people enter or leave employment; measures of the labour force also vary as people enter or leave the labour force. Figure 3.1 shows the main employment flows. People leave the unemployment pool as they are recruited by busi-

Box 3.2 Import penetration and unemployment

The circular flow of income model (Chapter 1) posits that if increased imports ('leakages') are matched by increased exports ('injections') then *real* balance in the foreign trade sector is maintained. However, if imports consistently exceed exports this causes problems not only in terms of maintaining external *monetary* balance (that is, balance of payments equilibrium) but also in terms of its impact on the internal real balance. Specifically, if import penetration (the proportion of total domestic consumption accounted for by imports) increases and is not matched by an equivalent amount of exports it will lead to lower domestic output and employment levels. This has been a particular problem in the UK in recent years, it has been argued, as import penetration has grown (up from 32 per cent in 1980 to 37 per cent in 1993) but the UK's large deficits in merchandise trade (see Box 6.3) have been only partially offset by surpluses in commercial services. Thus, it is suggested, the rise in UK unemployment from 2 million to 3 million in the period 1982–93 while mainly attributable to recessionary demand conditions has been exacerbated by the displacement of some domestic output by imports.

nesses or recalled after being temporarily laid off; while people join the unemployment pool as they are made redundant, are temporarily laid off, are dismissed or resign. Until the unemployed secure employment, their ranks may be swelled by new entrants to the labour force such as school and college leavers or re-entrants such as homemakers and carers returning to look for work after, say, rearing children. Meanwhile as people retire, return to education or simply become discouraged they will leave the labour force and cease to be unemployed (or employed). Any measure of the number unemployed (or the proportion of the labour force which is unemployed) taken at a particular point in time will reflect the relative balance of these various flows. For example, in the UK in 1993 the number of people unemployed at around 3 million reflected the net balance of over 4 million people who had become unemployed in that year and just under 4 million people who had ceased to be unemployed.

In practice, of course, 100 per cent full employment cannot be achieved. Inevitably there will always be people spending time in searching for and selecting new jobs, and structural changes in the economy – job losses in declining trades which require people to transfer to new jobs created in expanding sectors. Accordingly, a more realistic interpretation of full employment suggests itself: full employment is approximated when the number of persons *registered* as unemployed (that is, the *unemployment rate:*

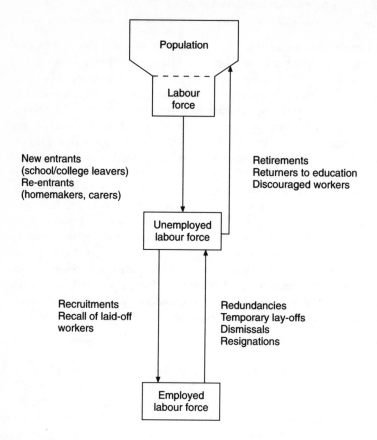

Figure 3.1 Employment flows

unemployed persons as a percentage of the labour force) is roughly equal to the number of notified job vacancies (that is, the *vacancy rate:* unfilled jobs as a percentage of the labour force). For example, in 1988, 1989 and 1990 UK unemployment rates at 8.1 per cent, 6.3 per cent and 5.9 per cent were *below* the vacancy rates for those years. (See Table 3.3.)

However, even these measures do not give an accurate picture, since some persons (for example, housewives) may fail to register as unemployed (a form of '*disguised*' *unemployment*), thus giving rise to understating of the unemployment figures, while not all available jobs are notified to the authorities, likewise giving rise to understating of the number of jobs on offer.

Overall unemployment measures tend to disguise the distribution of unemployment across society. For example, patterns of unemployment vary according to individual characteristics such as age, gender, ethnicity, qualification

Table 3.3 UK unemployment and vacancy rates, 1987–93 (%)

Rate	1987	1988	1989	1990	1991	1992	1993
Unemployment	10.0	8.1	6.3	5.9	8.0	9.8	10.3
Vacancy	8.3	8.8	7.7	6.1	4.2	4.2	4.7

Source: IMF, *World Economic Outlook,* 1994.

and experience, occupation and where people live. Evidence from the UK shows that higher rates of unemployment have been experienced in the northern regions than in the south, among the young, among minority ethnic groups, and among the least well qualified. Table 3.4 shows some labour market indicators, in particular unemployment rates for men and women, youth unemployment and the proportion of long-term unemployed in a number of countries. It is noteworthy that while unemployment rates among females are higher than the overall unemployment rate in Germany and Japan, female unemployment rates are below the average rate in the UK and USA. Part of this gender disparity in unemployment may be accounted for by the greater significance of part-time employment in the UK and USA in so far as many of these part-time jobs are filled by women. For example, in the UK the number of part-time employees has grown from 3.3 million in 1971 (15 per cent of all employees) to 4.5 million in 1981 (21 per cent of all employees) to 5.7 million in 1991 (26 per cent of all employees) and 5.9 million in 1993, men constituting only 15 per cent of the 5.9 million part-time work force. Again youth unemployment rates are higher than the national average rate in all countries except Germany, highlighting the difficulties which young people experience in finding jobs. Finally, the proportion of long-term unemployed (persons out of work for over one year) among the unemployed varies greatly, being high (over one-quarter) in Germany and the UK but lower in Japan and much lower in the USA. The low proportion of long-term unemployed in the USA may reflect the USA's more flexible labour markets and more numerous (often lower-paid) jobs, and its less generous unemployment welfare payments (such payments cease after six months of unemployment).

3.2 TRENDS IN UNEMPLOYMENT

Unemployment represents the non-utilisation of available labour resources. Conventionally, the amount of unemployment present in an economy is indicated, as noted above, by the *unemployment rate* – the number of registered unemployed persons as a percentage of the total labour force. Table 3.5 shows the annual unemployment rates for a number of leading industrial countries in recent years as well as the 'all industrial countries' average. Care must be taken in interpreting and comparing these figures. Notably the method of

Table 3.4 Labour market indicators, selected countries, 1989–93

Indicator	1989	1990	1991	1992	1993
Germany					
Labour force (% change)	0.7	2.3	1.8	0.9	−0.1
Participation rate[1] (%)	68.9	69.1	69.2	68.9	N/A
Unemployment rate (%)	7.9	7.2	6.3	6.6	8.2
Male	6.9	6.3	5.8	6.2	8.0
Female	9.4	8.4	7.0	7.2	8.5
Youth[2] (15–19 years)	5.4	5.0	4.5	5.0	6.4
Long-term unemployed[3]	31.4	29.7	28.3	26.6	N/A
Japan					
Labour force (% change)	1.1	0.9	1.2	1.1	N/A
Participation rate (%)	65.2	65.2	65.1	64.0	N/A
Unemployment rate (%)	2.1	2.1	2.1	2.2	N/A
Male	2.0	2.0	2.0	2.1	N/A
Female	2.2	2.2	2.2	2.3	N/A
Youth[2] (16–24 years)	4.4	4.3	4.3	4.5	N/A
Long-term unemployed	18.9	19.0	17.6	15.3	N/A
USA					
Labour force (% change)	2.3	2.0	2.1	2.2	N/A
Participation rate[1] (%)	66.5	66.4	66.0	66.3	N/A
Unemployment rate (%)	5.2	5.4	6.6	7.3	N/A
Male	5.1	5.5	6.9	7.6	N/A
Female	5.3	5.4	6.3	6.9	N/A
Youth[2] (16–24 years)	10.5	10.7	12.9	13.7	N/A
Long-term unemployed	5.8	5.6	6.3	11.2	N/A
UK					
Labour force (% change)	0.9	0.1	−0.6	−0.7	−0.7
Participation rate[1] (%)	80.1	80.3	79.8	78.9	78.5
Unemployment rate (%)	6.3	5.8	8.1	9.8	10.3
Male	7.7	7.1	10.7	12.9	14.0
Female	4.0	3.3	4.6	5.1	5.5
Youth[2] (16–24 years)	8.3	8.1	12.8	15.2	15.8
Long-term unemployed[3]	38.9	32.4	26.0	23.2	26.3

Definitions
1 Participation rate: labour force as per cent of population aged 16–64 years
2 Youth unemployment: unemployed persons as per cent of labour force of the same age group
3 Long-term unemployed: persons out of work for over one year as per cent of total unemployed.

Source: OECD Economic Surveys: *Japan* and *USA* (1993); *UK* and *Germany* (1994).

measuring the rate of unemployment differs somewhat between countries and is susceptible to change over time. In the UK, for example, where record rates of unemployment have proved to be politically sensitive, the formula for measuring unemployment has changed twenty-six times since 1976, most of the changes serving to reduce the measured unemployment rate.

Overall, unemployment rates have been much higher in the period 1986–93 than for the period 1976–85, the primary exceptions being Japan and the USA. All countries, to a greater or lesser degree, have been hit by the re-emergence of recessionary conditions post-1990 after a modest recovery from the 1979–81 recession. In both periods sharp increases in oil prices (the latter following Iraq's invasion of Kuwait) have played a significant part in damping down demand and increasing unemployment, exacerbated in recent years in the case of the USA by the authorities' concern to reduce the size of the budget deficit, by unification problems in the case of Germany and in the case of the UK the priority the authorities have given to securing low inflation. Only Japan has managed to keep the level of unemployment at very low levels (see Box 3.3).

Table 3.5 Unemployment rates, industrial countries, 1976–93 (%)

Country	Average 1976–85	1986	1987	1988	1989	1990	1991	1992	1993
USA	7.5	7.0	6.2	5.5	5.3	5.5	6.8	7.5	6.8
Japan	2.3	2.8	2.8	2.5	2.3	2.1	2.1	2.1	2.5
Germany	5.2	7.6	7.6	6.6	6.8	6.2	6.7	7.8	8.9
UK	7.1	11.1	10.0	8.1	6.3	5.9	8.0	9.8	10.3
All industrial countries	6.4	10.4	10.0	9.5	8.7	8.4	9.3	10.0	12.3

Source: IMF, *World Economic Outlook*, 1994.

The economic and social effects of high unemployment are significant and sufficiently disturbing to warrant an examination of the causes of unemployment and a search for policy solutions to combat unemployment. High unemployment represents a waste of resources in so far as the people unemployed could be productively employed in expanding the country's output of goods and services. In addition, where people are unemployed the state generally accepts an obligation to provide unemployment and social security benefits for them and their dependants to (partially) replace their lost employment income. These transfer payments generally place an additional burden on people who are still in work and paying taxes. Furthermore, higher unemployment reduces the government's tax receipts, since the unemployed are no longer earning incomes which can be taxed; and the effect of this, when combined with higher unemployment benefits, is often to increase the government's borrowing requirement.

Finally, there are various adverse social consequences for those who become involuntarily unemployed. Work provides an important source of social contacts for many people as well as reinforcing their sense of identity and social worth. When people become unemployed they can suffer feelings of isolation, boredom and worthlessness, and the stresses associated with such feelings can lead to illness and to the break-up of families. It has also been suggested that the alienation suffered by the unemployed can lead to increases in crime, particularly among young people. Such social consequences are particularly likely to emerge when people remain unemployed for long periods of time.

Such social pressures are experienced not only by the unemployed but also by those in employment who have to contend with the fear of becoming unemployed. Anxiety about the possible loss of one's job tends to increase during a recession, when widespread redundancies and lay-offs increase the risk. In addition, the impact of technology and changing employment practices has served to reduce the likelihood of anyone retaining a 'job for life' with the sense of security which it implies. Many more people are now employed on short-term contracts and so are exposed to additional anxieties about whether their contract will be renewed or whether they will be able to obtain a new one with another employer. Such anxieties can affect people's spending decisions, causing them to curtail their spending and save instead in case they lose their job, which in turn will tend to accentuate recessionary conditions.

Box 3.3 Unemployment in the UK, the USA and Japan

UK

Unemployment increased between 1990 and 1993 as the recession continued to deepen. Consumer spending fell in real terms and the deficit on the current account of the balance of payments was substantial. Thus a combination of falling demand and the displacement of some domestic output by imports exacerbated unemployment. Structural change (the run-down of the coal-mining industry, for example) has also contributed to unemployment. The fall in employment has affected virtually all sectors and regions of the economy, in contrast to the 1979–81 recession, which mainly affected the tradeable goods sector and the central and northern regions. The number of unemployed rose from 1.7 million in 1990 to nearly 3 million in 1993. The recession has tended to mask improvements in the flexibility of the UK labour market in recent years resulting from a series of reforms designed to increase trade union democracy and limit the exercise of trade union power (closed shops were banned, stricter rules for balloting members before strike action were introduced, and secondary picketing was banned), and improved work incentives (including cuts in marginal income tax rates), together with various training schemes aimed at reducing long-term unemployment and youth unemployment. Hopefully, these measures should help reduce the 'non-accelerating inflation rate of unemployment' (NAIRU) when the economy picks up.

Japan

Unemployment has remained low despite a recent downturn in industrial activity. (In 1992 Nissan, the car producer, for example, recorded its first domestic loss since 1945.) Over the longer term a buoyant domestic economy, strong export growth despite an appreciating yen and a corporate culture of 'lifetime employment' have kept the labour market tight and encouraged investment in labour-saving equipment and technologies. The recent advent of recession has been accommodated mainly by a reduction in the 'standard' working week (the Labour Standard Law of 1988 aims to reduce the standard working week to 40 hours – in 1991 it was forty-four hours) and a sharp fall in overtime working.

USA

The recession of the early 1980s was followed by several years of strong expansion and there was a sharp fall in the unemployment rate. However, with the return of recessionary conditions in 1990 unemployment increased and despite a modest recovery in 1991–2, activity has remained sluggish and unemployment has continued to rise. Fiscal and monetary policy have been directed primarily at bringing down the spiralling federal budget deficit, which has ruled out further anti-cyclical government spending. Labour markets in the USA are very flexible. Despite the fact, however, that real average hourly earnings for production workers *fell* by 7 per cent over the period 1979–89 this in itself was insufficient to provide a solid platform for maintaining employment once demand turned down.

3.3 CAUSES OF UNEMPLOYMENT

In explaining the causes of unemployment economists have turned their attention over recent decades from models which emphasise the sources of unemployment to models which concentrate on the behaviour of the participants in the labour market. As we shall see, both types of model have their merits and have important implications for the application of economic policy aimed at eradicating the problem of unemployment.

As previously mentioned, early theories of the causes of unemployment emphasised the *source* of the problem. These fell essentially into four main categories:

1 *Frictional unemployment*, the unemployment experienced where people are changing jobs and are unemployed for a short period of time. This type of unemployment is temporary. Frictional unemployment represents the irreducible minimum level of unemployment which will be experienced in a dynamic economy. The level of frictional unemployment will be influenced by the quality of the labour market arrangements for providing information about job vacancies.

2 *Demand-deficient unemployment* ('*Keynesian unemployment*'), the unemployment which arises when there is a failure of aggregate spending in the economy to match the economy's supply potential. Consider the national income model in Figure 3.2. The full employment level of national income is OY_F. A level of spending shown by the aggregate demand schedule AD will result in the achievement of full employment, AD intersecting the aggregate supply schedule at the full employment level of national income OY_F. A fall in aggregate demand shifts aggregate demand from AD to AD_1. In such a case, a fall in the level of aggregate demand leads to a new equilibrium at OY_1. This shortfall in spending will result in a level of actual output which is below potential GNP. Specifically, the intersection of AD_1 and the aggregate supply schedule results in an actual output level of OY_1 which is below the full employment level of national income (OY_F), leaving an 'output gap' of Y_1Y_F.

This analysis assumes that product prices and wages are inflexible in a downward direction. If product prices and wages fall in response to excess supply, then, as the classical economists contend, this will serve to increase the demand for products and labour, thus restoring full

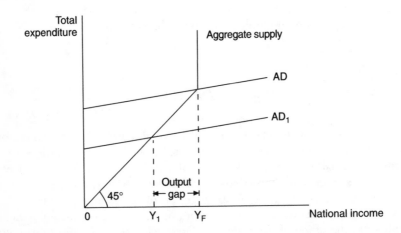

Figure 3.2 Demand-deficient unemployment

employment. However, Keynesians contend that because of the 'stickiness' of wages due to imperfect markets and institutional rigidities (see Section 3.4) the main impact of a fall in aggregate demand will be on the level of employment rather than on prices or wages.

3 *'Classical unemployment'*, the unemployment which is caused when the labour market fails to generate market-clearing wage rates. See Box 3.4 for a brief overview and Section 3.4 for a detailed analysis of this issue.

4 *Structural unemployment.* In addition to deficiencies in total demand, changes in demand patterns can cause unemployment. For example, *structural unemployment* is caused by the secular (long-term) decline in the demand for particular products, leading to the contraction of the industries which supply them, such as (in the UK) coal mining, shipbuilding and textiles. This problem may be exacerbated by the lack of labour mobility to other areas where jobs are available and the existence of a mismatch of skills between the skills held by the displaced workers and those required to gain new employment. To the extent that the industries concerned are concentrated in particular regions in a country, this can exacerbate *regional unemployment* as the decline of these industries in turn leads to a lower demand for the outputs of their local suppliers and serves to lower spending in the region as a whole. Structural and regional unemployment reflect the fact that there is not one uniform labour market; instead there are many interlocking and overlapping labour markets, with different markets for workers possessing different skills and available for work in different geographical regions. Also, short-term *seasonal* changes in demand can lead to the creation and elimination of jobs (for example, the loss of jobs in the UK tourist industry and the construction industry during the winter months). Finally, *technological unemployment* can be created where new plant, machinery or work practices improve labour productivity and lead to redundancies among workers.

Box 3.4 Wage rates, wage differentials and unemployment

The wage rate is the price paid by employers for labour used as a factor of production. In a competitive labour market the wage rate is determined by the demand for and supply of labour. The demand curve for labour as a factor input depends upon labour's marginal revenue product, that is, its contribution to earning revenues for firms. The demand curve is downward-sloping (D in Figure (a)) – the lower the price of labour the more employers will want to employ labour in the production process. The position and slope of the demand curve for a particular type of labour (for example, surgeons or office cleaners) will depend upon the productivity of the workers concerned and the demand for, and price elasticity of demand for, their product or service.

The supply curve (S) for labour is upward-sloping: the higher the wage rate the greater the amount of labour offered. The position and slope of the supply curve for labour will depend upon the skills of the particular workers concerned and their occupational and geographical mobility. The equilibrium wage rate is W_e, where the two curves intersect. In practice wage rates will be different for different types of work. For example (Figure (b)), a group of workers such as surgeons, whose skills are limited in supply and the demand for whose services is high, will receive a high wage rate; by contrast, office cleaners, who require little or no training or skills, are usually in plentiful supply in relation to the demand for their services, so their wage rates are comparatively low. The wage differential between these two groups is $W_s - W_o$.

Labour markets tend to work imperfectly. Trade unions may restrict the supply of labour and use their bargaining power to obtain increased wages; governments may stipulate minimum wage rates in order to enable workers to enjoy some basic standard of living. If, as a result, wage rates are pushed higher (W_m) than the market-clearing rate (W_e), the effect would be to create unemployment equal to $Q_1 Q_2$. Furthermore labour market imperfections will lead to wage 'stickiness', with wages not falling in response to an excess supply of labour, so that unemployment persists.

A variant on this theme is that wage increases (not matched by productivity gains) will, by fuelling cost-push inflation (see Chapter 4) make the country's products less price-competitive in international trade, with adverse effects on domestic jobs.

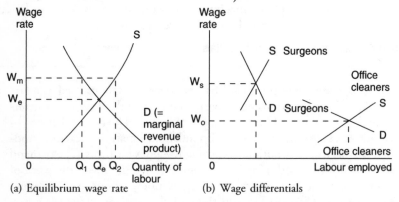

(a) Equilibrium wage rate   (b) Wage differentials

3.4 THE LABOUR MARKET – A BASIC MODEL

Modern approaches to unemployment, have focused, however, more on the way people in labour markets behave. Such models stress the microeconomic foundations of the macroeconomic problem of unemployment. It is argued that, by concentrating on the type of decisions made by firms which demand labour (shown by the labour demand function) and by people who supply labour (the labour supply function), such theories highlight the behavioural implications and consequences of government policy on unemployment.

In the labour market, portrayed in Figure 3.3, Ld represents the employers' demand for labour at different real wage rates, whereas Ls represents the willingness of employees to supply their labour at different real wage rates. Equilibrium occurs in the labour market at real wage rate OW1/P where labour demand equals labour supply, and the amount of employment is ON1.

However, given this depiction of the labour market, it is evident that at the equilibrium position there can be no unemployment. Indeed, unemployment (that is, an excess supply of labour at any real wage rate) can exist only if the market is restricted to maintain the real wage rate at a point like OW2/P, above the equilibrium wage rate. This might happen if either government or trade unions imposed a minimum wage rate above the equilibrium (classical unemployment).

The labour market depicted above does not reflect reality. At its equilibrium position it is not able to explain people who are between jobs

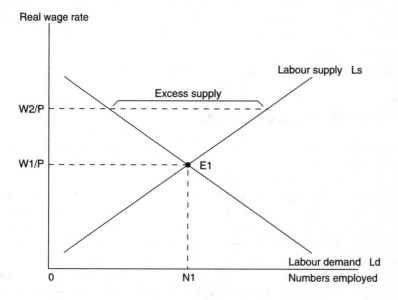

Figure 3.3 Labour market equilibrium with no market failure

(frictional unemployment) or those who are unemployable (mismatch of skills). Clearly such a model is deficient in explaining all the causes of unemployment. Much of this has to do with the fact that demand and supply analysis cannot easily replicate the workings of the labour market. The labour market is characterised by powerful institutions (trade unions and governments), social attitudes, and imperfect and costly information, which do not conform to the normal workings of a market as depicted by supply and demand analysis. Even more problematical is the fact that the parties involved in the exchange of labour have some choice about their level of involvement. For example, what may be an acceptable real wage rate to one employee may not be acceptable to another employee so that the latter will withdraw from the labour market.

Taken as a whole, these aspects of 'market failure', inherent within the labour market, produce a situation in which the wage and employment level is not determined solely by the (microeconomic) laws of supply and demand. In order to devise a more realistic model of the labour market, we must try and build into our simple model some of the above aspects of market failure. For example, the supply of labour is determined not only by the real wage (as in the simple model), but also by such factors as the level of unemployment benefit being paid or of trade union membership. Any extended analysis must recognise the fact that if unemployment benefit is high relative to the real wage being offered, then certain individuals (depending on their personal characteristics) will be unwilling to supply their labour. Similarly, any extended model must be able to incorporate the fact that the demand for labour is not only dependent on the real wage, but also dependent upon the cost of labour relative to capital. An increase in the cost of labour relative to capital is likely to result in employers switching to more capital-intensive production.

By adding such factors in the labour supply and labour demand functions we can show that, at the equilibrium position in the labour market, there will exist a certain amount of unemployment. This is what is known as the *natural rate of unemployment.*

The impact of introducing market failure is shown in Figure 3.4. For simplicity, it is assumed that there is no market failure in labour demand so that Ld = Ld*. Labour demand, Ld, and labour supply, Ls, represent the optimal choices people will make when there is no market failure (as in the simple model). The additional labour supply schedule, Ls*, represents the optimal choices people make when market distortions such as unemployment benefit are paid. Whereas the Ls curve shows the number of people who *want* to work, the Ls* schedule reveals the number of people who are *willing to accept* (rather than want) work at the current real wage rate offered. This schedule lies to the left of the Ls schedule because some people, although wanting to work, will find the real wage rate offered is not enough to persuade them to accept work. For example, some people

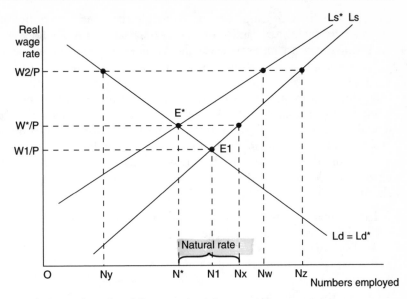

Figure 3.4 Impact of market failure on the labour market

may view the level of unemployment benefit along with increased leisure time as more than compensating for the real wage on offer with less leisure time.

Equilibrium in Figure 3.4 occurs at E* at the market-clearing real wage rate OW*/P and employment level ON*. The distance between the two supply schedules (Nx–N*) at the equilibrium wage rate represents the natural rate of unemployment. By definition the natural rate of unemployment is the rate of unemployment when the labour market is in equilibrium. Any factor which causes the Ls* schedule to shift to the right, other things being constant, will reduce market failure and hence reduce the natural rate of unemployment. At E* any unemployment is entirely voluntary. At the equilibrium real wage rate OW*/P, ONx people want to be in the labour force, but because of market failure only ON* want to accept offers; the remainder do not want to work at the equilibrium real wage rate. The natural rate of unemployment would seem to include both frictional and structural unemployment, both being voluntary in nature.

If the real wage rate is at a level above the equilibrium level, this is shown by wage rate OW2/P, which is above OW*/P. Total unemployment is now given by the distance Nz – Ny, that is, the excess of supply over demand. Nw – Ny of this relates to workers who would like to take jobs at the wage rate OW2/P but are unable to find them, since firms demand only ONy workers. Classical theory views such unemployment as voluntary. Workers by collectively deciding through their union to opt for the real wage rate OW2/P in excess of the equilibrium real wage rate have reduced the level of employment. Through the union's actions, unemployment has increased, and must be regarded as voluntary. Thus we also include classical unemployment in the natural rate of unemployment.

Keynesians, as previously explained, view this position differently. Unemployment in this sense is involuntary, caused by the combination of wage stickiness (which is beyond the control of workers or the unions) and a low level of demand in the economy. As such, unemployment is characterised more by disequilibrium in the labour market than as an equilibrium process, as put forward in the natural rate of unemployment analysis.

Disequilibrium in this sense is caused by a combination of the following types of market failure which stop the labour market reaching its market-clearing equilibrium:

1 Labour market segmentation, which occurs when employers discriminate because of skills, gender or age.
2 Trade union practices.
3 Pay bargaining methods and employer practices.
4 Mode of production and type of goods produced.
5 Size of the public sector.
6 Labour mobility problems.

Clearly, total unemployment can be divided into two different categories. First, equilibrium or natural rate unemployment. Equilibrium in the labour market results in a level of unemployment which is voluntary by nature and dependent upon the degree of union power, incentives in the labour market, skill mismatches and labour turnover. Second, disequilibrium or demand-deficient unemployment. The combination of low levels of aggregate demand and factors inherent in the labour market which make it (and wages in particular) slow to adjust results in unemployment being a disequilibrium process and involuntary by nature.

Such a division clearly has implications for how governments should tackle the problem of unemployment. In the short run at least (that is, rather than waiting for wage and price reductions to occur in the long run) Keynesian demand-deficient unemployment could be dealt with by an active fiscal and monetary policy to boost aggregate demand to its full employment level. In contrast, the natural rate of unemployment, being voluntary by nature, needs to be tackled by affecting labour market incentives. Thus policies should be aimed at the supply side of the market to induce more people into work.

In recent years the focus of most governments' policy has been on reducing the natural rate of unemployment (moving the LS* nearer to the LS schedule). However, evidence suggests that in the UK (between 1981 and 1987), while two-thirds of unemployment was accounted for by factors which had caused the natural rate of unemployment to increase, the other one-third was attributable to a lack of demand in the economy, that is, the old-style Keynesian demand-deficient unemployment. Thus if a balanced view is to be offered of possible policy options, we must consider policies aimed at both the supply and the demand sides of the economy.

3.5 POLICIES TO REMOVE UNEMPLOYMENT

The labour market models outlined above (backed by unemployment figures) indicate that the natural rate or labour market failure should be the target for policy action to reduce persistent unemployment. A reduction in voluntary unemployment can be achieved by reducing the impact of market failure in the labour market. In terms of Figure 3.4 many of these policies will result in a shift to the right of the Ls* schedule. They include the following:

1 Training schemes.
2 Reduce wage-based taxes.
3 Reduce the size and duration of unemployment and social security benefits.
4 Increase labour mobility.
5 Reduce trade union power.
6 Reduce wage rigidity.

The provision of training and re-training facilities is aimed at decreasing the degree of skills mismatch and also improving the mobility of labour. The geographical mobility of labour could also be aided by improving information flows and reducing regional disparities, notably in terms of house prices, e.g. by giving some assistance with moving expenses.

In order to encourage workers to actively seek work, measures designed to entice workers back into the labour market (a reduction in the marginal rates of income tax) and measures to coerce people back into the work force (a reduction in the size, duration and coverage of benefit schemes) have been suggested.

Finally, 'real wage' unemployment can be reduced by improving the flexibility of the labour market by, for example, limiting the power of trade unions to enforce a 'closed shop' and other restrictive labour practices. Collectively these measures may serve to increase the general level and efficiency of resource use in the economy, thus improving the output potential and competitiveness of the country vis-à-vis international trade partners.

However, as previously indicated, some market rigidities may not be insurmountable, nor is all unemployment caused by supply-side factors and in that sense voluntary. As a result, the traditional remedy for demand-deficient unemployment is for the authorities to boost spending by reflationary fiscal policy and monetary policy measures – for example, tax cuts and interest rate cuts to increase consumer spending, and increases in government expenditure on the provision of roads, schools, etc. In terms of Figure 3.2 the aim would be to bring about a shift in the aggregate demand schedule from AD_1 to AD so that aggregate demand would inter-sect the aggregate supply schedule at the full employment level of national income, OY_F. Box 3.5 outlines the main policies for dealing with unem-ployment advocated by the OECD.

In order to ensure the maximum impact of demand management techniques to stimulate demand and employment, it is advisable that the policies are actively targeted at those industries with spare capacity; those industries which are labour-intensive (such as construction); and those industries which do not involve many imports.

Various policy measures may be adopted to remove unemployment caused by changes in demand patterns or supply-side deficiencies. Investment incen-tives (grants, subsidies, tax breaks, etc.) can be used generally to increase the start-up of new businesses and industries and the expansion of existing businesses and industries, to assist in the removal of 'structural' and 'technological' unemployment (industrial policy). More particularly, such incentives can be targeted to remove 'regional' unemployment by encourag-ing new investment in depressed areas (regional policy).

3.6 CONCLUSION

Unemployment, as the Western world economies have increasingly come to recognise, is a growing problem. The multi-faceted nature of unem-ployment makes its reduction difficult to achieve, especially with the present priority given to curbing the level of inflation. However, as is increasingly being recognised, unemployment involves not only a waste of economic resources in terms of output forgone, and additional expense in terms of benefit payments, but also has wider social implications. Whether the current belief that an environment of low inflation is a prerequisite of sustainable growth and falling unemployment is hotly debated amongst economists. This is an issue we tackle in the next chapter.

3.7 IMPLICATIONS FOR BUSINESS

Demand-deficit unemployment is symptomatic of recession in the economy and hence a generally unfavourable business climate for companies. In situ-ations of low and falling sales companies may be forced to put employees on short-time working or lay workers off, temporarily or permanently. In this way companies may aggravate unemployment, reacting to a situa-tion beyond their control. Even the 'lifetime' employment philosophy was jettisoned by many Japanese companies in the early 1990s as the economy moved into recession and, because of rising labour costs and the appreci-ation of the yen, some companies moved production to offshore locations.

In reacting to falling demand a company must consider a number of factors. Initially, some view must be taken on the severity and likely dura-

Box 3.5 Policies to deal with unemployment

In June 1994 the Organisation for Economic Co-operation and Development (OECD), which represents the twenty-four main indus-trialised nations, issued a report on policies to deal with the 35 million people who were unemployed in the twenty-four OECD member states (equal to 8.5 per cent of their labour force). The OECD pointed out that this unemployment 'represents an enormous waste of human resources, reflects an important amount of inefficiency in economic systems and causes a disturbing degree of social distress'.

The central problem, according to the OECD, is insufficient ability among the industrialised nations to adapt to change. This situation must be rectified if countries are to overcome the jobless problem.

The study makes it clear that Europe's weak employment growth but high productivity and the US experience of creating large numbers of low-skilled, low-productivity jobs over the past two decades are two sides of the same coin. Neither pattern of job creation is desir-able. Only Japan has adjusted relatively well to such changes as glob-alisation and the spread of new technologies but it too is now having to deal with substantial problems.

The OECD report made more than sixty recommendations, most of them concerned with reforming labour markets. They include: macroeconomic stability, faster diffusion of technological know-how, increased flexibility of working hours, nurturing entrepreneurship, making wages and labour costs more adaptable to market conditions, reforming employment security provisions, making labour market policies more pro-active, improving skills and competences, and reforming benefit and tax systems, to ensure that social objectives are achieved in ways that impinge less on the efficient functioning of labour markets.

tion of adverse trading conditions. If, for example, the lack of demand is expected to be short-term, then firms may decide not to reduce the size of their workforce. On the other hand, if the shortfall in demand turns out to be more protracted than originally envisaged, firms will face a more complex decision. In particular, they will need to consider the trade-offs between the savings on their labour bill by reducing their workforce, their investment in their existing labour force (training expenses, etc.) and the cost of training new employees in the future as demand picks up.

Supply-side considerations may force companies to reduce the size of their labour force. For example, high-cost labour may be replaced by cheaper capital inputs, or firms may rationalise their operations to improve their efficiency. For example, Xerox, the US document processing company, announced in 1993 that it was to reduce its worldwide workforce by 10,000, about 10 per cent of its employee levels, while BBA, the UK automotive components concern, was to reduce the size of its European labour force by 3,000, some 15 per cent of its total European workforce. Since labour is an *input* into the production process, the cost of labour and the skills and competences of the workforce are important elements in enabling firms to remain competitive. It is now generally accepted that, in the case of internationally traded goods, merely increasing domestic demand to 'mop up' unemployment will fail unless local products are competitive against trade competitors. In this context, policies aimed at making the labour market more flexible and adaptable to change can improve both employment prospects and the competitiveness of industry. The long-term priority, however, must be to upgrade labour skills and competences by investment in education and training to create new high-paid jobs rather than vulnerable low-paid unskilled work.

Government policies to redress unemployment both nationally and regionally may present opportunities for firms to improve their own competitive position. For example, the UK government's current emphasis on measures promoting labour market flexibility is aimed at simultaneously improving employment prospects *and* firms' cost effectiveness. The government has taken the view that this policy would be prejudiced if it were to endorse the European Union's social chapter, which imposes additional 'social wage' burdens on industry (see Box 9.6). Similarly, in the case of governmental regional policies to reduce unemployment, opportunities exist for firms to relocate to areas where financial 'sweeteners' are available. For example, the Japanese vehicle producers Nissan received grants totalling some £35 million for locating a car assembly plant in the Tyne and Wear district of north-east England.

QUESTIONS

1 Outline and comment on recent trends in unemployment in the main industrial countries.
2 What is demand-deficient unemployment? What measures can the authorities use to remove demand-deficient unemployment?
3 Explain the terms 'natural rate of unemployment' and 'market failure' as applied to the labour market.
4 Discuss the various supply-side policies the authorities can adapt to make labour markets more 'flexible'.
5 Distinguish between 'frictional', 'Keynesian', 'classical' and 'structural' forms of unemployment.

Chapter 4

Inflation

Inflation as an object of policy interest has shifted to centre stage over the last decade in the UK and in many other developed market economies. Given the significant increase in inflation over the last twenty years, the weighting given to the control of inflation relative to employment and growth in the policy-maker's priorities has increased in the UK and elsewhere. For example, throughout the 1980s Margaret Thatcher and her successive chancellors stressed that the reduction and elimination of inflation were and should be the overriding goal of UK economic policy; inflation was 'public enemy number one', as it was put in one Budget speech. In pursuit of this goal, Mrs Thatcher was prepared to pay a high economic price, in terms of unemployment and lost output (albeit in her view it was a short-term price).

The first part of this chapter explains why recent governments have placed such a high priority on inflation control. Their enthusiasm presumably reflects a belief that inflation imposes real costs on society and a belief that the costs of 'squeezing inflation out of the system' are less than the benefits which will follow as a consequence. Second, we explain the divisions among economists about how to analyse the causes of inflation and how to control it.

4.1 WHY GOVERNMENTS SEEK TO CONTROL INFLATION

Inflation can be defined as an increase in the *general level* of prices in an economy that is *sustained* over time. The annual increases in prices may be small or gradual (creeping inflation), or large and accelerating (hyper-inflation). The rate of inflation can be measured, using, for example, a consumers' price index which shows the annual percentage change in consumer prices (see Box 4.1). Alternatively broader measures of inflation may be employed which incorporate the prices of capital goods as well as the prices of final consumer goods, such as the GDP deflator price index, which is used to convert money GDP into real GDP. (See Box 5.2.)

Box 4.1 Price indices and the measurement of inflation

Inflation can be measured over time using a price index which comprises a weighted average of the prices of selected goods and services. One commonly used price index is the *retail price index* (RPI), which measures the average level of the prices of a typical 'basket' of the sort of goods and services bought by final consumers. Each item in the index is weighted according to its relative importance in total consumers' expenditure (see below). Starting from a selected base year (index year = 100), price changes are then reflected in changes in the index value over time. Thus, taking the example of the UK, the current RPI base year is 1987 = 100; in 1993 the index value stood at 141, indicating that retail prices, on average, had risen 41 per cent between the two dates. Such price indices can be used to measure the rate of inflation. Another commonly used index of prices is the *wholesale price index,* which records the price of a 'basket' of goods measured in terms of wholesale prices.

Weightings of products included in the UK retail price index

Food	144
Catering	45
Alcoholic drink	78
Tobacco	35
Housing	164
Fuel and light	46
Household goods	79
Household services	47
Clothing and footwear	58
Personal goods and services	39
Motoring expenditure	136
Fares, etc.	21
Leisure goods	46
Leisure services	62
Total	1,000

In theory, zero inflation may be possible if price rises in some *individual* goods and service markets are exactly offset by a fall in the prices of other goods and services, and inflation may become negative if, overall, price falls exceed price rises. In practice, these are 'special cases'. The experience of the world economy in the period since 1945 indicates that some inflationary pressure is likely to be ever-present and that while price increases may 'slow down', either of their own accord or because of the application of anti-inflationary policies, *complete* price stability is unlikely to be attained.

There are some economists who argue that a modest increase in the price level (accompanied by rising profitability) is positively beneficial in that it encourages investors to invest more and provides incentives for industry. High rates of inflation are, however, to be avoided, since high inflation rates reduce the 'purchasing power' of money (that is, a given unit of money will buy fewer real goods and services as their prices rise) and introduce various 'distortions' into the economic system. In particular, inflation can have adverse effects on income distribution (people on fixed incomes suffer), lending and borrowing (lenders lose, borrowers gain), speculation (diversion of saving away from industry into property and commodity speculation) and international trade competitiveness (exports become more expensive, imports cheaper). Of primary concern to many economists is that inflation generates uncertainty. This is undesirable on both equity and efficiency grounds. Specifically, uncertainty hinders the working of the price mechanism (it blurs signals and distorts incentives on which the market economy depends), makes it harder to draft contracts, and makes planning for the future more complex. In broader terms, some economists have argued that inflation, far from being the alternative to unemployment (as in the Phillips curve), is the cause of it. This issue focuses on much of the political debate about inflation and unemployment, and forms the basis of the second part of this chapter.

Hyper-inflation is particularly serious because people lose confidence in the use of money as a store of value, as a means of dealing with deferred payments and as a means of exchange, and the economic system is liable to collapse. Many commentators have advocated the use of indexation to eliminate the problems of inflation by linking increases in wages, profits, etc., to changes in the price index. However, indexation is merely a means of living with inflation (a second best solution), not a means of curing it (the best solution).

4.2 TRENDS IN INFLATION

The priority given to the containment and reduction of inflation within the overall framework of macroeconomic policy is often a matter of economic expedience and political 'judgement'. Some governments – for example, successive Conservative administrations in the UK – have accorded the control of inflation the highest priority even though this has meant tolerating higher levels of unemployment. The strategic thinking behind their policy has been the view that only by getting inflation down to low levels can a sustainable, non-inflationary growth in output, with the attendant creation of jobs, be achieved. Germany too has attempted to keep a tight rein on inflation, but it has proved difficult in the face of the spiralling costs of integrating West and East Germany, post-1990. Table 4.1 shows inflation rates for a number of leading industrial countries in recent years as well as the 'all industrial countries' and the 'all developing countries' average. In contrast to unemployment rates, inflation rates have been much lower in the period 1986–93 than in the period 1976–85 in the industrial countries. The developing countries in general have, however, experienced much higher rates of inflation, particularly those countries which have had problems with declining export earnings from primary produce and higher oil import costs which have forced them to increase their international debt levels. In the period since 1973 world inflation has largely been driven by cost pressures (the major increase in oil prices of 1973, 1979 and 1989, in particular, and wage increases 'accommodated' by monetary expansion; see below) rather than by 'excess demand'. The lower rates of inflation experienced in the 1980s and the early 1990s compared with the 1970s have been largely due to recessionary conditions, which have moderated wage demands and (alongside productivity gains) limited increases in unit labour costs (see Table 4.2), while many countries have pursued anti-inflationary fiscal and monetary policies.

4.3 CAUSES OF INFLATION

There are two main explanations of why inflation occurs: the presence of excess demand at the full employment level of national output which 'pulls' prices up (demand-pull inflation); and an increase in factor input costs (wages and raw materials) which 'pushes' prices up (cost-push inflation). Figure 4.1 summarises the main causes of inflation and the relations between these causal factors. Excess aggregate demand can result from an increase in aggregate demand and/or a decrease (or slow increase) in aggregate supply, causing an imbalance in demand and supply. Rapid increases in money supply can also increase aggregate demand and lead to excess demand if

Table 4.1 Inflation rates, selected countries, 1976–93 (%)

Country	Average 1976–85	1986	1987	1988	1989	1990	1991	1992	1993
UK	10.5	3.6	4.1	4.6	5.9	8.1	6.8	4.7	3.0
USA	7.2	1.9	3.7	4.1	4.8	5.4	4.2	3.0	3.0
Germany*	4.0	−0.1	0.2	1.3	2.8	2.7	4.5	4.9	4.7
Japan	4.7	0.9	0.1	0.7	2.3	2.8	3.3	1.7	1.3
All industrial countries	7.9	2.4	3.2	3.4	4.4	4.9	4.5	3.3	2.9
All developing countries	25.7	28.3	35.7	53.7	61.9	65.5	35.9	38.8	45.9

* Germany: West Germany before 1990.
Source: IMF, *World Economic Outlook*, 1994.

they leave households with more money than they wish to hold, encouraging them to increase their spending. Excess demand in turn 'pulls' prices up, as too much money 'chases' too few goods and services. Cost-push causes of inflation reflect the main cost elements involved in producing goods and services, namely raw material, labour wages and profits for capital providers. Increases in raw material prices, increases in profit margins and increases in wage rates can cause materials cost push, profit push or wage push respectively. However, the direction of causation is not necessarily just one way, and as price levels increase, materials suppliers, businesspeople and workers will seek to adjust their materials prices, profit margins and wages to compensate for inflation as they seek to maintain their real (inflation-adjusted) incomes. These motives lie at the heart of the wage–price spiral, with workers demanding wage increases to offset the cut in their living standard caused by rising prices; and businesspeople in turn raising prices to reflect the increased wage costs involved in production, in order to protect their profit margins; which in turn leads to further wage demands, etc.

Table 4.2 Hourly earnings, productivity and unit labour costs in manufacturing, 1976–93, annual percentage change

Country	Average 1976–85	1986	1987	1988	1989	1990	1991	1992	1993
Hourly earnings									
UK	12.5	7.9	7.5	8.0	9.0	9.7	9.3	6.5	4.7
USA	7.6	4.0	2.3	3.9	3.9	5.2	5.5	4.2	2.8
Germany	6.0	5.0	5.2	3.9	4.2	5.7	7.3	7.1	5.8
Japan	5.5	2.3	1.1	3.2	6.7	6.5	5.8	4.6	2.7
All industrial countries	9.1	4.6	3.8	4.6	5.6	6.3	6.4	5.0	3.3
Productivity (output per employee)									
UK	3.1	3.8	5.5	5.4	4.3	1.9	2.5	4.9	7.1
USA	1.9	2.6	6.5	2.4	0.6	1.7	2.1	4.1	5.1
Germany	3.6	0.9	1.9	4.2	3.3	3.5	2.9	1.4	2.3
Japan	4.2	0.0	4.1	7.4	4.5	2.8	1.5	−3.7	−1.6
All industrial countries	3.2	1.8	4.8	4.1	2.3	2.0	2.0	2.2	2.9
Unit labour costs (approximate hourly earnings/productivity growth)									
UK	9.3	4.0	1.9	2.5	4.6	7.7	6.7	1.5	−2.3
USA	5.5	1.4	−3.9	1.6	3.4	3.5	3.3	0.2	−2.2
Germany	2.3	4.0	3.3	−0.2	1.1	2.1	4.3	5.6	3.4
Japan	1.2	2.4	−3.0	−3.8	2.0	3.5	4.3	8.6	4.7
All industrial countries	5.8	2.8	−0.9	−0.4	3.2	4.2	4.3	2.8	0.4

Source: IMF, *World Economic Outlook*, 1994.

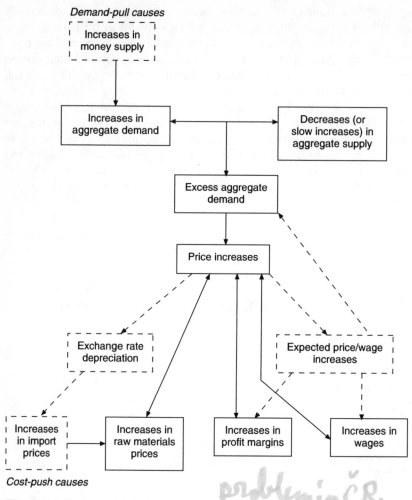

Figure 4.1 Causes of inflation

Figure 4.1 depicts two other major inflationary forces at work. First, where a country's rate of inflation exceeds that of its major competitors its exports are likely to fall and its imports to rise, leading to depreciation of the exchange rate of its currency. A falling exchange rate will lead to increases in import prices, further increasing materials costs. Second, public expectations about future rates of inflation will have an effect upon price setting and wage increases, which not only compensate for current inflation but also offset expected inflation. Inflationary expectations will be influenced by the rate of price increases in the present and the immediate past. In turn, inflationary expectations can influence aggregate demand, for when people expect inflation to accelerate they will tend to bring their spending plans forward, buying before goods go up in price, thus adding to the pressure of current demand. Using the aggregate demand/aggregate supply framework, we can analyse demand-pull inflation in terms of movements in the aggregate demand schedule, and cost-push inflation in terms of movements in the aggregate supply schedule. In order to do so it is useful to depict the level of national income in relation to price levels, as in Box 4.2.

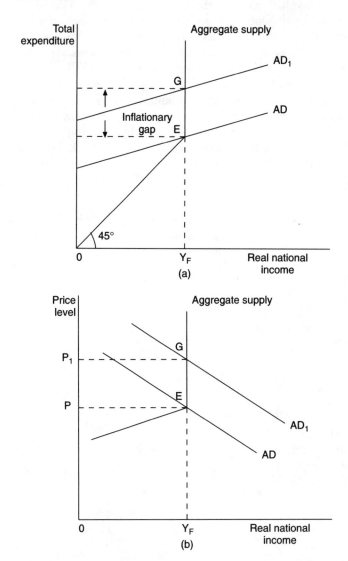

Figure 4.2 Demand-pull inflation

Box 4.2 National income and the price level

The equilibrium level of national income can be depicted in terms of the intersection of the aggregate demand schedule and the aggregate supply schedule at particular price levels. This version of the aggregate demand schedule parallels at the macro level the demand schedule for an individual product, though in this case the schedule represents demand for all goods and services and deals with the general price level rather than with a particular price. Similarly, the aggregate supply schedule parallels at the macro level the supply schedule for an individual product but, again, represents the supply of all goods and services and deals with the general price level rather than a particular price. In Figure (a) aggregate demand equals aggregate supply at the equilibrium price level OP. At any price level above this, say OP_1, aggregate supply exceeds aggregate demand and the resulting excess supply will force the price level down to OP. At price levels below OP, say OP_2, aggregate demand exceeds aggregate supply and this excess demand will force the price level up to OP.

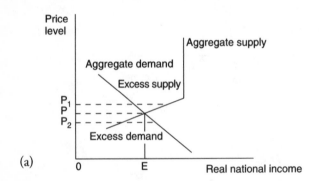

(a)

The equilibrium level of real national income and the price level will change if there is a shift in the aggregate demand schedule. For example, if aggregate demand rises from AD to AD_1, the result is an increase in the equilibrium real income level from OE to OE_1 and an increase in the price level from OP to OP_1.

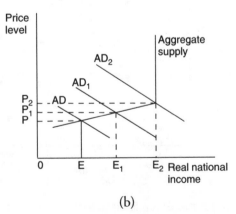

(b)

The equilibrium level of real national income and the price level will also change if there is a shift in the aggregate supply schedule. For example, as in Figure (c), if aggregate supply increases from AS to AS_1 (because of an increase in the labour force or the capital stock, etc.) the result is an increase in the equilibrium real income level from OE to OE_1 and a fall in the price level from OP to OP_1.

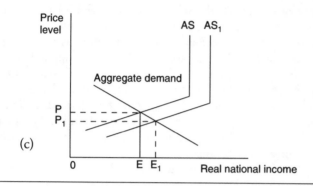

(c)

4.3.1 Demand-pull inflation

Demand-pull inflation occurs when there is an excess of total spending (aggregate demand) at the full employment level of national income (potential gross national product). This is illustrated in Figure 4.2(a), where aggregate demand and aggregate supply are expressed in terms of total spending and national income (see Chapter 1) and 4.2(b), where aggregate demand and aggregate supply are expressed in terms of price levels and national income (see Box 4.2). Once the economy reaches the full employment level of national income (OY_F) output cannot expand further and at this level of output the aggregate supply schedule becomes vertical. If aggregate demand was at the level indicated by AD the economy would be operating at full employment without inflation (at point E). However, if aggregate demand were at a higher level such as AD_1 the excess aggregate demand would create an *inflationary gap* (equal to EG), pulling price upward. In terms of Figure 4.2(b) an inflationary gap shows up as the difference between the price level (OP) corresponding to the full employment level of aggregate demand (AD) and the price level (OP_1) corresponding to the higher level of aggregate demand (AD_1) at national income level OY_F.

Monetarists suggest that excess demand is particularly associated with an excessive expansion of the money supply; that is, demand-pull inflation reflects a situation of 'too much money chasing too little output'. This contention is often expressed in terms of the quantity theory of money, which is set out below.

4.3.2 The quantity theory of money and the general level of prices

The *quantity theory of money* posits a direct relationship between the money supply and the general price level in an economy. The basic idea underlying the quantity theory was first developed by Irving Fisher in 1911. The Fisher equation states that:

$$MV \equiv PT$$

where M is the money stock, V is the velocity of circulation of money (the average number of times each pound changes hands in financing transactions during a year), P is the general price level and T is the number of transactions or the total amount of goods and services supplied.

The above relationship is true by definition because total money expenditure on goods and services (MV) in a period must equal the money value of goods and services produced (PT), and the four terms are defined in such a way that the identity must hold. However, the identity can be converted into a testable equation by assuming that the velocity of circulation of money is constant or changes slowly.

Economists at Cambridge University reformulated the traditional quantity theory of money to emphasise the relationship between the stock of money in an economy (M) and final income (Y), of the form $MV \equiv Y$. The income velocity of circulation (the Cambridge equation) is thus:

$$V = \frac{Y}{M}$$

where V is the average number of times the money stock of an economy changes hands in the purchase of final goods and services. For example, taking Y as gross national product, if a country has a GNP of £5,000 million and an average money stock (M) over a year of £1,000 million, then V is 5. Velocity cannot be observed directly and is thus determined using Y and M, figures which may be calculated from government statistics.

The term V in the Cambridge equation is not the same as V in Fisher's traditional quantity theory of money. In Fisher's equation, $MV \equiv PT$, rearranged to give:

$$V = \frac{PT}{M}$$

the number of transactions in the period, T, includes all transactions involving real goods and services plus financial transactions. In the Cambridge equation, PT (where P is the average price level) is replaced by Y, which contains not all transactions but only those generating final income. This formulation allowed the Cambridge economists to emphasise real income (that is, final goods and services).

The classical economists argued that velocity of circulation was constant because consumers have relatively constant spending habits and so turn money over at a steady rate. This argument converts the identity into an equation that leads to the quantity theory, which expresses a relationship between the supply of money and the general price level. If V and T are constant then $M = P$ and change in M = change in P.

The modern exponents of the quantity theory (such as Milton Friedman) do not necessarily hold that the velocity of circulation is fixed, but they argue that it will change only slowly over time as a result of financial innovations like the spread of bank accounts and cheque payments, and the growing use of credit cards. They also point out that in a fully employed economy there is a maximum amount of goods and services being produced and which therefore can be exchanged, so that the number of transactions, T, is determined by real supply-side considerations like productivity trends. With V and T fixed or changing slowly, the price level is determined by the stock of money, M. Any increase in the money supply feeds directly into an increase in demand for goods and services (aggregate demand). It follows that if the money supply (M), and hence aggregate demand, increase over time faster than the supply capacity of the economy (T), the result will be a rise in the general price level, P (inflation). Keynesian economists, by contrast, argue that the velocity of circulation is unstable and changes rapidly, and may offset changes in the money stock.

4.3.3 Cost-push inflation

Cost-push inflation reflects a situation of rising prices caused by increases in factor input prices which are independent of the state of demand for final goods and services. Thus prices may rise even when the economy is operating at

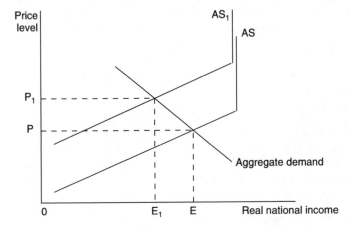

Figure 4.3 Cost-push inflation

output levels below the full employment level of national income. In Figure 4.3 the initial price level is shown as OP and the equilibrium level of national income as OE. Suppose now there is an increase in factor input prices across the economy. It is reflected in a shift in the aggregate supply schedule from AS to AS$_1$. As a result the equilibrium level of national income falls from OE to OE$_1$ and the price level increases from OP to OP$_1$.

Factor input costs may rise because raw materials and energy costs increase, owing to worldwide shortages or the operations of cartels (in oil, for example), or where a country's exchange rate falls, serving to increase the cost of imported raw materials; or because wage rates in the economy increase at a faster rate than output per person (productivity). (See Table 4.2 and Box 4.3.) In the latter case institutional factors such as the use of comparability and wage differential arguments in collective bargaining and the persistence of restrictive labour practices can serve to push wages up

Box 4.3 Non-inflationary wage increases

It is important to note that wage increases are not necessarily inflationary *per se*. Wage increases must be looked at alongside productivity gains. If wage increases are 'financed' or 'absorbed' by an increase in productivity (output per employee) then prices need not be increased. The figures below show a situation where a wage increase in a carpet firm is exactly matched by an increase in productivity, leaving unit costs/prices unchanged. Complications can arise, however, when not all the increase in productivity is attributable to the labour input; for example, the productivity gain may stem largely from investment in new machinery. Thus part of the value added is attributable to the capital input. If labour appropriates the *whole* of the productivity gain the capital cost of the investment will reduce the firm's unit profits or require it to put its prices up.

Wage rate	Output rate
1 £10 per hour Labour cost per square metre of carpet = £10	1 m^2 of carpet per hour
2 £10.30 per hour 3 per cent wage increase Labour cost per square metre of carpet *unchanged* at £10 (£10.30 divided by 1.03)	1.03 m^2 of carpet per hour 3 per cent productivity increase

Therefore: no need to increase price

and limit the scope for productivity improvements. Faced with increased input costs, producers try to pass on increased costs by charging higher prices in order to maintain profit margins. If this is done across the economy it can result in cost-push inflation (see Boxes 4.2 and 4.3).

Monetarists, however, suggest that 'cost-push' is not a truly independent theory of inflation – it has to be 'financed' or 'accommodated' by money supply increases. Suppose, initially, a given stock of money and given levels of output and prices. Assume now that costs increase (for example, higher wage rates), causing suppliers to put up prices. Monetarists argue that the increase in prices will not turn into an inflationary process (that is, a *persistent* tendency for prices to rise) unless the money supply is increased. The given stock of money will buy fewer goods at the higher price level and real demand will fall. However, if the government increases the money supply this enables the same volume of goods to be purchased at the higher price level. If this process of increasing the money supply continues, cost-push inflation is validated and will become persistent.

The value of analysing the causes of inflation using the aggregate demand and supply framework is that it enables us to discuss appropriate policies to deal with inflation. Specifically, this framework has become the basis of a policy debate between monetarists and Keynesians about the efficacy of demand management policies in controlling inflation.

4.4 INFLATION THEORY AND POLICY

A central issue deriving from the above analysis is whether governments can influence the movements of the aggregate demand and aggregate supply schedules in such a way as to maintain full employment at low levels of inflation. In other words, is there potential for governments to play an active role in the running of an economy? This issue reveals one of the sharpest distinctions between economic policy of the 'orthodox' Keynesian variety as operated in the period 1945–80 and the more monetarist policies followed by some of the leading industrial countries since the early 1980s.

4.4.1 Orthodox demand management

Demand management formed the basis of economic policy after 1945. An integral part of the policy was the manipulation of the level of aggregate demand, involving a trade-off between unemployment and inflation (often described in terms of the Phillips curve, as depicted in Figure 4.4). Belief in the Phillips curve relationship underpinned much of the macroeconomic policy of the 1950s and 1960s, when policy appeared to involve a choice of evils. Governments had to choose how much inflation to tolerate when the cost was unemployment – they had to trade off inflation against unemployment. Thus, in terms of Figure 4.4, an expansion of aggregate demand

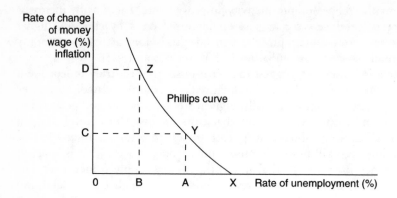

Figure 4.4 Phillips curve

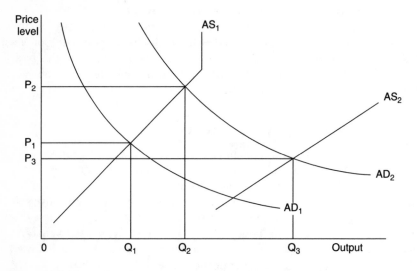

Figure 4.5 Unemployment and inflation trade-offs

would serve to reduce unemployment from OA to OB but only at the cost of higher wage increases (and thus higher inflation) as wages increase from OC to OD, the economy being moved along the Phillips curve from point Y to point Z. Figure 4.5 provides another way of depicting this trade-off in terms of aggregate demand and aggregate supply. An expansionary demand management policy (AD_1 to AD_2) would increase output from OQ_1 to OQ_2 and reduce unemployment, but at a cost, that cost being higher inflation as prices rise from OP_1 to OP_2. To counter these inflationary impulses, governments of the day tried to manipulate aggregate supply by imposing wage restraint (incomes policies). This it was hoped would move the aggregate supply schedule from AS_1 to AS_2 thus leading to a new equilibrium posi-tion in which output was higher (OQ_3) and inflation (OP_3) lower than the original equilibrium.

The focus of the economic debate was whether governments could induce such a beneficial change. The failure to achieve wage restraint (that is, the failure of incomes policies) and the resultant 'stagflation' (high unemploy-ment combined with high rates of inflation) of the 1970s raised questions about the ability of governments to induce such a beneficial change using demand management techniques. These in turn lent increasing credibility to contrasting monetarist ideas on the causes of inflation.

4.4.2 Monetarist critique of orthodox (Keynesian) demand management

The essential point of the new monetarist doctrine was that demand management was counterproductive. Demand management, although bene-ficial in the short-run, was actually counterproductive in the long term. The essence of the argument can be stated in terms of the expectations-augmented Phillips curve as portrayed in Figure 4.6. It may be argued that there is not just one Phillips curve but a whole set of such curves like P_0,

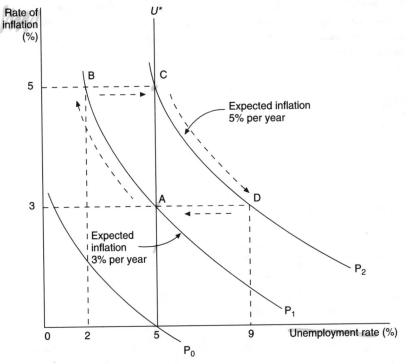

Figure 4.6 Expectations-augmented Phillips curve

P_1 and P_2 in Figure 4.6, each curve corresponding to a different expectation about inflation rates. In this case P_0 corresponds to an expected inflation rate of 0 per cent per year (stable prices), P_1 corresponds to expected inflation of 3 per cent per year, while P_2 corresponds to expected inflation of 5 per cent per year. The vertical line U^* shows the 'natural rate of unemployment' which would be established by the interaction of supply and demand in the labour market. In so far as U^* corresponds to the point where Phillips curve P_0 cuts the horizontal axis, it also shows the non-accelerating inflation rate of unemployment (NAIRU).

Suppose that currently people expect inflation to be 3 per cent per year and that the economy is therefore on Phillips curve P_1, say at point A, with inflation of 3 per cent and unemployment of 5 per cent. If the government seeks to reduce unemployment below 5 per cent by stimulating aggregate demand the initial short-term effect is to move the economy along Phillips curve P_1 from point A to point B and unemployment falls from 5 per cent to 2 per cent. However, at point B inflation has now increased from 3 per cent to 5 per cent and after a while businesspeople and wage earners will adjust their inflationary expectations to the new higher inflation, tending to increase their prices and wage rates. In the longer term, the monetarists argue, unemployment will revert to its 'natural rate' of 5 per cent and the economy will move to point C on Phillips curve P_2, which corresponds to inflationary expectations of 5 per cent per year. The effect, therefore, of stimulating aggregate demand is simply to raise rates of inflation in the economy, without any permanent reduction in unemployment. Furthermore, monetarists argue, over the longer term the ratcheting up of

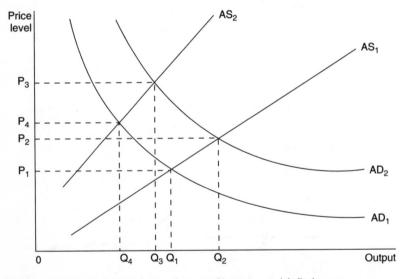

Figure 4.7 Monetarist analysis of unemployment and inflation

inflationary expectations will tend to disrupt the functioning of markets and cause the underlying natural rate of unemployment to increase, moving U* to the right.

Figure 4.7 emphasises the above point in terms of aggregate demand and aggregate supply. Suppose that output was originally OQ_1, where AS_1 and AD_1 intersect. To reduce unemployment the government increases its spending and the money supply so as to shift the aggregate demand curve from AD_1 to AD_2. Both orthodox and monetarist analyses agree that the effect will be to increase output from OQ_1 to OQ_2 and so reduce unemployment, albeit at a cost in terms of inflation as prices rise from OP_1 to OP_2. However, while this is the end of the 'orthodox' story, monetarist analysis has another crucial stage: the aggregate supply curve shifts upwards to AS_2 (because of the upward revision of inflationary expectations) so that output is lower at OQ_3 than it was originally and prices are higher at OP_3. The monetarist analysis, in other words, rejects the view that aggregate supply and aggregate demand are independent of each other. Shifting the AD curve outwards causes firms to expect inflation, which will shift the AS curve inwards as firms reduce output. Governments can reduce unemployment in the short term but the cost is not only inflation but higher long-term unemployment. Thus it is argued by monetarists that unemployment was high in the 1980s as a consequence of misguided efforts to reduce it, via demand management, in the 1950s and 1960s.

Central to this hypothesis was the role of inflationary expectations in the work of Milton Friedman. Friedman suggested that demand inflation may feed upon itself, creating an inflationary spiral involving the interaction of rising final prices and rising input costs. For example, an initial sharp increase in the prices of goods and services caused by an expansionary demand management policy (increasing AD_1 to AD_2 in Figure 4.7) can lead to a demand for higher money wages by trade unions concerned to protect their members' living standards (cost-push inflation movement in the AS schedule, from AS_1 to AS_2). If conceded, higher wage costs are soon likely to prompt producers to put their prices up to protect their profit margins. The higher prices in turn produce further demands for wage increases, and so on. Over time price–cost increases tend to be self-reinforcing and are exacerbated by expectations of yet further increases. Where inflation is expected or 'anticipated' this will cause economic decision-makers, whether they be individuals, trade unions or businesses, to adapt their current behaviour – for example, wage bargainers instead of relating their current wage demands solely to the current inflation rate may attempt to secure an 'additional' increase now in order to allow for anticipated future rates of inflation over the period of the wage settlement (one year, two years, etc.).

Employing this analysis, monetarists put forward the view that the era of demand management in the 1950s and 1960s caused the period of stagflation in the 1970s. They argued that the era of demand management in the 1950s and 1960s had created a belief among firms and trade unions that governments were committed to the idea of full employment. As a result trade unions ceased to believe that the threat of unemployment need constrain wage demands, and their demands were agreed to by firms whose belief in full employment suggested that the increased costs could be passed on in higher prices, because high demand would be ensured. Hence the belief in full employment led to cost increases, and so to upward movements of the AS curves.

Thus higher inflation (induced by demand management) leads to a higher expected level of inflation and so to an adverse shift of the AS schedule. The higher the expected increase in inflation the larger will be the move in the AS schedule. In turn the larger the move in the AS schedule the less effective will demand management (movements in the AD schedule) be.

4.4.3 Monetarist policy

Monetarists suggested a different remedy for inflation which was adopted as the basis of government policy in a number of countries, including the UK. What emerged was a government policy which took the control of inflation as its main priority, supplemented by strong supply-side measures. The rationale was that only by getting inflation down to low levels and liberalising the supply side of the economy could a sustainable, low-inflationary growth of output, with the attendant creation of jobs, be achieved. Expressed in terms of Figure 4.6, if the economy was initially at point C on Phillips curve P_2, corresponding to expected inflation of 5 per cent per year, and with 5 per cent unemployment, then the government could act to deflate demand. This would serve to increase unemployment above its 'natural rate' in the short term, increasing unemployment from 5 per cent to 9 per cent, as the economy moved along Phillips curve P_2 from point C to point D. However, in moving from C to D inflation falls from 5 per cent to 3 per cent and this lower level of inflation will cause businesspeople and wage earners to revise their expectations of inflation downward from 5 per cent to 3 per cent. Thus the economy moves from point D to point A on Phillips curve P_1, which corresponds to lower expected inflation of 3 per cent; and as businesspeople and wage earners revise their pricing and wage bargaining behaviour unemployment contracts back to its 'natural rate'. The effect of government policy is thus to reduce long-term inflation by means of a short, sharp shock in the form of (temporarily) increased unemployment.

The same monetarist argument is illustrated in terms of aggregate demand and aggregate supply in Figure 4.7. Starting with price OP_3 and output OQ_3, if the government reduces aggregate demand from AD_2 to AD_1 output falls from OQ_3 to OQ_4 and unemployment rises. However, such a deflationary policy induces not only a fall in the rate of demand inflation but also a downward reappraisal of people's inflationary expectations. As a result of overall lower inflation the aggregate supply starts to shift outwards from AS_2 to AS_1 so that in the end output is higher, at OQ_1, and unemployment lower. Few economists would disagree that this will happen 'in the end' or indeed that it has happened in the UK but the question is how long it will be before the full benefits are obtained and whether they are worth the cost (i.e., lost output and unemployment).

4.5 POLICIES TO CONTROL INFLATION

Most countries have experienced inflation over recent decades, though the extent of it has varied greatly from one country to another (see Box 4.4). The traditional prescription to remove inflation caused by *excess demand* is for the authorities to reduce spending by deflationary fiscal and monetary policy measures; for example, tax increases and reductions in government expenditure and the money supply. In view of the desirability of maintaining investment spending so as to add to capacity and improve competitiveness on the supply side of the economy (see Chapter 5), ideally the brunt of these measures should be borne by consumer demand and 'non-essential' government spending (particularly if excess demand has been exacerbated by large public sector borrowing requirements). In terms of Figure 4.8 the aim would be to bring about a shift in the aggregate demand schedule from AD_1 to AD so that aggregate demand would be just sufficient to purchase the full employment level of national income OY_F at the lower price level of OP, thus removing the 'inflationary gap'. In the monetarist view while fiscal policy may go some way to removing excess demand a fundamental requirement is a reduction in the money supply to eliminate 'surplus' liquidity available for financing or 'accommodating' undesirable levels of spending.

Tackling cost-push influences is more problematic, since some inflationary pressures may arise outside the immediate domestic system (for example,

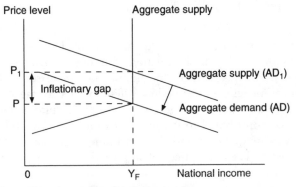

Figure 4.8 Removing demand-pull inflation

in imported raw materials and foodstuff prices) and others, such as the role of expectations in wage bargaining, can be changed only over the medium to longer term. Inflationary expectations may be 'wound-down', it is suggested, if the government is seen to be taking a hard line on inflation and inflation rates actually do come down. Some economists, however, recommend that a *prices and incomes policy* may be necessary to 'break' the inflationary spiral. A prices and incomes policy is a *direct* means of halting or slowing down the inflationary spiral of price–wage rises, in contrast to deflationary monetary policy and fiscal policy, which work *indirectly* to achieve the same result. The basic rationale of a prices and incomes policy is that, whereas deflationary monetary and fiscal policies can control

Box 4.4 Inflation in the UK, Japan and the USA

Inflation rates in the main industrial economies were much lower in the 1980s and early 1990s than in the 1970s, largely as a result of recessionary conditions and lower energy prices.

UK
Inflation rates (see chart) reached extremely high levels in the first half of the 1970s, mainly as a result of the cost-push impulses of the quadrupling of the price of oil in 1973, the UK's entry in that year to the European Community, which led to a substantial increase in food prices and a wages 'explosion' in response to the increased cost of living. Inflationary pressures decelerated over the period 1976–8 but then inflation took off again as a result of a further large increase in oil prices in 1979 and an increase in value-added tax from 8 per cent to 15 per cent. This resulted in the UK's worst post-1945 recession, leading to double-digit unemployment rates. Inflation rates remained at relatively modest levels down to 1988, when a boost to demand by tax cuts and financial deregulation propelled it upwards. However, after peaking in 1990 the inflation rate has fallen to low levels.

Japan
In contrast to most other countries, Japan has been singularly successful in keeping both inflation and unemployment in check. Although Japan was hard hit by the oil price increases of 1973 and 1979, inflation rates in the period 1984–93 have averaged around 2 per cent. Moderation in wage rate increases (despite a tight labour market) has contributed to keeping inflation rates low, and in recent years lower energy prices and the continuing appreciation of the yen have served to keep the prices of imported raw materials and foodstuffs down.

USA

Inflation averaged around 8 per cent in the USA over the period 1974–83, higher than in Germany or Japan but less than the in UK and the average inflation rate for all industrial countries. Inflation rates remained modest in the 1980s despite a substantial increase in the size of the federal budget deficit, aided by lower energy and food prices. Since 1990 a slow-down in wages growth has also helped keep inflation in check.

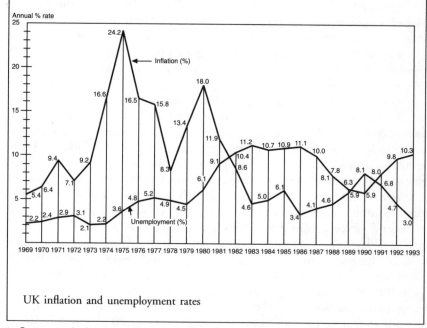

UK inflation and unemployment rates

inflation only by increasing the rate of unemployment, a prices and incomes policy, if applied rigorously, can check inflation *and* maintain high levels of employment.

A prices and incomes policy can be operated on a voluntary or a statutory (compulsory) basis. In the former case, an appeal is made to the collective sense of responsibility of firms not to increase their prices 'unduly' and to trade unions to 'moderate' their demands for wage increases. The very vagueness of such exhortations, however, means that they are usually given short shrift by vested interests. A statutory policy has more chance of success, certainly in the medium term if it is backed by strong penalties for non-compliance. Typical elements of the statutory approach include: (1) an initial, brief (six months to one year) standstill or 'freeze' on all price, wage, dividend, etc., increases; (2) a following period (usually 'phased' to allow the progressive relaxation of controls) in which either (a) general 'norms' are laid down for permitted price and wage increases, for example limiting them to, say, 3 per cent per annum, or (b), more specifically, formulas are etablished for linking permitted price and wage increases to, for example, in the case of a price rise, to non-absorbable cost increases, or in the case of a wage rise to increases in productivity. This latter approach requires the establishment of some regulatory body (such as the National Board for Prices and Incomes or the Price Commission and the Pay Board, which formerly operated in Britain) to ensure that proposed price and wage increases are indeed justified.

Proponents of a prices and incomes policy see it as a useful way of 'defusing' inflationary expectations, thereby removing the danger of accelerating inflation rates, by publishing pay and price norm targets. On the other hand it must be recognised that because such a policy interferes with the operation of market forces it is likely to produce distortions in factor and product markets.

Finally, it may be possible to take the 'sting' out of inflation and reduce its distortions by a policy of *indexation*. Indexation provides for the *automatic* adjustment of income payments in proportion to changes in a general price index. For example, wages and pensions can be linked to the retail price index so that, as retail prices increase year by year, wages and pensions increase in the same proportion so as to maintain their value in real terms. Indexation can be useful in helping people to 'live with inflation' without suffering hardship and it can play a part in bringing inflationary expectations down. If the economic system were entirely 'closed' and sealed off from international influences then indexation might prove a viable long-term means of ameliorating inflation. However, by itself it does not tackle the forces driving inflation, and it is these which have powerful international repercussions. Thus, although domestically, in the short term, inflation can be 'bought off' by indexation, unless an attempt is made to remove the root causes the longer-term effects may well be disastrous. (See Box 4.5.)

Specifically, in an 'open' economy it is imperative in the interests of maintaining domestic output and employment at high levels for a country to remain internationally competitive (see Chapter 6 and Sections 10.2–3).

4.6 CONCLUSION

Inflation can, if unchecked, become a serious economic problem with insidious effects upon the efficient functioning of the economy. There are many possible causes of inflation, several of which may act simultaneously to accelerate inflation. Furthermore controversy about the relative strength of the causes of inflation has led to problems in developing appropriate policy responses to deal with inflation.

4.7 IMPLICATIONS FOR BUSINESS

Inflation is generally disliked by the business community, as it causes a number of inconveniences and distortions. Regular renegotiation of contracts with suppliers and the adjustment of list prices are but two of the administrative hassles.

In times of inflation a company will need to keep a close eye on the value of its assets. Historic cost accounting procedures are unreliable in times of rapid inflation, seriously overestimating the real profitability of the firm and underestimating the replacement cost of the firm's fixed assets in terms of current market prices. Moreover, by undervaluing the firm's net worth it can make the firm more vulnerable to an unwanted take-over bid. Regular revaluations of the firm's assets to reflect current prices is imperative if these anomalies are to be removed. One relatively simple means of inflation-adjusting a firm's accounting results is the *current purchasing power method*. This method uses a price index number to adjust the calculated profit figure from the profit and loss account and to express it in real terms. A more detailed approach is the *current cost accounting method*. This produces a supplementary current-cost profit and loss account. In these current-cost accounts the deduction from revenue for cost of sales is based upon the replacement cost of the goods sold, while depreciation provisions are calculated on the replacement cost of fixed assets and not on their historical cost.

Faced with increases in labour and materials costs, a company will need to consider whether to pass these costs on by charging higher prices for its products or to absorb them.

Concurrent improvements in a firm's efficiency and productivity may permit it to absorb cost rises, enabling it to hold its prices down. This may well be an important consideration for firms operating in a highly price-competitive market. However, firms are likely to reach a point when further increases in input costs can no longer be contained and must be passed on in higher prices. Rising demand often allows scope for firms to improve profit margins by increasing prices, and even relatively inefficient firms may well be in a position to secure higher profits. Again, as emphasised earlier, due note must be taken of whether these profit gains represent a 'real' improvement in the firm's profit position or merely an inflationary increase.

Inflation can erode the price competitiveness and profitability of companies trading internationally. This is particularly the case under a regime of *fixed exchange rates*. If a country's inflation rate increases more rapidly than other countries' it can serve to reduce the price competitiveness of firms, both in export markets and in their domestic market (see Chapter 10). To illustrate: assume initially that goods produced by a UK supplier are priced

at £1 and the same goods produced by a US manufacturer are priced at
$1. If the exchange rate between the dollar and pound is £1=$1 the product
is equally competitive in both markets. Assume now that, because of cost
inflation in both countries, the price of the goods produced in the UK
doubles to £2 but that the price of the goods produced by the US firm
rises by only 50 per cent to $1.50. At an *unchanged* exchange rate of £1=$1,
the UK goods exported to the USA are now priced at $2 in the local
currency, compared with the $1.50 charged by the US firm, thus making

Box 4.5 Inflation, Brazilian style

Brazil has had rampant inflation for a number of years and has
attempted to take the 'sting' out of it by daily or monthly indexation. The on-going 'inflationary culture' has, however, damaged the
economy. For firms cash management has become a critical element:
'Our main challenge is to ensure that money earned from sales all
around the country reaches our Rio HQ as rapidly as possible in
order to invest it in the money markets' (Finance Director, BAT
Industries subsidiary, *Financial Times*, February 22 1993). The preoccupation of firms with investing cash in the money market has had
a negative impact on investment in capital formation. The country's
growth of real GDP has averaged less than 1 per cent since 1987 and
the quality of Brazil's infrastructure has declined alarmingly.

Since 1987 various measures have been used to tackle inflation (see
graph). In 1993, however, the incoming Franco government elected
to make growth its priority, cutting interest rates to restore business
confidence and increasing government spending. A new tax on bank
cheques was introduced not only to cover increased spending but also
to reduce the size of the government's overall budget deficit with the
aim of limiting money supply growth. In 1994, however, further
currency reform was instigated when the government introduced yet
another currency – the 'real'.

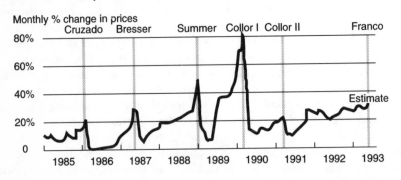

Stabilization programmes: main measures
Cruzado (February 1986): price freeze; new currency - the cruzado.
Bresser (June 1987): price freeze; public spending controls; devaluation.
Summer (January 1989): price freeze; new currency - the new cruzado; interest rate increase.
Collor I (March 1990): price freeze; new currency - the cruzeiro; abolished wage indexation; tax reform; assets tax; public spending cuts; import controls freed.
Collor II (January 1991): price freeze; abolished some daily indexation; free wage bargaining; tariff cuts.

Inflation in Brazil and presidential regimes since 1985
Source: Financial Times, 30 April 1993.

them uncompetitive in the US market. By the same token, the US goods imported into the UK are now priced at £1.50 in the local currency, compared with their UK competitor's price of £2. Suppliers may, of course, attempt to hold prices down by reducing their profit margins but clearly there are limits to what can be absorbed in the way of profit erosion. More generally, the government may attempt to redress a loss of external competitiveness by devaluing the exchange rate against other currencies, or (under a *floating exchange rate* regime) allowing the exchange rate to depreciate in value against other currencies.

QUESTIONS

1 Outline and comment on recent trends in inflation in the industrialised countries.
2 What do you understand by the terms 'demand-pull' inflation and 'cost-push' inflation? What policies can governments use to combat each of these forms of inflation?
3 How do monetarists view inflation? How would a monetarist government set about controlling inflation?
4 Discuss the role of expectations in the inflationary process.
5 What is the relationship, if any, between inflation and unemployment?

Chapter 5

Economic growth

Policy-makers rarely set explicit targets for the long-term well-being of an economy. Targets such as the doubling of living standards every twenty-five years would be seen as over-ambitious, yet such a target would only entail an annual growth rate of less than 3 per cent. Over the period 1976 to 1985 Japan, for example, averaged 4.2 per cent growth and 4.4 per cent growth over the period 1986 to 1991 before falling into recession, so that Japan was comfortably meeting the twenty-five-year doubling target.

The aim of the present chapter is to emphasise the role of macroeconomic policy in the long-term growth of the economy, as against policies aimed at countering short-term fluctuations in income and output. The policy framework changes from a situation where in the short run a country's potential gross national product is constrained by the availability of economic resources (labour and capital) to the long run, where a country is able to produce more goods and services through an increase in the quantity of resource inputs available to it and more efficient use of those resources. It should, however, be noted that although economic growth is desirable in itself, as a means of increasing the standard of living, it can bring with it various problems – for example, the exhaustion of finite natural resources and exacerbate problems of environmental pollution. (See Box 5.1.) Both these issues have come to the fore in recent years, with governments (both nationally and through international agreements) being concerned to conserve resources (for example, by setting limits on fishing catches) and imposing more exacting pollution control standards (for example, requiring motor cars to have catalytic converters to reduce sulphur emissions).

In the present chapter we look, first, at the measurement of economic growth and recent international growth trends. Second, we discuss in some detail the major determinants of economic growth, and how different countries have performed in relation to these factors. This analysis gives some indication of the long-term growth potential of the leading world economies and their need for a long-term economic policy, which we discuss in the final section.

Box 5.1 Environmental issues

In recent years the emphasis on the pursuit of economic efficiency and growth at all costs has been tempered by a recognition that protection of the environment should be given greater priority. At the international level concerns such as global warming and its effects on the earth's ozone layer, control of pollution and conservation of natural habitats and species of wildlife found expression at the 'Earth Summit' in Rio in June 1992. This conference, attended by 172 countries, agreed on the need to take active measures to control toxic emissions (e.g. motor car exhaust fumes, chemical discharges, etc.) and the protection of wildlife.

The European Union has also been active; for example, all cars manufactured in the EU are now required to incorporate catalytic converters to minimise sulphur emissions. The introduction of an energy tax is high on the EU's agenda, although some members (e.g. the UK) felt that environmental protection should be left to the discretion of the individual members.

The 'polluter pays' principle, embraced at the Rio conference, that companies which pollute the environment should bear the costs of the damage they cause and should be encouraged to invest in producing technologies which limit harmful side effects, is gaining widespread acceptance. For example, in the UK the Environmental Protection Act 1990 holds the producer of waste legally responsible for its safe handling and disposal. The range of this legislation, and the competitive changes it is provoking in many industries, mean that more companies are now making environmental management part of their overall strategic thinking.

More generally, the 'green' movement is educating consumers to demand environmentally-friendly products (e.g. biogradable washing powders) and packaging materials (e.g. aluminium beer cans which can be recycled).

In the last analysis the increased economic costs of protecting the environment have to be traded against 'quality of life' considerations. However, attention to pollution control can itself produce economic benefits. For example, making aluminium from recycled scrap requires only 5 per cent of the energy used in processing virgin aluminium. This has knock-on effects into other areas – around 70 per cent of the aluminium used in electrical engineering and virtually all aluminium automotive castings are made from recycled aluminium scrap, thus serving to reduce production costs in these industries.

5.1 MEASUREMENT OF ECONOMIC GROWTH

Measures of the money value of the output of an economy over time can convey a misleading impression of economic growth unless the effects of inflation are allowed for to reveal *real* output changes (see Box 5.2). Thus economic growth is defined as the growth of the *real* output of an economy over time and can be measured in terms of an increase in real gross national product (GNP) or real gross domestic product (GDP) over time, or in terms of an increase in income per head over time. The former two measures reckon the expansion of output in absolute terms, the latter relates the expansion of output to the concurrent growth of population. The difference is important, as one measure without the other can give misleading indications of the extent of growth. Most notably, countries experiencing rapid population growth often have higher growth records in terms of real GDP. However, growth measured as an increase in income per head may reflect lower growth rates, by comparison with other countries. (See Box 1.1.)

Box 5.2 Real and money GNP

Real GNP or GDP is important because it represents the output of *physical* goods and services, not their money values. An economy may appear to produce more goods and services because money GDP (measured in *current* prices) has increased, but this may simply reflect price increases (inflation) without any increase in physical output (measured in *constant* prices). For example, the table shows that although the UK's GDP measured in current prices increased between 1990 and 1991, there was actually a decline in the UK's GDP measured in real terms. A GNP and GDP 'deflator' is used to remove the influence of price changes and record only real changes by reworking longitudinal data on a constant price basis.

UK gross domestic product

Year	Constant (1990) prices (£ billion)	Current prices (£ billion)
1990	418	550
1991	409	574
1992	537	597
1993	549	630

Source: UK National Income Accounts, 1994.

Even so, real GDP per person is often a very imperfect indicator of the income of the typical individual within a country, since many countries have a very unequal income distribution, with a few people earning high incomes and many people earning low incomes. Thus it is possible for such countries to have fairly high *per capita* real income while many of their citizens are really quite badly off. (See Box 5.3.)

There are also problems with the use of gross domestic product (GDP) and gross national product (GNP) as measures of growth. In particular, GDP (and GNP) are very incomplete measures of *economic* output. GDP measures the net output, or value added, of an economy by measuring goods and services purchased with money. It omits output which is not bought and sold, such as goods and services produced in the 'black market' or the housekeeping services rendered by unpaid housewives, and which is therefore unmeasured. To the extent that such elements of the economy are significant GDP will be understated. This is particularly important when measuring the output of developing countries, where a large proportion of the population are involved in subsistence farming rather than specialising in cash crops for market sale. The self-sufficient peasant farmers in such countries consume most of their crops themselves rather than selling them, making it difficult to measure the agricultural output of such economies. On the other hand, GDP may overstate the true output of an economy by neglecting externalities such as pollution and congestion. The pollution created in producing goods and services reduces the net economic welfare that the economy is producing and ideally should be subtracted from GDP. Ironically, in most countries' GDP accounts the goods produced to protect people from pollution and the work of service industries involved in cleaning up pollution are counted as part of national output.

5.2 TRENDS IN ECONOMIC GROWTH

Table 5.1 shows the growth in real GDP of the USA, Japan, Germany and the UK, together with the 'all industrial' and 'all developing' countries averages for the period 1976–93. On a more global level, the world economy has experienced three broad eras of growth since the 1960s: the rapid growth of the 1960s, the slowdown in the 1970s and early 1980s, and the higher growth rates of the mid-1980s to early 1990s.

5.2.1 Era of rapid growth, 1960–73: reasons for rapid growth

1 Inter-sectoral shifts in labour – shifts in labour from low-productivity to high-productivity sectors of the economy.
2 Liberalisation of world trade, mainly through the General Agreement on Tariffs and Trade (GATT), which reduced barriers to trade like tariffs and quotas.

Table 5.1 Real GDP, selected countries, 1976-93, annual % change

Country	Average 1976–85	1986	1987	1988	1989	1990	1991	1992	1993
USA	2.9	2.9	3.1	3.9	2.5	1.2	−0.7	2.6	3.0
Japan	4.2	2.6	4.1	6.2	4.7	4.8	4.3	1.1	0.1
Germany	1.6	2.3	1.5	3.7	3.6	5.7	1.0	2.1	−1.2
UK	1.9	4.3	4.8	5.0	2.2	0.4	−2.2	−0.6	1.9
All industrial countries	2.2	2.9	3.1	3.8	4.0	2.8	0.9	0.9	1.6
All developing countries	4.5	5.0	5.7	5.3	4.0	3.7	4.4	5.9	6.1
Eastern Europe and former USSR	3.8	3.6	2.8	5.3	3.0	−2.0	−11.6	−18.2	−11.9

Source: IMF, *World Economic Outlook*, 1994.

3 Low energy prices.
4 Transfer of technology; mainly from the USA to Japan and Western Europe.

5.2.2 Reasons for the slow-down, 1973–84

1 Oil price increases (1973 and 1979) led to balance of payments problems in oil-importing countries which forced them to deflate their economies in order to curtail imports.
2 Deflation led to lower investment and hence slower growth in the capital to labour ratio and slower growth in technology.
3 Anti-inflation policies in the form of high interest rates and tight fiscal policies checked demand and growth.
4 The more limited scope for productivity improvements in the service sector. (This constraint has become important as the service sector has grown as a proportion of GDP).

Most industrial countries experienced higher growth rates between 1984 and 1990. Since 1990 most of the industrialised economies have suffered recessionary conditions which have stunted growth. The emergence of a 'world' recession in most of the Western world stands in stark contrast to the growth rates of certain developing countries, particularly Asian countries (Hong Kong, Singapore, China, Taiwan, Thailand), which have generally been higher than those of the advanced industrial countries. This reflects their greater scope for increasing manufacturing output and productivity as they 'industrialise' their economies and reduce their dependence on agricultural commodities and basic raw materials. In this sense we may hypothesise that in the future we can expect a growing convergence

Box 5.3 Distribution of income and wealth in the UK

The distribution of national income among households in the UK is seen to be very unequal when national income is classified into five quintile groups according to size of household income, as below:

Personal distribution of original income in the UK, 1991

Quintile groups of households	Original income (%)
Top fifth	42.0
Second fifth	24.7
Third fifth	17.2
Fourth fifth	10.1
Bottom fifth	6.0

Original income: income before payment of tax and receipt of state benefit in cash, e.g. pensions, and kind, e.g. health and education.

Source: Social Trends, 1994.

The size of incomes differs for a variety of reasons, including differences in people's natural abilities, educational attainment, special skills and inherited wealth.

Marketable wealth is also very unequally distributed in the UK, as the figures below show:

Distribution of marketable wealth in the UK, 1991

Wealth owners	Wealth owned (%)
Most wealthy 1%	18
Most wealthy 5%	37
Most wealthy 10%	50
Most wealthy 25%	71
Most wealthy 50%	92

Total marketable wealth £1,694 billion. Total wealth includes land and buildings (net of mortgage debt), consumer durables, stocks and shares, bank and building society deposits and other financial assets.

Source: Social Trends, 1994.

between the economic performance of the developed and the developing countries.

However, many of the poorer developing countries face severe problems in achieving even modest rates of economic growth and raising living standards. In such countries, low living standards mean that people are unable to save much and virtually all the nation's resources are needed to feed and clothe the population, leaving few resources for investment. Thus these countries are locked into a poverty cycle whereby low living standards lead to low investment and low investment means that living standards remain low. Unless investment funds can be attracted from overseas investors or from international agencies like the World Bank, such countries cannot break out of the poverty trap. However, such countries are often heavily in debt and their international indebtedness makes it difficult for them to borrow more. (See Chapter 10.) Furthermore such countries often have little industry, inadequate education and training facilities, and a poor economic infrastructure (few or poor roads, ports, airports, power stations, etc.) which all serve to impede their growth. Developing countries are often heavily dependent upon agriculture both to feed their population and as the basis of their exports; low agricultural yields limit their output, while the poor world prices for their (cash-crop) agricultural exports limit their foreign exchange earnings. Finally, rapid population growth means that, even when such countries achieve modest growth rates, with more mouths to feed their *per capita* incomes rarely rise.

5.3 DETERMINANTS OF ECONOMIC GROWTH: AN OVERVIEW

Economic growth is a multi-faceted process involving complex input–output interactions. The physical ability of an economy to produce more goods and services over time is dependent on a number of factors (as depicted in Figure 5.1), including:

1 An increase in the quantity and quality of natural resources.
2 An increase in the quantity and quality of the labour force.
3 An increase in the quantity and quality of investment in capital goods.
4 Efficient allocation of these factor inputs as between various end uses, such as to maximise their contribution to the expansion of output.
5 Technological advance – the development and introduction of innovative production processes, techniques, equipment and products.
6 Education and training of workers to improve their productivity.
7 Improved management to organise the more productive deployment of resources.

Whether or not an economy is actually able to achieve its growth potential is dependent on one further consideration:

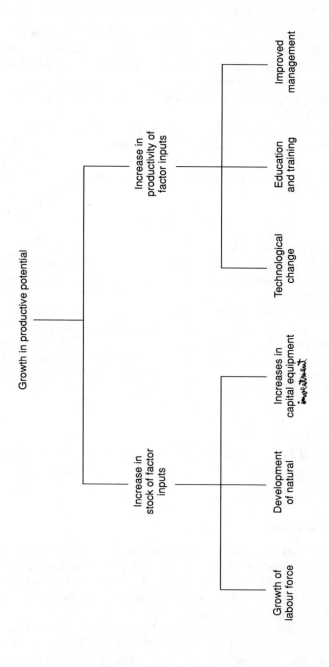

Figure 5.1 Causes of economic growth

8 The level of aggregate demand – it is necessary to have a level of demand sufficient to ensure the full utilisation of the increased production capacity of the economy.

In sum, various supply-side factors combine to raise the slope of the potential output line for the economy over time from, say, 2 per cent to 3 per cent (Figure 5.2a), and shift the aggregate supply curve rightward from AS to AS_1 in Figure 5.2b. However, the stimulus of rising demand is required to ensure that output potential is fully realised, for example, from AD to AD_1 in Figure 5.2b.

When discussing the contributors to the growth process, it is convenient, conceptually, to invoke the concept of the *production function* in the form:

$$Q \text{ depends on Labour and Capital}$$

or

$$Q = A\,(L,\ K)$$

where Q is real output expressed as a function of labour and capital inputs L and K. The production function shows the maximum output that can be produced using specified quantities of inputs, given the existing technical knowledge.

Output may be increased by increasing the input of productive factors; alternatively, any increase in output not explained in terms of factor augmentation must stem from changes in the value of A. The coefficient A may thus be regarded as a productivity source of growth and will include such important influences as innovation and technical change, cultural and social factors, fiscal influences and so forth.

5.3.1 Labour

The impact of labour on economic growth can either be in terms of its quantity (the size of the work force) or its quality (the skills of the existing work force).

5.3.1.1 Labour force

Employment may increase for three reasons. First, there may be population growth. Second, a larger fraction of a given population may be in employment (especially with the increased participation of women in the work force). Third, the labour input will depend on the hours worked as well as on the number of people working.

In most industrial countries there has been only relatively modest growth in the size of the total labour force, although the USA and Japan have recorded sizeable increases (see Table 5.2), while at the same time there has

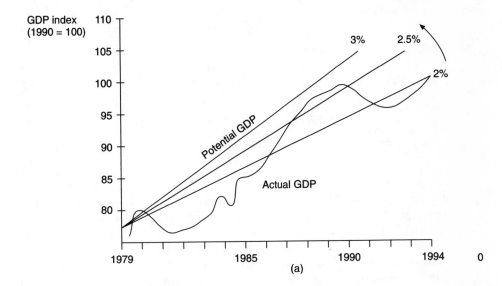

(a)

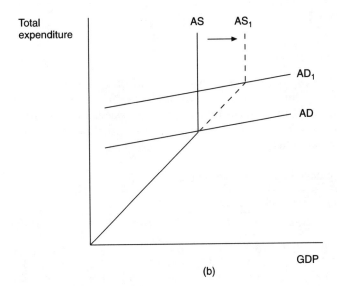

(b)

Figure 5.2 Economic growth: (a) actual and potential GDP, (b) aggregate demand and supply

Table 5.2 Labour force, selected countries, 1977 and 1992

Country	Year	Total (millions)	Male (%)	Female (%)
USA	1977	99	59	41
	1992	125	55	45
Japan	1977	54	62	38
	1992	64	59	41
Germany	1977	26	62	38
	1992	31	60	40
UK	1977	26	61	39
	1992	29	57	43

Source: International Labour Office, 1994.

been a fall in the number of hours worked per week and an increase in holiday periods. Thus, for many countries, increases in the labour input have made only a relatively small contribution to growth.

However, the contribution of labour needs to be looked at in combination with that of investment or the capital input, since it is the 'enrichment' of labour productivity (output per employee) which this provides that contributes the critical element in expanding growth potential. Thus it is something of a misnomer to talk exclusively of the productivity of labour; rather it is the combination of capital and labour that is the key factor. (See Box 5.4.)

5.3.1.2 *Labour productivity*

'Productivity' is the relationship between the output of an economic unit and the factor inputs which have gone into producing it. Conventionally, productivity is measured in terms of output per employee, and an increase in productivity occurs when output per employee is raised. Table 5.3 shows the growth in labour productivity in the manufacturing sector for a number

Table 5.3 Labour productivity in manufacturing, 1976–93

Country	Average 1976–85	per cent change 1986	1987	1988	1989	1990	1991	1992	1993
USA	1.9	2.6	6.5	2.4	0.6	1.7	2.1	4.1	5.1
Japan	4.2	0.0	4.1	7.4	4.5	2.8	1.5	−3.7	−1.6
Germany	3.6	1.0	1.9	4.2	3.3	3.5	2.9	1.4	2.3
UK	2.6	3.8	5.4	5.4	4.3	1.9	2.5	4.9	7.1
All industrial countries	3.2	2.0	3.8	5.2	3.6	1.8	1.9	2.6	2.7

Source: IMF, *World Economic Outlook*, 1994.

Box 5.4 Economic growth and productivity

Employing more people can increase output. Equally, increasing the productivity (conventionally defined in terms of *output per employee*) of the existing labour force can be an important means of raising output levels. This is a more complicated issue than it seems at first. Productivity may be held back by poor worker motivation, restrictive labour practices (for example, inter-union 'demarcation' rules leading to gross overmanning) and inefficient work organisation on the part of management. Thus it may be possible to improve productivity in particular instances by providing better work incentives (profit-related pay) reorganising work tasks (job rotation, etc.) and securing management–worker co-operation in respect of job flexibility (removal of demarcation restrictions, etc.).

While improvements in the quality of the labour input *per se* can help increase productivity, a more decisive element is the use of more and better plant and equipment, that is, *capital*. Thus it is something of a misnomer to talk exclusively of the productivity of labour; rather it is the combination of capital and labour which is the key factor. (The fact that 'units' of labour are more identifiable and more easily measured than capital items is the reason for the use of a labour-orientated measure of productivity.)

The important contribution that capital makes to increasing output and productivity can be illustrated thus:

1 Suppose, initially, that the assembly of a motor car is a labour-intensive operation; it takes a team of ten men working with a minimal amount of capital (spanners and screwdrivers only) one whole day to assemble one car.

2 The firm now invests in hydraulic lifting gear (capital deepening) and this cuts down considerably the amount of time taken in aligning parts for assembly, reducing the time it takes to complete the assembly operation to, say, one-tenth of a day. The same team of men are now able to assemble ten cars a day – their productivity has gone up tenfold.

3 The firm introduces a continuous flow assembly line with automatically controlled machines (again, capital deepening), which one man can operate. Output increases to, say, fifty cars a day; the productivity of the remaining man has increased from one car a day (a tenth part of ten cars) to fifty.

Just as important, nine men have been 'released' from the team. Either they too could all be put to work on a similar automated assembly line (capital widening), in which case the total output of the ten men is now 500 cars per day (ten times fifty), compared with fifty before. Alternatively, they could be redeployed outside the car industry, thereby helping to increase output in other sectors of the economy.

of the main industrial countries for the period 1976–93. The UK and the USA, it will be noted, have managed to achieve substantial productivity gains in the 1980s. In the case of the UK the initial improvement in productivity in this period was associated with a substantial reduction in the numbers employed. The swingeing cut-backs in the recessioniary period of 1979–83, when a large number of inefficient plants were closed, led to a dramatic fall in jobs in the UK manufacturing sector. This produced an automatic lift in productivity: output fell by less than employment, thus raising the output per head of the remaining workforce. Secondly, investment in new technology, particularly the application of computer-aided manufacturing systems, has improved productivity by upgrading the capital stock. Thirdly, the productivity improvement in part reflects the impact of the government's 'supply-side' policies, aimed at removing such restrictive working practices as overmanning and demarcation limitations on labour flexibility.

Despite the substantial increase in labour productivity in the UK in recent years, the 'productivity gap' remains a problem in some areas. An 'internal' report by Ford on its European car plants, for example, revealed striking differences in productivity performance, as exemplified in Table 5.4, which compares Ford's Dagenham plant with those in Belgium and Spain. Additionally, the report was critical of the Dagenham plant's quality record, which, along with its lower productivity, made it the least efficient of Ford's six assembly plants in Europe. The main explanation of this state of affairs was given by the report as continued labour disruption and consequent unreliability of supply. The report was more optimistic about future prospects, however, noting the emergence of a different attitude in the plant, based upon an environment of teamwork: 'Recently, there has been a marked improvement in employee relations in most areas of the organisation. We have been able to achieve changes to production shifts, work allocation and levels of employment, without major conflict. The changes have been brought about by a combination of actions ranging from a more open management style, and a willingness to involve all personnel in the changes.'

Another example of the 'productivity gap' is provided by a National Institute study comparing clothing manufacturers in Britain and West Germany in the late 1980s. On the face of it, Britain with its long tradition of clothing manufacture and relatively low labour costs might have

Table 5.4 Selected Ford plants in Europe, 1988

Plant/car model	Hours per car	Vehicles per employee
Valencia (Spain): Fiesta	33	38
Genk (Belgium): Sierra	40	34
Dagenham (England):		
Fiesta	57	22
Sierra	67	22

Source: Ford Motor Co. Ltd.

been expected to perform well in comparison with West Germany, which has little tradition in this field and high labour costs. However, the study found the level of productivity of the German clothing industry to be some 20 per cent higher than in Britain. A number of reasons were advanced to explain this difference in productivity performance. First, there were marked differences in the age of the machinery and equipment in use, with that in West Germany tending to be more modern. Three-quarters of the machines there were less than five years old, while in Britain three-quarters of the machines were more than five years old. Secondly, the incidence of machine breakdowns was lower in West Germany than in Britain, resulting in less disruption of production. Thirdly, the West German industry used more sophisticated production planning techniques, enabling delivery dates to be met more reliably than in Britain. Fourthly, and most important, West Germany's success was attributed to the high standards of training and the resultant skills of the workforce. Thus the quality of the workforce must also be of prime importance.

5.3.1.3 Labour quality

Human capital is the skill and knowledge embodied in the minds and hands of the population. Experience, education and training promote productivity and growth because they improve the ability of the labour force to produce, using a given level of technology, and they enable the state of technology to progress more rapidly, so leading to the faster introduction of more advanced production techniques.

Comparative international statistics on education and training are difficult to compile because of the substantial differences between countries in educational traditions and structures. What evidence there is indicates that, in terms of education expenditure per head and as a proportion of GDP, the UK is about average for the European Union. However, there is a difference between the UK and most other EU countries in the allocation of funds as between general education and vocational (that is, practical) training. The UK educational system as a whole has placed little emphasis on engineering and technological training. There is a much lower incidence of technical education and qualifications throughout the workforce in the UK than among major competitors. (See Table 5.5.) The neglect of applied engineering and technological skills by the educational infrastructure has been further compounded by the low status accorded to the engineering profession by industry itself.

5.3.2 Capital

Productive capital is the stock of machinery, buildings and inventories with which other factors of production combine to produce output. For a given labour force, an increase in total capital and in capital per worker will increase output. However, capital depreciates over time. A certain amount of new investment is required merely to maintain the existing capital stock intact; and with a growing labour force, an even higher level of investment is required if capital per worker is to be maintained. With yet faster investment, capital per worker will increase over time, thereby increasing the output each worker can produce. Thus an increase in capital per worker is one of the principal ways in which output per worker and *per capita* income are increased.

Thus investment in plant, machinery and equipment is one important means of raising a country's growth potential. Gross fixed capital formation (GFCF) fell in most of the leading industrial countries in the decade after 1973, a situation largely reflecting the persistence of recessionary conditions and an accompanying fall in corporate profitability. In the mid and late 1980s capital formation has increased strongly in most countries. Table 5.6 gives details of gross fixed capital formation as a proportion of GDP and growth in real GDP over the period 1985–93 for seventeen countries. Although it is to be expected that higher investment will lead

Table 5.5 The skills gap: numbers qualifying in engineering and technology, 1985 (000)

Qualification	UK	France	Germany	Japan*	USA*
Higher degree	3	6	5	5	3
First degree	14	15	21	30	19
Technicians	29	35	44	27	17
Craftsmen	35	92	120	44	na

* Numbers for Japan and USA reduced in proportion to UK population.

Source: National Institute *Economic Review*, February 1989.

Table 5.6 Investment, saving and GDP growth rates, selected countries, 1985–93

Country	Investment as % of GDP	Growth in real GDP (annual %)	Savings as % of GDP
Japan	31	4.1	33
Switzerland	28	2.1	29
Austria	25	2.8	26
Finland	25	1.4	25
Norway	25	2.1	29
Germany	23	2.6	26
Australia	23	2.6	22
Italy	21	2.5	21
Canada	21	2.3	22
France	20	2.5	21
Netherlands	20	2.5	24
Ireland	20	4.1	27
UK	19	2.1	17
Denmark	19	1.8	22
Belgium	18	2.4	21
Sweden	18	1.2	21
USA	16	2.2	14

Source: World Bank, *World Development Report*, 1994.

to higher growth, there is no strong correlation between the investment/GDP ratio and the rate of economic growth achieved. Japan had the highest investment ratio and the fastest rate of growth. Ireland achieved the same rate of growth but had an investment ratio only two-thirds that of Japan. Some countries which invested at the same rate had markedly different growth performances (for example, Belgium and Sweden, Austria and Finland). Clearly, investment is a necessary, but not a sufficient, condition of high growth potential.

Investment by companies can differ between countries because of institutional differences in the financing of companies. For example, in Germany and Japan investment has been encouraged by the fact that most shares in the major industrial companies are held by banks and trading groups, which have taken a 'long-term' view of their investments in and loans to such companies. By contrast, in the UK and USA, it is alleged, companies have focused their attention on a short-term return on capital, rather than committing resources to longer-term investment projects, in order to maintain the stock market valuation of their shares and avoid take-overs.

One important factor in securing growth is the efficiency of investment. Failure to achieve productivity growth could be due, for example, to the fact that too much investment occurs in areas where the potential for productivity gains is limited, or to the fact that, even when the scope for productivity gains is high, nonetheless productivity is held back by inefficient management and restrictive labour practices.

In some countries (most notably the less developed countries) capital formation may be held back by a lack of savings, or the channelling of savings into relatively unproductive uses (for example, investment in real estate). In some cases the inadequacy of domestic savings may be overcome by overseas borrowing or by attracting foreign capital (for example, inward investment by multinational companies – Chapter 9).

Table 5.6 indicates that there are considerable variations in international savings ratios. Japan and Switzerland, for example, exhibit a much higher propensity to save than either the UK or the USA. In part these differences reflect differences between countries with regard to society's deep-seated attitudes towards thrift and the acquisition of wealth, as well as business philosophies regarding retention of profits versus dividend pay-outs.

5.3.3 Land and raw materials

Many countries, including the UK and Japan, are not especially well endowed with natural resources and import the bulk of their raw material requirements. However, provided these imports can be financed by exports of finished goods and services, a domestic shortage of natural resources rarely acts as a brake on economic expansion.

Having briefly discussed the major factor inputs, we turn now to the role of technical knowledge.

5.3.4 Technical knowledge

Technical advances come through *invention*, the discovery of new knowledge, and *innovation*, the incorporation of new knowledge into actual production techniques. Investment is the main way in which new technology and new products are developed and introduced. Technological advance frequently involves the scrapping of existing capital and its replacement by superior plant and equipment. Innovation thus contributes to new capital formation and can reduce supply costs and establish product leadership. Technological innovation is therefore an important means of improving international competitiveness and growth potential. Table 5.7 shows research and development spending by a number of leading industrial countries. It will be noted that, as a proportion of GDP, UK research and development (R&D) spending is below that of the country's industrial competitors, and the 'research gap' between the UK and the other countries has widened in recent years. In absolute terms (because of the UK's lower level of GDP) total R&D spending is much lower than in the USA,

Table 5.7 Spending on research and development, selected countries, 1987–92

Year	UK	Germany	Japan	USA
Total gross expenditure on R&D £ (billions)				
1987	9	15	24	72
1988	10	16	28	79
1989	11	18	32	85
1990	12	19	38	90
1991	12	22	43	98
1992	13	23	43	100
Total gross expenditure as % of GDP				
1987	2.2	2.9	2.6	2.9
1988	2.2	2.9	2.7	2.8
1989	2.2	2.9	2.8	2.8
1990	2.2	2.7	2.9	2.8
1991	2.1	2.6	2.9	2.8
1992	2.1	2.5	2.8	2.7

Source: OECD Science and Technology Indicators, 1994.

Japan or Germany. In 1992 the business sector in the UK accounted for a lower percentage of total R&D spending (67 per cent) than in Germany (74 per cent), Japan (73 per cent) and the USA (72 per cent). Moreover, some 44 per cent of UK government spending was defence-related (which produces very little in the way of industrial spin-offs), compared with 12 per cent in Germany and only 5 per cent in Japan.

5.4 DEMAND AND ECONOMIC GROWTH

A sustained expansion of aggregate demand is an important prerequisite in facilitating economic growth, since a high and rising level of demand, by putting pressure on existing levels of capacity utilisation and increasing corporate profitability, will encourage increased investment in new capacity and technologies, thus serving to expand the underlying growth potential of the economy. By contrast, recessionary conditions of the kind besetting the world economy for much of the period since 1973 are not conducive to growth. Although realised (that is, actual) growth can be very rapid in the recovery phase of the business cycle, this is merely a 'catching up' process, bringing into operation mainly existing unused productive capacity, and it will be halted once the full employment ceiling has been reached. Thereafter, sustainable growth will be dependent on the underlying growth rate of capacity and productivity.

The pattern of demand can also have a significant bearing on a country's underlying growth potential and the sustainability of realised growth. (See Box 5.5.) Investment and export-led growth can have particularly

Box 5.5 Demand and output

USA (current prices, $ billions)

	1992	1989	1990	1991	1992	1993	
		% change from previous period (1987 prices)					
Private consumption	3,342	1.9	1.5	-0.4	2.6	N/A	US growth has been modest; a massive federal budget deficit was the main stimulus to growth, serving to offset a falling-off of investment and a continuing deficit on the balance of payments
Government consumption	945	2.0	3.2	1.5	-0.1	N/A	
Gross fixed investment	726	0.3	-2.3	-8.0	6.5	N/A	
Total domestic demand	5,013	1.8	0.8	-1.4	2.9	N/A	
Exports	578	11.9	8.2	6.4	6.4	N/A	
Imports	661	3.8	3.6	0.5	8.7	N/A	
GDP at market prices	4,986	2.5	1.2	-0.7	2.6	N/A	

Japan (current prices, trillion yen)

	1992	1989	1990	1991	1992	1993	
		(1985 prices)					
Private consumption	265	4.3	3.9	2.2	1.7	N/A	Japanese growth was strong in the early 1990s, underpinned by export demand, but has slowed as consumption and investment have fallen. There is still a large surplus on the balance of payments.
Government consumption	44	2.0	1.9	1.7	3.4	N/A	
Gross fixed investment	145	5.9	5.0	2.7	-1.0	N/A	
Total domestic demand	454	5.8	5.0	2.7	0.6	N/A	
Exports	47	9.0	7.3	4.9	4.0	N/A	
Imports	36	17.6	8.6	-4.5	0.0	N/A	
GDP at market prices	465	4.7	4.8	4.0	1.3	N/A	

Germany *(current prices, DM billions)*

	1993	*(1990 prices)*				
	1993	*1989*	*1990*	*1991*	*1992*	*1993*
Private consumption	1,793	2.7	5.4	3.6	2.3	0.1
Government consumption	623	-1.7	2.1	0.8	1.5	-1.3
Gross fixed investment	679	6.5	8.7	6.5	4.2	-3.3
Total domestic demand	3,095	3.4	5.1	3.7	2.1	-1.2
Exports	655	11.4	11.0	12.1	3.7	-6.1
Imports	642	8.4	11.6	12.6	3.9	-9.6
GDP at market prices	3,107	3.4	5.1	3.7	2.1	-1.2

The main stimulus to growth was the expansion of investment demand and exports, though both investment and export growth slackened from 1992 onwards.

UK *(current prices, £ billions)*

	1993	*(1990 prices)*				
	1993	*1989*	*1990*	*1991*	*1992*	*1993*
Private consumption	406	3.2	0.6	-2.2	0.0	2.5
Government consumption	136	1.4	2.5	2.4	0.7	-0.5
Gross fixed investment	93	5.5	-3.4	-9.8	-1.6	0.8
Total domestic demand	636	3.3	-0.1	-2.7	-0.2	1.6
Exports	158	4.7	5.0	-0.9	3.0	3.1
Imports	166	7.4	0.5	-5.4	6.3	3.5
GDP at market prices	794	2.3	0.4	-2.2	-0.6	1.9

The falling-off in investment and consumption demand has had a depressant effect on the economy. The size of the balance of payments deficit has been reduced but remains a major obstacle to the achievement of faster economic growth

Source: OECD, *Economic Outlook, Japan and USA,* 1993; *Germany and UK,* 1994.

beneficial effects. Investment, we have noted, is not only a component of aggregate demand but a key factor operating on the supply side of the economy in increasing capacity and productivity. Thus, unlike consumption, investment adds to both demand and supply. Exports, like investment, constitute an injection into aggregate demand (representing foreign demand for domestically produced output), enabling a higher level of import absorption to be attained without attendant balance of payments problems. For some countries growth may require a substantial increase in imports of natural resources and capital equipment, while increased consumption may lead to an increase in imports of finished manufactures. Japan and Germany have both felt the benefits of high investment and export growth, which have enabled them to achieve a high overall rate of economic growth combined with balance of payments surpluses in most of the post-1945 period (see Table 2.1). By contrast, the UK, with its relatively weaker investment and productivity record, has been trapped for much of this period in a 'stop–go' cycle, with short, consumption-led booms tending to suck in an unaffordable volume of imports which has then required the authorities to deflate domestic demand, bringing growth to a halt. In more recent times, although greater exchange rate flexibility has allowed the UK authorities more latitude in this respect, the growing 'openness' of the UK market to international competition (GATT tariff cuts and UK membership of the European Union free trade bloc) has served to expose the chronic weaknesses of the UK economy, particularly the manufacturing sector. Expanding demand to promote growth has merely served to bring in more imports of manufactured goods which have displaced UK manufacturing output. The fact that, even in the recent recession, import penetration (the proportion of domestic demand accounted for by imports) has continued to rise forcibly underscores the point that poor international competitiveness may severely stunt a country's growth prospects. This highlights the extent to which a country's growth rate may be constrained by its balance of payments. Rapid growth in a relatively open economy will suck in imports and cause a balance of payments deficit, which may in turn force the government to check the growth in demand in order to restore balance of payments equilibrium.

5.5 POLICIES TO ACHIEVE HIGHER ECONOMIC GROWTH

Economic growth is a longer-term phenomenon requiring an increase in factor inputs and more efficient use of inputs in order to increase supply capacity and productivity. Conventional demand management policies can facilitate the growth process in so far as a high and rising level of aggregate demand will act as a stimulus to investment. However, it is mainly the 'supply side' of the economy itself which requires attention if higher rates of economic growth are to be achieved. The authorities may use a variety of industrial policies to enlarge supply capacity and increase productivity. In market economies they can range from 'indicative planning' mechanisms to more *ad hoc* and selective 'supply-side' measures.

5.5.1 Indicative planning

Indicative planning is a method of controlling the economy that involves the setting of long-term objectives and the mapping out of programmes of action designed to achieve those objectives. Unlike a centrally planned economy, indicative planning works through the market rather than seeking to replace it. To this end the planning process specifically brings both sides of industry (the trade unions and management) and the government together. Indicative planning has been tried in a number of countries, including the UK, Japan and France.

The only occasion when a comprehensive indicative planning approach has been tried in the UK was in 1965, when a 'National Plan' was formulated (which set a target economic growth rate for the economy of 3.8 per cent over the period 1964–70) and a variety of planning agencies (the National Economic Development Council [NEDC], and Economic Development Committees [EDC] for individual industries) were used to draw up and co-ordinate action programmes. The National Plan itself, however, was abandoned in 1966 after being overtaken by events (a balance of payments crisis forced the government to introduce a package of deflationary measures), but the NEDC and the EDCs continued to function on a less formal basis down to 1992, when they were abolished.

The NEDC pre-dated the National Plan, having been established in 1962 by a Conservative government concerned at the poor economic performance of the UK in comparison with other leading industrial countries. The NEDC met monthly to discuss issues of general concern to the economy and to establish a consensus view of the economic threats and opportunities facing the country. The NEDC had no formal mechanisms for planning the economy or directing resources into specific industries, etc., but instead worked informally to secure collective commitment to particular courses of action which at the same time preserved the integrity of each interest group.

While the NEDC took a general view of the economy, the EDCs operated at the grass-roots level. There were thirty-five EDCs for various industrial sectors – for example, the Food and Drink Manufacturing EDC, the Footwear EDC, the Office Systems EDC, etc., each comprising, like the NEDC, members drawn from management, the unions and government. Their remit was to assess the performance of their sector and agree on steps to overcome problems and develop opportunities. EDCs published periodic reports on their sectors, giving guidance on ways of improving performance and competitiveness in functional areas like marketing, production and R&D, which were designed to act as catalysts of change.

In Japan economic policy-making in the period since 1945 has revolved around a series of five-year 'economic plans' formulated by the Economic Council and the Economic Planning Agency. Such planning involves a process of consultation with other state agencies and departments (for example, the Ministry of Finance, responsible for the annual budget, the Ministry of International Trade and Industry, responsible for industrial structure and foreign trade, the Ministry of Construction, responsible for public works programmes, the Ministry of Health, responsible for social security programmes, and the National Land Agency, responsible for land utilisation) to draw up a set of interlocking action programmes designed to achieve the central objectives of the economic plan; for example, the 1988–92 economic plan had as its main aims an economic growth rate of 3.25 per cent, an unemployment rate target of 2.5 per cent, an inflation limit of 1.5–2.0 per cent and a reduction (unspecified) in the country's massive balance of payments surplus.

French indicative planning has been based for several decades upon a series of five-year national plans which provide a comprehensive, co-ordinating structure for industry and commerce. Through the indicative plan firms are able to base their investment plans upon a common shared set of expectations about future growth prospects. The planning process also serves to identify possible constraints on economic growth so that the government can take steps to overcome these constraints. In addition French governments have generally pursued policies of support for selected firms such as Renault which operate in key strategic or high-technology industries. Selective assistance is given to such firms in the form of subsidies, preference in public procurement policies or protection from foreign competition in order to build them up as 'national champions'.

5.5.2 Supply-side measures

Governments may adopt various supply-side policies to increase the stock of factors of production and to improve the efficiency of resource use by promoting the flexibility of markets in responding to demand changes. These policies include:

1 Financial incentives to increase capital investment in plant and equipment and promote similar investment in process and product invention and innovation.
2 Education and training policies to improve the supply of requisite skills.
3 More competition in the financial and industrial sectors to improve the efficiency of capital and product markets.

4 Privatisation and reduced government control of industry (deregulation) to encourage industrial efficiency.

5 Regional policy assistance, private rented accommodation and portable pensions to encourage labour mobility.

6 Lower tax rates and fewer social security benefits as incentives encouraging people to work harder and take risks.

7 Curbs on the power of trade unions, so as to improve the flexibility of labour markets.

8 Wider share ownership and assistance to the self-employed in order to promote an 'enterprise culture'.

5.6 CONCLUSION

The success of Japan, in particular, has highlighted the benefits governments may derive from directing some of their economic policy towards long-term targets. The range of policies open to governments and the potential benefits emphasise the growing importance that is now attached to long-term planning. Among these government policies to promote growth, incentives to encourage investment, improve productivity and foster research and development are particularly important in accelerating economic growth.

5.7 IMPLICATIONS FOR BUSINESS

Economic growth, characterised by a strong expansion of output and buoyant demand conditions, provides an ideal climate for firms to expand their sales and profitability. Rising demand fosters increased investment in plant and equipment and stimulates process and product innovation.

The policies pursued by governments to achieve higher growth rates such as income tax cuts to boost consumer spending and investment incentives for businesses may lead to a 'virtuous circle' of rising demand, output and profitability, continuing for some years. The sustainability of high growth rates, however, must be looked at in the context of business cycle tendencies, where, for example, external 'shocks' such as the oil price increases of 1973, 1979 and 1990 may bring a sharp return to recessionary conditions. In the case of some countries, the UK in particular, balance of payments weaknesses may force the authorities to limit the rate of domestic expansion.

While 'easy' sales expansion can be achieved in times of boom, firms need to be mindful of the need to remain efficient and competitive so as to underpin their viability in harsher times. However, for exporting companies and multinational companies with extensive global business operations it may be possible to offset the vagaries of the business cycle in any single economy by *geographical diversification*. Moreover, with the slowing down of growth rates in the older industrialised countries in the 1980s and early 1990s, much attention has been directed towards growth prospects in the emergent economies of Southern Asia and Eastern Europe. ICI, the UK chemical multinational, for example, is to establish a new paint plant in Bangkok as part of its Asian expansion programme. The Asian Pacific region represented nearly a quarter of ICI's paint division's turnover in 1993. Demand for paints in the Asia–Pacific region totalled some 4.6 million tonnes in 1993 and is expected to expand, in line with the projected growth rates of the region's economies, to 8 million tonnes by the year 2000. In 1992 ICI opened its largest single product plant, a £150 million complex producing pure terephthalic acid, in Taiwan.

QUESTIONS

1 Outline and comment on recent trends in economic growth in the industrialised countries.
2 Indicate the main determinants of economic growth, discussing in particular the role of investment in the growth process.
3 What policies can governments adopt to increase the rate of economic growth?
4 Why do growth rates differ between countries?
5 What do you understand by the term 'productivity'? What can a government do to improve the productivity of its economy?

Chapter 6

Balance of payments

All countries, to a greater or lesser degree, are dependent on international trade, exporting some of their domestic output of goods and services to other countries in exchange for imports of goods and services from them. Likewise, many countries invest in other countries and, by the same token, receive inward investment into their own economies. In so far as countries operate with different domestic money systems, trade and capital flows between countries need to be *financed* by an exchange of currencies in the foreign exchange market. Collectively these transactions give rise to the *balance of payments*. To ignore the impact of such major influences on the domestic economy, particularly in economies where the foreign trade sector accounts for a high proportion of gross domestic product, would be misleading.

In a world where international trade and capital flows have great practical significance, it is important to extend macroeconomic analysis to deal with the open economy. Indeed, in open economies a country's international trade performance can have a major impact on the domestic economy and vice versa. Since 1950 Japan and Germany, for example, have benefited from export-led growth, with a strong export performance serving to underpin domestic prosperity, and high levels of domestic investment and innovation, in turn assisting further export expansion. By contrast, the UK for much of this period has been trapped in a 'stop–go' cycle of economic activity, characterised by short-lived import-led consumption booms leading to balance of payments crises, followed by long periods of low growth. Thus it is important to view the balance of payments as the 'monetary' mirror of the 'real' economy, that is, strong economies tend to have a strong currency and balance of payments position, and vice versa.

The aim of this chapter is to emphasise that the international environment is not something that can conveniently be discussed separately from other aspects of macroeconomics: in open economies it is intrinsic to the way such economies work. The structure of the balance of payments and the removal of payments imbalances, particularly trading deficits and surpluses, are considered in this chapter in the context of macroeconomic management.

The factors underlying international trade and investment and related exchange rate and foreign exchange matters are discussed more extensively in Chapters 7–10.

As a starting point, the different components of the balance of payments and the international performance of some of the leading industrial countries are examined.

6.1 THE BALANCE OF PAYMENTS

The balance of payments is a statement of a country's trade and financial transactions with the rest of the world over a particular period of time, usually one year. Table 6.1, taking Japan as an example, shows a 'standard' presentation of the balance of payments as used by the International Monetary Fund to present comparative international balance of payments data. The account is divided up into two main parts, the first recording current transactions and the second relating to capital transactions.

The current transactions account shows the country's 'profit or loss' in day-to-day dealings. It is made up under a number of headings. The 'trade balance' indicates the difference between the value of exports and the value of imports of *goods* such as raw materials, fuels, foodstuffs, semi-processed products and finished manufactures. (Such items are often referred to as 'visible' trade, since movements of goods can be directly recorded as the goods cross national frontiers.) The *services* component of the current account includes earnings from and payments for commercial services such as banking, insurance, transport and tourism. The 'income' component of the account covers receipts and payments in respect of interest, rent, dividends and profits from overseas direct and portfolio investments and loans. 'Other transfers' include government receipts and spending on overseas administration, defence, etc. (Services, income and other transfers are collectively referred to as 'invisibles', since in the main they cannot be recorded at national frontiers and details of such transactions need to be compiled from records submitted by banks, companies, etc., to the authorities.)

Major determinants of the size of the current account are income, relative prices (the price of domestically produced goods relative to the price of similar goods produced abroad), and other factors such as consumer preferences, quality of the goods, delivery dates, etc.

A country's current account position reflects not only the *volume* of imports and exports of goods and services traded but also the relative *prices* of imports and exports, that is, the 'terms of trade' (see Box 6.1).

The capital transactions account records a variety of dealings relating to the acquisition and sale of financial assets. A broad distinction is drawn between 'long-term' and 'short-term' capital transactions (although the distinction can at times be arbitrary). The former relate principally to direct

Table 6.1 Balance of payments data, Japan, 1986-92 (US$ billions)

Transactions	1986	1987	1988	1989	1990	1991	1992
Current							
Merchandise exports	205.59	224.62	259.77	269.55	280.35	306.58	330.87
Merchandise imports	−112.77	−128.20	−164.77	−192.66	−216.77	−203.49	−198.47
Trade balance	92.82	96.42	95.00	76.89	63.58	103.09	132.40
Services:							
Credit	23.54	28.85	35.03	39.70	40.83	44.65	48.31
Debit	−35.45	−48.42	−63.53	−75.01	−81.97	−85.04	−89.73
Income:							
Credit	30.16	50.81	76.75	104.21	125.13	143.94	145.75
Debit	−23.18	−36.96	−59.52	−84.52	−106.18	−121.24	−114.47
Other transfers (net)	−2.06	−3.68	−4.12	−4.28	1.48	−12.49	−5.38
Current account	85.83	87.02	79.61	56.99	35.87	72.91	117.64
Capital							
Long-term capital direct investment (net)	−14.25	−18.75	−34.73	−45.22	−46.29	−29.37	−14.52
Portfolio investment (net)	−102.04	−91.33	−52.75	−32.53	−14.49	−35.45	−28.41
Other long-term capital	−15.79	−23.90	−29.61	−16.01	7.70	33.43	12.15
Total long-term capital	−132.08	−133.98	−117.09	−93.76	−53.08	31.39	−30.78
Short term capital (net)	58.60	88.61	50.87	45.83	31.54	−103.24	−75.77
Errors and omissions	2.49	−3.71	3.13	−21.82	−20.92	−7.68	−10.46
Overall balance	14.84	37.94	16.52	−12.76	−6.59	−6.63	0.63

Source: IMF, *Balance of Payments Statistics Yearbook*, 1993.

investment (for example, the establishment of a new factory or take-over of a foreign firm), portfolio investment (for example, the purchase of overseas government bonds by a pension fund) and the provision and receipt of foreign aid. 'Short-term' capital movements (inflows and outflows of capital) in the main relate to interbank dealings in foreign currencies and can be highly volatile, reacting to interest rate differentials between financial centres and 'speculative' runs on weak currencies.

Major determinants of the size of the capital account are expectations of exchange rate changes; the nominal interest rate differentials between countries; and differences in the expected rate of return on real investment opportunities in different countries.

The summation of all these items (including 'errors and omissions' –

Box 6.1 Terms of trade

The terms of trade are a price index that shows a country's export prices relative to its import prices. It is constructed by taking an index of prices received for exports, on the one hand, and an index of prices paid for imports, on the other, and then dividing the first by the second, as depicted in the figures for the UK. An improvement in a country's terms of trade occurs if its export prices rise at a faster rate than import prices over time, and a worsening of the terms of trade if export prices rise more slowly than import prices.

Superficially, an improvement in a country's terms of trade may be considered to be beneficial: in foreign exchange terms, a given quantity of exports will now finance the purchase of a greater quantity of imports, or, to put it another way, a given quantity of imports can now be purchased for a smaller quantity of exports. A critical factor in this regard, however, is the price elasticity of demand for exports and imports. If, for example, export demand is price-elastic, then price rises (which make the country's exports less competitive in world markets) will result in a more than proportionate fall in export volume, thus lowering foreign exchange receipts and adversely affecting domestic output and employment.

UK terms of trade
(1990=100)

Index	1988	1989	1990	1991	1992
Export prices	92	97	100	101	104
Import prices	94	98	100	101	102
Terms of trade	98.6	98.8	100.0	100.0	101.4

balance of payments accounting is still a very imprecise task, given the millions of transactions involved!) will show whether the country is in balance of payments surplus or deficit. In the case of a deficit, the deficit can be financed by drawing on the country's stock of 'international reserves' of gold and foreign currencies (see Chapter 10) and/or increased borrowing of foreign currencies, while in the case of a surplus the 'extra' foreign exchange generated can be used to bolster the reserves position or to reduce borrowings.

The relative importance of the main components of the balance of payments can vary substantially as *between* different countries (see Table 6.2), depending on their industrial structure, trade dependence and competitiveness, and these components (and sub-categories therein) can also change in relative importance for *individual* countries over time (see Table 6.3). In recent years Japan has recorded large surpluses in merchandise trade, with export earnings on manufactured goods far exceeding payments for imports of raw materials, oil and foodstuffs. By contrast, the UK has been continuously in deficit on merchandise trade, a situation aggravated by the disappearance of the traditional surplus in manufactured goods (this section has been in deficit since 1982). The UK has traditionally generated large surpluses on 'invisible' items, benefiting especially from the City of London's pivotal role as a financial services centre, and from earnings on overseas investments, and these earnings in the past have usually been sufficient to cover merchandise deficits and provide foreign exchange to finance capital exports. Japan, by contrast, has traditionally been a net importer of services and has relied on merchandise surpluses to cover net payments for services. In addition, Japan's strong trade balance has enabled it to finance an increase in direct and portfolio investment, with Japanese companies becoming increasingly prominent investors in the USA and the European Union.

The balance of payments can also be looked at from a geographical perspective. In absolute terms most countries tend to have a diverse range of import sources and, likewise, export to a large number of countries. However, in many cases regional proximity and the formation of free trade blocs such as the European Union (EU) have tended to increase the relative importance of a narrower range of trade (and investment) partners. For example, even before the formation of the North American Free Trade Agreement in 1989 over 70 per cent of Canadian exports went to the USA,

Table 6.2 Components of balance of payments, selected countries, 1992 (US$ millions)

Component	USA	Germany	Canada	Switzerland	UK
Current account	−66,300	−25,560	−23,012	13,419	−20,714
of which:					
Merchandise	−96,140	+32,870	+8,183	−251	−24,618
Services	+42,320	−33,510	−11,450	+7,208	+5,835
Investment Income	+20,400	+7,060	−20,007	+9,440	+7,087
Long-term capital	−17,610	+38,610	+10,571	−9,175	−18,203
of which:					
Direct investment	−32,420	−8,980	+2,015	−3,864	+3,362
Portfolio investment	+14,190	+49,520	+8,248	−2,936	−24,222
Short-term capital	+54,190	+29,470	+3,218	+487	+35,533
Overall balance (allowing for errors and omissions)	−42,060	+43,020	−5,807	+4,420	−2,085

− Net outflow of foreign exchange. + Net inflow of foreign exchange.

Source: IMF, *Balance of Payments Statistics Yearbook*, 1993.

Table 6.3 UK merchandise trade, 1979–93 (£ million)

Category	1979	1981	1983	1985	1987	1989	1991	1993
Food, beverages and tobacco	-2,933	-2,281	-8,029	-3,723	-4,030	-4,310	-3,950	-4,178
Basic materials	-2,375	-2,086	-2,598	-2,842	-2,977	-3,591	-2,580	-2,779
Oil, lubricants, etc.	-1,089	+2,731	+6,300	+6,506	+2,903	+31	-52	+1,487
Semi-manufactures	+626	+1,338	-139	-417	-1,950	-4,347	-1,196	+892
Finished manufactures	+2,084	+3,159	-2,594	-3,348	-6,343	-12,918	-2,431	-8,892
Other goods	+344	+391	+523	+479	+815	+452	-75	+261
Totals	-3,342	+3,251	-1,537	-3,345	11,582	-24,683	-10,284	-13,209

– Net outflow of foreign exchange. + Net inflow of foreign exchange.

Source: UK Balance of Payments, 1993.

while trade between member countries of the EU has increased markedly. In 1993 around 53 per cent of UK merchandise trade was with EU partners, while in the case of Ireland, Belgium and Portugal over 70 per cent of their merchandise trade was intra-Community. (See Chapter 8.)

6.2 BALANCE OF PAYMENTS ADJUSTMENT: THE CURRENT ACCOUNT

From a policy perspective, the balance of payments reflects a country's economic strengths and weaknesses and the establishment of comparative advantage and specialisation in certain types of economic goods. So long as deficits in particular categories of goods or services are matched by surpluses generated elsewhere, then in foreign currency terms the balance of payments will remain broadly 'in balance' over a run of years. In an unregulated world it is highly unlikely that external balance will always prevail. Balance of payments deficits and surpluses will occur but, provided they are small, balance of payments disequilibrium can be readily accommodated. What is to be avoided, to use the IMF's definition of a serious payments problem, is a 'fundamental disequilibrium' where a country is *persistently* in surplus or persistently in deficit. Clearly, there is more pressure on a deficit country to take action to remedy the situation, since the financing of deficits requires the country to run down its stock of gold and foreign currency reserves or increase its borrowings, and there are limits to both these courses of action. Surplus countries are under no immediate imperative to take remedial action but may accept that they have an international 'responsibility' to ease the problems facing their trade partners. That is, countries are interdependent – one country's surplus is another country's deficit – so effective adjustment requires all trade partners to participate in removing payments imbalances, otherwise protectionism is likely to rear its head.

A balance of payments current account disequilibrium can arise in a number of ways. For example, a payments deficit could occur as a result of a boom in domestic demand leading to a surge in imports and a fall in exports as exportable goods are diverted to the home market. On the other hand, the deficit could reflect underlying weaknesses in the economy. For example, if a country's inflation rate is significantly higher than those of its trade partners, then (under a fixed rate system) there could be a growing deterioration in its price-competitiveness, leading to higher imports and a loss of export sales. Similarly, the country may suffer a fall in non-price competitiveness through inability to match trade partners in product innovation. Structural long-term (i.e. supply-side) weaknesses (low investment in modern plant, R&D, etc.) can lead to a growth in 'import penetration' (see Box 3.4) *even when* the economy is in recession, so that the orthodox prescription of demand deflation in this case would have only a marginal impact. The continuing Japanese trade surplus despite very substantial appreciation of the yen provides an interesting example of both a strong domestic industrial base providing a platform for export success and an 'artificially' low propensity to import reinforced by various non-tariff obstacles to imports.

A number of measures can be used by a country to remedy a payments imbalance. These are discussed below (Sections 6.3 onwards), assuming for expository purposes that the country operates under a fixed exchange rate regime (see Chapter 10) and the problem it faces is a payments deficit.

By way of introduction it is important to understand the concept of the 'equilibrium rate of exchange'. Figure 6.1 shows the equilibrium rate of exchange between the UK pound and US dollar, indicating that UK–USA trade is in balance of payments equilibrium at the exchange rate of £1 = $2.80. It will be noted that the demand schedule for pounds is downward-sloping, indicating that a fall in the value of the pound against the dollar makes *UK goods cheaper* in exchange terms and *increases American demand for pounds* with which to buy such goods. (For example, if the dollar price of £1 falls from $3 = £1 to, say, $2 = £1, UK goods costing £1 can now be bought for $2 instead of $3.) The supply schedule for pounds is upward-sloping, indicating that an increase in the value of the pound against the dollar makes *US goods cheaper* in exchange terms and *increases the supply of pounds* offered by UK citizens and companies to obtain dollars in order to buy US goods. (For example, if the dollar price of £1 rises from $1 = £1 to $2 = £1 US goods costing $1 can now be bought for an outlay of 50p instead of £1.)

Let us assume now that US demand for UK goods falls (owing to a change in taste, or a switch to other countries' products), leading to a *shift* in the demand schedule for pounds from DD to D_1D_1 in Figure 6.2. Under

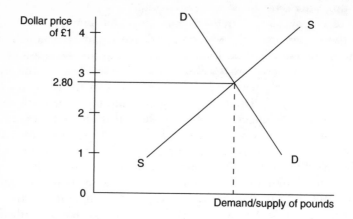

Figure 6.1 Equilibrium rate of exchange between the pound sterling and the US dollar; S supply of pounds in exchange for dollars to buy US goods (imports), D demand for pounds in exchange for dollars to buy British goods (exports)

a *floating exchange rate system* this would cause the exchange value of the pound to fall (depreciate) against the dollar to a new exchange value of $2.40, thereby restoring equilibrium in the demand and supply of the currencies. Assume, however, that the UK and the USA are members of a *fixed exchange rate system* so that initially the exchange rate remains unchanged at $2.80 = £1.

In that case the fall in American demand has reduced the volume of UK exports, leading to an 'exchange gap' of XY. In the short term, the UK central bank will need to 'support' the existing exchange rate by selling XY amount of dollars out of its reserves.

The deficit in the UK's payment position may be temporary and self-correcting. However, if it persists corrective measures may be required. There are three main mechanisms for restoring balance of payments equilibrium under a fixed exchange rate system: external price adjustments, internal income and price adjustments and trade/foreign exchange restrictions.

6.3 EXTERNAL PRICE ADJUSTMENTS

An external price adjustment involves an alteration in the exchange rate between currencies which is dependent upon the particular exchange rate system in operation. Under a fixed exchange rate system it is usual to talk of devaluations and revaluations of exchange rates rather than depreciation and appreciation of exchange rates, as under a floating exchange rate system. In the case of a trade deficit a devaluation/depreciation of the exchange rate will make exports cheaper and imports more expensive, while in the

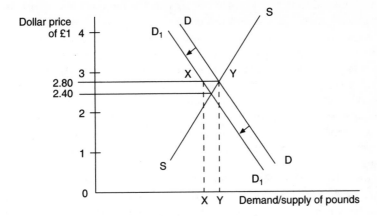

Figure 6.2 Fall in US demand for UK goods; XY dollar gap

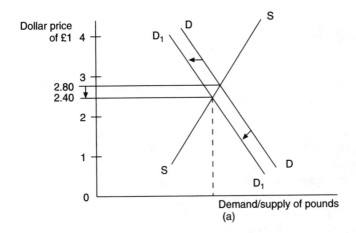

UK domestic price of a product	Exchange rate	Price of the UK product exported to US
£1	£1 = $2.80	$2.80
£1	£1 = $2.40	$2.40

(b)

Figure 6.3 Devaluation

case of a trade surplus a revaluation/appreciation of the exchange rate will make exports dearer and imports cheaper in foreign currency terms. In our example, Figure 6.3(a) shows a devaluation of the pound, with the exchange rate between the dollar and the pound being re-pegged at a new (lower) value of $2.40 = £1. This serves to make exports cheaper and imports more expensive in foreign currency terms. For example, with regard to exports, in Figure 6.3(b) the devaluation of the pound from $2.80 to $2.40 would allow UK exporters to reduce their prices by a similar amount, thus increasing their competitiveness in the US market (and other foreign markets), although in some cases exporters may choose not to reduce their prices by the full amount of the devaluation in order to boost unit profit margins.

It must be emphasised that the 'workability' of devaluation (and for that matter of depreciation under a floating exchange rate system) depends on a number of factors, in particular the price elasticity of demand for exports and imports – they must sum to more than 1 for a positive overall effect. Specifically, the elasticity values for a successful devaluation, for example, are:

Demand for imports is price-elastic $(e \geqslant 1)$
Demand for exports is price-elastic $(e \geqslant 1)$

How successful the devaluation is thus depends critically on the reaction of import and export volumes to the change in prices implied by the devaluation. If trade volumes are relatively responsive to price changes (price-elastic) the devaluation will be successful; that is, an increase in import prices results in a more than proportionate fall in import volumes, reducing the total amount of foreign currency required to finance the import bill, while the decrease in export prices results in a more than proportionate increase in export volume, bringing about an increase in total foreign currency earnings on exports.

By contrast, if trade volumes are relatively inelastic to price changes the devaluation will not succeed; that is, an increase in import prices results in a less than proportionate fall in import volume, increasing the total amount of foreign currency required to finance the import bill, while the decrease in export prices results in a less than proportionate increase in export volume, bringing about a fall in total foreign currency earnings on exports. There are, however, a number of other factors which influence the eventual outcome of a devaluation.

Firstly, resources must be available and sufficiently mobile to expand export production and provide output to replace imports. Secondly, domestic inflation needs to be contained, otherwise *internal* prices rises will nullify the *external* price reduction (see Boxes 6.2 and 6.3). Thirdly, if the demand for imports tends to outstrip export growth over time then there will be persistent pressure for the exchange rate to be devalued. However, devaluation will offer only a temporary cure, as it does not in itself tackle the underlying weaknesses of the economy. Thus a devaluation/ depreciation of a currency usually needs to be accompanied by appropriate internal price and income adjustments (as indicated in Section 6.4).

Even if all these factors are favourable the effects of a devaluation will still take time to work through. Usually there will be a tendency for the balance of payments deficit to worsen initially, following a devaluation, before then improving (the so-called J curve effect). This is because the full adjustment of trade volumes to devaluation involves a time lag: there is an immediate fall in export prices and a rise in import prices so that current exports earn less foreign exchange and current imports absorb more foreign exchange, thereby increasing the size of the payments deficit (the downturn of the J curve). Over time, however, the lower export prices will increase overseas demand and export earnings will rise, while higher import prices will reduce domestic demand, leading to an improvement in the balance of payments (the upturn of the J curve).

Additionally, various political considerations may affect a government's willingness to devalue the currency. First, devaluation may be seen as reflecting the government's failure to manage the economy effectively. Second, devaluation requires other countries to accept the realignment of exchange rates within the system. Assent may not be forthcoming if the devaluation is seen as harmful to their own trading interests.

6.4 INTERNAL PRICE AND INCOME ADJUSTMENTS

Internal price and income adjustment involves the use of deflationary and reflationary monetary and fiscal policies to alter the prices of domestically produced goods *vis-à-vis* products supplied by other countries so as to make exports cheaper and imports more expensive, in the case of a deficit, and exports more expensive and imports cheaper in the case of a surplus. Figure 6.4(a) shows how, after a fall in US demand for UK goods (DD to D_1D_1) causes a deficit (XY), domestic deflation serves to reduce UK demand for US goods (shifting the supply schedule of pounds from SS to S_1S_1) and increase US demand for UK goods (shifting the demand schedule for pounds from D_1D_1 to D_2D_2) restoring equilibrium at an *unchanged* exchange rate of $2.80 = £1.

Domestic deflation works in a dual way: the *price effect* – deflation slows down UK domestic price rises *relative* to US domestic prices, thereby reducing import demand and increasing export demand; the *income effect* – lower UK incomes reduce the demand for imports, and a lower level of domestic demand releases resources which can be used to increase exports.

Deflation thus serves to make exports cheaper and imports more expensive in foreign currency terms. For example, with regard to exports,

Box 6.2 Exchange rates, inflation and international competition: an example

1 Assume that initially a particular product X, which is manufactured in both the UK and the USA, is competitive in both the UK and the US markets at the prevailing exchange rate of £1 = $2.80, i.e. UK domestic price = £1, US domestic price = $2.80.
2 Assume now that the pound is devalued to £1 = $2.40 in order to remove an *overall* payments deficit.

Effects

UK exports cheaper. UK price of the product is still £1 but Americans can now buy it for $2.40 instead of $2.80 (although British exporters may choose to increase the local currency price to boost profits, e.g. they might increase the price to, say $2.70 in the US market, boosting unit profits but still undercutting the price of the equivalent US product).

Imports dearer. The price of the US product in the UK market rises to £1.14 (although US exporters may choose to 'absorb' the currency rise by reducing their unit profit margins).

But

3 *Domestic (UK) inflation may nullify devaluation* (that is, internal price rises may offset external price reduction).

Assume that the UK domestic price of product X goes up by 25 per cent to £1.25, but that the US product's price is unchanged.
   The cost to Americans of importing the UK product now rises to $3 (that is, $2.40 for £1 *plus* an extra 60 cents for the 25p increase), making it uncompetitive against the US version selling at $2.80.

Box 6.3 Depreciations/devaluations and trade performance

A fall in the exchange rate value of a country's currency makes its exports cheaper in foreign currency terms and its imports more expensive. If export and import volumes are price-elastic, then (over time) exports should increase relative to imports, thus helping to remove a payments deficit. As emphasised in the text, a number of 'back-up' conditions are required for this to happen, in particular the need to ensure that a fall in external prices is not *offset* by an increase in domestic prices.
   The charts below contrast recent US and UK experience. Since the mid-1980s the trade weighted exchange rates of the US dollar and

UK pound hcve depreciated by some 25 per cent and 10 per cent respectively (Chart (a)). Allowing for the rise in domestic prices (chart (b)), however, while the *real* exchange rate of the dollar fell, the real exchange rate of the pound rose. The reason for higher UK domestic prices is explained largely by increases in wage costs (chart (c)). In the UK real wages have increased by some 26 per cent since the mid-1980s while US real wage rates have fallen by 10 per cent. Overall, the favourable exchange rate value of the dollar has brought about a significant improvement in the USA's merchandise trade performance (chart (d)). US export volumes increased some 20 per cent faster than import volumes over the period 1985–92; by contrast, UK export volumes fell by 9 per cent relative to import volumes over this period.

Obviously it is too simplistic to focus solely on price competitiveness as a determinant of trade performance. The continued strong expansion of Japanese exports despite a large appreciation of the yen indicates that the ability to offer innovative and technologically sophisticated products is equally important.

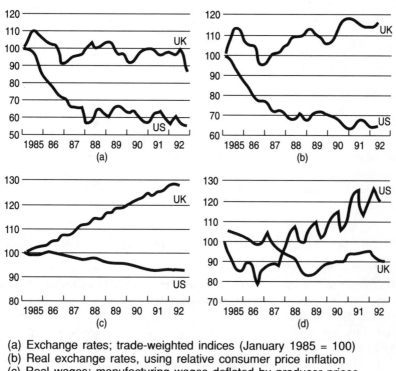

(a) Exchange rates; trade-weighted indices (January 1985 = 100)
(b) Real exchange rates, using relative consumer price inflation
(c) Real wages: manufacturing wages deflated by producer prices
(d) Trade performance: merchandise export/import ratio

Source (a)–(d): Datastream, *Financial Times*, 26 October 1992

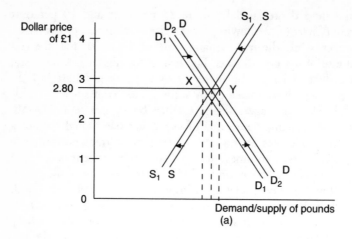

Figure 6.4 Deflation

UK domestic price of a product	Exchange rate	Price of the UK product exported to US
£1	£1 = $2.80	$2.80
88p	£1 = $2.80	$2.45

(b)

Figure 6.4 Deflation

in Figure 6.4(b), if it was possible to reduce the domestic price of a UK product from £1 to, say, 88p, as shown in Figure 6.4(b), given an unchanged exchange rate, that would allow the dollar price of the product in the US market to be reduced to $2.45, thereby improving its price competitiveness *vis-à-vis* US products and other foreign imports.

6.5 TRADE AND FOREIGN EXCHANGE RESTRICTIONS

Balance of payments adjustment can also involve the use of various trade restrictions such as tariffs and quotas and restrictions on foreign exchange transactions in order to affect the price and availability of goods, and of the currencies they are purchased with. In general, given the post-1945 emphasis on trade liberalisation programmes at both the international (through GATT) and the regional level (through the formation of various 'free trade' blocs), many of these restrictions have either been outlawed or their use has been severely constrained by the danger that 'beggar-my-neighbour policies' will provoke retaliatory action, with mutually destructive results. Nevertheless, national self-interest often prevails, with countries resorting to less visible means of protecting their economies such as subsidies, local content rules, etc. (see Chapter 7).

Figure 6.5 illustrates the use of a tariff as a means of removing a payment deficit. In Figure 6.5(a) D represents domestic demand for imports of particular goods, say textiles, S is the world supply price of textiles, and OQ is the current volume of imports. By applying a tariff of the amount T, the authorities are able to increase the price of textiles to domestic buyers from OP to OP_1, reducing the volume of imports from OQ to OQ_1. In Figure 6.5(b), after a fall in US demand for UK goods causes a deficit (XY), tariffs can be used to reduce UK demand for US goods, shifting the supply schedule for pounds from SS to S_TS_T, thereby restoring balance of payments equilibrium at the unchanged exchange rate of $2.80 = £1.

Import demand may be highly price-inelastic, however, and import volumes may fall only slightly even when high tariff rates are imposed. Thus, for some products, the use of trade quotas may represent a more practical means of reducing imports. Under a quota arrangement the government directly restricts the volume of permissible imports to a specified maximum level.

Finally, exchange controls may be used to limit the availability of certain foreign currencies. By cutting off the supply of foreign currency the authorities can reduce the volume of imports to a level compatible with the foreign currency earned by the country's exports. In Figure 6.6, after a fall in US demand for UK goods causes a deficit (XY), the authorities 'ration' the available supply of dollars earned by UK exports (OX) among UK importers, who demand the amount OY, shifting the supply schedule of pounds from SS to S_1S_1, securing balance of payments equilibrium at an unchanged exchange rate of $2.80 = £1.

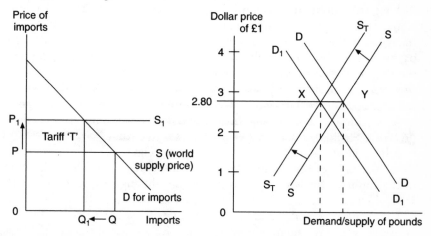

Figure 6.5 Tariff: (a) import volumes, (b) currency effect

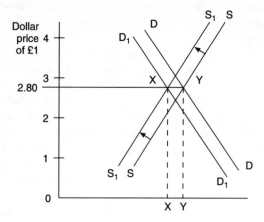

Figure 6.6 Exchange controls; XY dollar gap

6.6 INTERNAL–EXTERNAL BALANCE

The priority accorded by governments to the achievement of balance of payments equilibrium will depend, in part, on the size of the country's payments deficits or surpluses, and on the relative importance of the foreign trade sector in the country's gross domestic product. Some countries are highly dependent on foreign trade as an income generator, while for others the foreign trade sector is much less significant in this regard (see Table 6.4).

Furthermore, attention to the balance of payments needs to be looked at alongside the government's domestic economic objectives. Clearly, the opening up of an economy presents further difficulties for policy-makers. Although the domestic economy may be in equilibrium, external considerations may suggest that the economy's overall position is unsatisfactory. In that case the three mechanisms discussed above for securing balance of payments equilibrium are unlikely to be used in isolation. Depending upon the state of the economy, it will more usually be the case that they will be *combined* in various ways. The internal–external balance model provides a useful conceptual framework for examining combinations of policy measures aimed at achieving both full employment and price stability ('internal balance') and balance of payments equilibrium ('external balance').

A brief illustration of the model is given in Figure 6.7. The vertical axis shows the ratio of international prices to domestic prices. This is an index of the country's foreign competitive position: the higher one moves up the scale, the larger are exports and the smaller are imports. On the horizontal axis is domestic real demand, which increases from left to right. The two curves shown in the figure represent, respectively external balance (EE) and internal balance (DD).

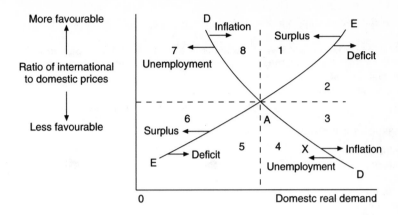

Figure 6.7 Internal–external balance model

The EE curve has a positive slope, indicating that the more unfavourable the international price ratio becomes, the lower domestic real demand must be to maintain balance of payments equilibrium. Positions to the left of the curve and above it represent payments surplus; to the right and below, deficit. Thus, as shown in Figure 6.8, if for example the level of domestic real demand is X, the ratio of international to domestic prices must be at level P to secure external balance. If it is not, the result is a surplus or a deficit in the balance of payments.

The DD curve has a negative slope, indicating that the more unfavourable the international price ratio becomes the higher domestic real demand must be to maintain full employment. Positions to the right of the curve and above represent price inflation; those to the left and below,

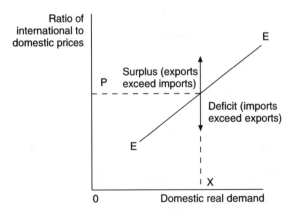

Figure 6.8 External balance

Table 6.4 Trade dependence: selected countries, 1990–2

Trade dependence ratios vary markedly between countries, depending on such things as their basic resource endowments, the range and sophistication of their domestic industries and governments' trade policies.

	Exports as % of GDP	Imports as % of GDP
Developed countries		
Australia	18	18
Belgium	69	66
Canada	26	28
Denmark	37	29
France	23	22
Germany	33	26
Greece	23	34
Italy	18	18
Japan	10	9
Netherlands	52	46
New Zealand	31	28
Norway	43	35
Sweden	33	30
Switzerland	36	32
UK	23	25
USA	11	12
Developing countries		
Brazil	10	6
Cameroon	15	17
Chile	32	30
Ecuador	31	27
Egypt	29	32
Ghana	16	25
Hungary	36	39
Indonesia	29	27
Israel	31	45
Jamaica	45	53
Kenya	27	32
Korea (South)	31	31
Kuwait	35	49
Malaysia	80	74
Mexico	16	17
Pakistan	17	21
Poland	21	22
Taiwan	44	41
Thailand	37	43

Source: Europa World Yearbook, 1994.

unemployment. Thus, as shown in Figure 6.9, if for example the ratio of international to domestic prices is P, domestic demand must be at level X to secure internal balance. If it is not, the result is unemployment or inflation.

Where the EE and DD curves intersect (point A) the country is in general equilibrium. All other positions represent disequilibrium. However, from only a few of these disequilibrium positions can the country attain the two policy objectives of internal and external equilibrium using just a single policy variable – specifically, from only those positions located on the horizontal and vertical dotted lines drawn through the intersection in Figure 6.7. In the situations shown by the horizontal line to the right of point A, for instance, the ratio of international to domestic prices is appropriate but domestic real demand is too high, resulting in both inflation and a balance of payments deficit. Deflation of demand alone would therefore suffice to realise both goals. In situations shown by the vertical line below point A, domestic real demand is just right but domestic prices are uncompetitive, resulting in both a balance of payments deficit and unemployment. A currency devaluation alone would therefore suffice to realise both goals. However, these are special cases. In all other situations both domestic demand and the international price ratio are inappropriate. As a result, the two policy objectives are in conflict, and the separate policy variables must be combined if they are to be effective. For example, if the economy is operating in zone 4 at position X it is experiencing both a balance of payments deficit and unemployment. If these two problems were considered in isolation the payments deficit would require demand to be cut (deflation) to reduce imports, whereas conversely unemployment would necessitate an increase in demand (reflation). Thus the problem encountered at position X cannot be solved by one policy variable alone. Given

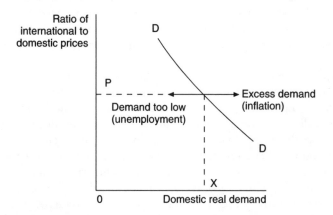

Figure 6.9 Internal balance

the more pressing problem of the balance of payments deficit, reflected in the fact that position X is much further from the EE curve than the DD curve, the appropriate policy response is a combination of currency deval-uation/depreciation and deflation. Devaluation makes imports more expen-sive and exports cheaper, not only moving the economy nearer to balance of payments equilibrium but also stimulating growth and jobs in the export sector, thus 'mopping up' unemployment. However, one of the side effects of devaluation is that it can be inflationary – hence the need to combine devaluation with deflation of the appropriate strength.

6.7 CONCLUSION

Attention to the balance of payments is an integral part of macroeconomic management, particularly for countries heavily involved in international trade and investment. Since by its very nature the balance of payments involves dealings with foreign countries, a country must be mindful of the impact of its own policies on the position of other countries. This broader influence of international trade and international investment is discussed in Chapters 7–10.

6.8 IMPLICATIONS FOR BUSINESS

A country's balance of payments represents the aggregate outcome of millions of individual cross-border exports and imports of goods, services and financial assets. Ideally, a country's balance of payments should be broadly in 'equilibrium' over a run of years, with deficits and surpluses cancelling themselves out over the long run. Failure to eliminate a long-standing surplus or deficit can cause serious friction between countries which may, in turn, adversely affect firms' trading interests. The conflict between the USA and Japan over Japan's massive current account surplus with the USA is a case in point, with the USA threatening trade sanc-tions unless Japan is prepared to 'open up' its economy further to US exports.

However, it is important to understand the *mechanisms* underlying persistent deficits and surpluses. In the final analysis the ability of a free-enterprise economy to pay its way internationally without recourse to protectionism depends fundamentally on its comparative advantages (see Chapter 7) and the competitiveness of its domestic firms and industries. A current account deficit, for example, could reflect a failure on the part of a significant number of a country's firms and industries to supply goods and services at competitive prices, or to supply the kind of product buyers demand, because of cost inefficiencies, low productivity, lack of investment in innovation, etc. However, it must also be recognised that a deficit can arise from, or can be exacerbated by, failure on the part of government to provide an appropriate monetary framework. For example, the government may have 'fixed' its exchange rate too high against other currencies and it may have failed to devalue the currency as appropriate to restore price competitiveness.

QUESTIONS

1 Indicate the structure of the balance of payments, commenting on the nature and significance of each sub-group of transactions identified.
2 Would you agree that it is relatively unimportant that individual sub-groups of the balance of payments are in deficit provided that *overall* the balance of payments is in equilibrium?
3 What is meant by the term 'equilibrium rate of exchange'? Indicate the factors that are likely to cause a change in the equilibrium rate of exchange.
4 Outline the 'mechanics' of an external price adjustment in restoring balance of payments equilibrium, and discuss the conditions necessary for this to be successfully achieved.
5 Discuss how 'deflation' can assist in the removal of a balance of payments deficit.
6 Indicate the nature and significance of the internal–external balance model. What combination of measures would you recommend to secure both internal and external balance if the economy was operating inside zone 4? Zone 8?

Chapter 7

International trade
1 Facts and theories

As the previous chapter has recognised, international trade is becoming increasingly important to the economic well-being of a nation. With the advent of global markets, facilitated by the removal of tariffs, etc., through the General Agreement on Tariffs and Trade (GATT), expansion of international trade has moved to the top of most governments' and businesses' agendas. An understanding of the basis of international trade flows and trade policy is essential.

International trade involves the exchange of goods and services between countries through exports and imports. Such cross-frontier trade is generally based on the comparative advantages which countries have in supplying particular products, providing the basis of an international division of labour (location of production).

Strictly speaking, of course, in the case of *market* economies it is not countries as such that trade but rather a multitude of private enterprise firms. This is an important distinction, for, as we shall see in Chapter 9, while countries remain relatively 'fixed' entities over time, firms, specifically multinational firms, can deploy their resources *between* countries, replacing, for example, arm's-length exporting to a foreign market by investment in manufacturing capacity in that market.

Inter-country variations in comparative advantage are reflected both in terms of their differential cost structures (i.e. price competitiveness) and in terms of their different skill levels (i.e. product differentiation competitiveness). These, in turn, are determined in large measure by a country's basic factor endowments (natural resources, labour and capital) and degree of economic maturity (level of *per capita* income, general cost and price levels, scientific and technical skills, etc.). Resource availability and skills indicate the product range which a country is technically capable of supplying, while *relative* cost, price and product differentiation factors dictate which of the products in the range it is economically appropriate for the country to produce, i.e. those products in which it has a comparative advantage over other countries. Through international trade, countries can capitalise on their economic strengths, thereby improving their real living standards.

International trade can bring both consumption and production gains to a country. Such trade enables countries to consume some goods and services more cheaply by importing them, and also to obtain some resources and products from other countries which would otherwise be totally unavailable because domestic producers are unable to supply them (for example, a scarce raw material or a high-technology product). International trade promotes production efficiency by encouraging the reallocation of resources away from areas of the economy best serviced by imports into industries where the country enjoys a comparative advantage over its trade partners.

Consideration of the benefits of international trade suggests that the optimisation of such benefits is best achieved by conditions of free trade (that is, the absence of restrictions on trade such as tariffs and quotas). In practice, however, the benefits of international trade are often unequally divided between countries, and this inevitably tends to produce situations where national self-interest is put before international obligations, resulting in the unilateral imposition of protectionist measures. In addition, the manner in which world trading patterns have developed has not benefited certain developing countries which have specialised in a narrow range of raw materials for which world demand has grown slowly.

The chapter begins by looking at the facts. Who trades with whom and in what commodities? The second part of the chapter examines why international trade takes place. This section recognises that various aspects of international trade may be unacceptable to some countries.

7.1 TRENDS IN INTERNATIONAL TRADE

Over the long-term, rising *per capita* incomes in the leading industrial countries, the continuing industrialisation of many developing countries and governments' commitment to free-trade policies have all served to increase international trade. Table 7.1 gives details of the growth in world exports of merchandise (that is, trade in goods) in value and volume terms for the

Table 7.1 World merchandise trade and output, 1960–92: average annual percentage change

	Exports		
Year	Value	Volume	Output
1960–9	9.2	8.6	6.0
1970–9	20.3	6.2	4.8
1980–90	6.0	4.1	2.7
1991	1.6	3.0	0.0
1992	5.9	4.0	1.0

Source: GATT, 1993.

Table 7.2 Shares in world trade, 1950–92, by value (%)

Trading bloc	1950	1960	1970	1980	1992
Developed market economies	61	66	71	62	71
Developing countries	31	22	18	29	22
East European and socialist countries	8	12	11	9	7
of which:					
USA	22	20	19	14	13
European Union	28	33	37	34	39
European Free Trade Association	5	6	6	5	7
Japan	1	3	6	6	8
Central and Latin America	12	8	5	5	4
Africa	5	4	4	5	2
Asia	13	9	8	18	15

Source: United Nations, GATT, 1993.

period since 1960. Although the recessionary impact of the oil price increases of 1973 and 1979 served to slow down the rate of growth of international trade in the 1980s, world exports have continued to expand at a more rapid rate than world output.

7.1.1 Regional distribution of merchandise trade

International trade in goods is dominated by the developed countries, a situation explained largely by the preponderance of manufactures in world exports and imports (see Section 7.1.2). Since 1950, as Table 7.2 shows, the developed countries have steadily increased their share of total world trade, from 61 per cent in 1950 to 71 per cent in 1992, the only interruption of this trend occurring in the 1970s, when the oil price increases of 1973 and 1979 temporarily boosted the world market share of the oil-exporting developing countries. Western Europe, particularly the European Union bloc, has increased in relative importance and in 1992 accounted for around 46 per cent of total world trade. Japan too has significantly increased its share of world trade. It will be noted that the developing countries' share of world trade declined between 1980 and 1992 after increasing (mainly in the case of oil producers) in the 1970s. Some Asian countries (Korea, Singapore, Taiwan and Hong Kong), however, have continued to increase their share of world trade (see Table 7.3) while Central and Latin America and Africa have declined in importance; likewise the share of East European (mainly communist) countries and socialist countries has declined, after peaking in the early 1960s.

Table 7.3 gives details of the twenty-five leading exporters and importers of goods in 1979 and 1992. Together these countries accounted for some

85–6 per cent of total world exports and imports. A number of countries increased their merchandise export ranking substantially between 1979 and 1992, these being mainly the newly industrialising countries of Asia and the Pacific rim – China, Hong Kong, Korea, Taiwan, Singapore and Malaysia in particular. The older industrial countries, however, continue to dominate the higher rankings. In general, the leading importing countries are those countries (the USA, Germany, Japan, France, the UK, Italy, the Netherlands and Canada) which are also the major exporting countries, a fact explained largely by the increased degree of intra-product specialization in manufactures (see below).

Table 7.4 indicates the extent to which a particular region's exports comprise *intra-regional* trade (that is, trade between the various countries making up that region) as compared with *inter-regional* trade (that is, trade between different regions). It will be noted that in the case of the world's largest region in international trade, Western Europe, 72 per cent of Western European countries' exports were intra-regional (up from 68 per cent in 1986) while in the case of the world's second largest region in international trade, Asia, 47 per cent of Asian countries' exports were intra-regional (up from 37 per cent in 1986). The growing proportion of intra-regional trade, fuelled by regional trade alliances and their discrimination against non-members (for example, the European Union's Common Agricultural Policy), has led to fears in GATT that further 'polarisation' of trade flows may undermine attempts to develop a broader-based multilateral trade framework.

The relative importance of various trade partners to *individual* countries can vary substantially, reflecting traditional historical associations and the commodity composition of a country's exports and imports as well as membership of a free trade area. For example, UK exports to other European Union countries accounted for 53 per cent of total UK exports in 1992 (up from 42 per cent in 1979).

7.1.2 Product composition of merchandise trade

Table 7.5 gives details of the product composition of world merchandise trade. Around a quarter of world merchandise trade in 1992 consisted of primary products, principally foodstuffs and fuels, while manufactures accounted for nearly three-quarters of total merchandise trade. Within the manufactures sector it will be noticed that over half of all trade consisted of machinery and transport equipment. Over the long term, trade in primary products has declined in importance, while trade in manufactures has increased. These developments are a reflection of changed patterns of demand and the introduction of new technologies and products.

Demand has become more diverse and sophisticated, with rising *per capita* income in the older industrialised countries, and their industrial structures have become more specialised, which has led to a trade flow increasingly

Table 7.3 Leading exporters and importers in world merchandise trade, 1979 and 1992

Rank			1992 Value	1992 Share
1979	*1992*	*Country*	*(US$ billion)*	*(%)*
Exporters				
1	1	USA	448	12.0
2	2	Germany*	430	11.5
3	3	Japan	340	9.1
4	4	France	236	6.3
5	5	UK	190	5.1
6	6	Italy	178	4.8
8	7	Netherlands	140	3.8
10	8	Canada	134	3.6
11	9	Belgium and Luxembourg	123	3.3
27	10	Hong Kong	120	3.2
34	11	China	85	2.3
22	12	Taiwan	81	2.2
29	13	Korea, South	77	2.1
13	14	Switzerland	66	1.8
19	15	Spain	64	1.7
32	16	Singapore	63	1.7
12	17	Sweden	56	1.5
9	18	Saudi Arabia	49	1.3
37	19	Mexico	46	1.2
25	20	Austria	44	1.2
28	21	Australia	42	1.1
38	22	Malaysia	41	1.1
30	23	Denmark	40	1.1
–	24	Russian Federation	37	1.0
27	25	Brazil	36	1.0
Total exporters			3,166	85.0
Total, World†			3,731	100.0

Continued

characterised by the interchange of differentiated manufactured products within the same product group. Thus, for example, as Box 7.1 shows, the USA and Germany are both substantial exporters and importers of auto-motive and textile products. Trade in manufactured goods has been greatly facilitated by the removal of tariffs and other obstacles at the GATT level and by the establishment of free-trade areas.

The slower growth in primary produce trade has been variously attrib-uted to the low income elasticity of demand for a substantial number of foodstuffs, economies in the use of raw materials or their replacement by synthetics, and the protectionist policies of the developed countries. The relative importance of various products for *individual* countries in their export and import structure can differ markedly, reflecting differences in

Table 7.3 Continued

Rank			1992 Value	1992 Share
1979	*1992*	*Country*	*(US$ billion)*	*(%)*
Importers				
1	1	USA	554	14.3
2	2	Germany*	409	10.6
3	3	France	240	6.2
4	4	Japan	233	6.0
5	5	UK	222	5.6
6	6	Italy	189	4.9
7	7	Netherlands	134	3.5
10	8	Canada	129	3.3
8	9	Belgium and Luxembourg	125	3.2
21	10	Hong Kong	123	3.2
13	11	Spain	100	2.6
15	12	Korea, South	82	2.1
11	13	China	81	2.1
20	14	Singapore	72	1.9
24	15	Taiwan	72	1.9
25	16	Switzerland	66	1.7
16	17	Mexico	62	1.6
12	18	Austria	54	1.4
29	19	Sweden	50	1.3
19	20	Australia	44	1.1
44	21	Thailand	41	1.1
18	22	Malaysia	40	1.1
30	23	Denmark	34	0.9
22	24	Saudi Arabia	32	0.9
–	25	Russian Federation	31	0.9
Total importers			3,219	84.4
Total, World[†]			3,855	100.0

Source: GATT, 1993.

[*] Refers to the Federal Republic of Germany after unification.

[†] Discrepancy between export and import figures due to recording differences.

their basic factor endowments and technological capacity. For example, many developing countries are highly dependent on one or two primary products or on labour-intensive, low-technology manufactures. In 1992, as Table 7.6 shows, crude petroleum accounted for 90 per cent of Angola's exports and 73 per cent of the Congo's exports; coffee accounted for 85 per cent of Burundi's exports and 80 per cent of Rwanda's exports; sugar and honey accounted for 75 per cent of Cuba's exports and for 76 per cent of Réunion's exports; base metal ores accounted for 90 per cent of Guinea's exports; and tobacco accounted for 66 per cent of Malawi's exports.

In consequence of their concentration on a limited range of exports many developing countries have heightened their exposure to cyclical price

Table 7.4 Shares of intra-and inter-regional trade flows in each region's total exports, selected regions, 1992(%)

	Destination					
Origin	North America	Latin Amercia	Western Europe	Africa	Asia	Other
North America	33	13	22	2	25	5
Latin America	47	17	20	1	9	6
Western Europe	7	2	72	3	7	9
Africa	14	2	56	7	10	11
Asia	26	2	19	2	47	4

Source: GATT, 1993.

Table 7.5 Composition of world merchandise exports by product, 1992 (%)

Agricultural products	**12.0**
Food	9.5
Raw materials	2.5
Mining products	**12.2**
Ores, minerals and non-ferrous metals	3.1
Fuels	9.1
Manufactures	**72.8**
Iron and steel	2.8
Chemicals	9.0
Other semi-manufactures	7.7
Machinery and transport equipment	37.3
Textiles	3.2
Clothing	3.6
Other consumer goods	9.2

Source: GATT, 1993.

fluctuations and secular price falls and this has exacerbated their foreign debt problems (see Chapter 11). By contrast, developed countries have a significantly more diversified export structure, tending to produce a very wide range of manufactured products (see Box 7.2).

Over time, the product composition of countries' import and export structures may change, reflecting, for example, a country's drive for industrialisation, general trade liberalisation and gains/losses in international competitiveness (see Table 7.7). In general, developing countries have been characterised by a fall in the proportion of their exports accounted for by agricultural products and an increase in exports of manufactures (for example, Argentina, Barbados, the Dominican Republic, India).

Box 7.1 Leading exporters and importers of automotive and textile products, 1980 and 1992

Exporters	Share of world exports (%) 1980	1992	Importers	Share of world imports (%) 1980	1992
Automotive products					
Japan	19.8	21.7	USA	19.5	21.3
Germany	21.0	20.5	Germany	5.9	11.0
USA	12.7	11.2	Canada	8.3	6.9
Canada	7.0	8.5	France	5.2	6.1
France	9.9	8.0	Italy	5.3	5.9
Belgium/Luxembourg	4.9	5.2	UK	5.5	5.8
UK	5.8	4.7	Belgium/Luxembourg	5.2	5.2
Spain	1.8	4.3	Spain	0.8	3.5
Italy	4.5	3.5	Netherlands	2.5	2.4
Sweden	4.8	2.1	Mexico	1.4	2.1
Textiles					
Germany	11.3	11.9	Hong Kong	5.1	10.3
Hong Kong	3.2	8.9	Germany	11.7	10.1
Italy	7.4	8.7	USA	4.3	6.7
China	4.5	7.3	China	1.9	6.2
Korea	4.0	7.0	France	7.0	6.1
Taiwan	3.2	6.5	UK	6.1	5.7
Japan	9.2	6.1	Italy	4.5	4.6
Belgium/Luxembourg	6.4	5.5	Japan	2.8	3.4
France	6.1	5.4	Netherlands	3.9	3.0
USA	6.7	5.0	Belgium/Luxembourg	4.0	2.9

Source: GATT, 1993.

Table 7.6 Main exports of selected developing countries, 1992

Country	Product	% of total exports accounted for by main product
Angola	Crude petroleum	90
Iran	Crude petroleum	88
Iraq	Crude petroleum	90
Libya	Crude petroleum	82
Nigeria	Crude petroleum	91
Oman	Crude petroleum	88
Qatar	Crude petroleum	73
United Arab Emirates	Crude petroleum	73
Bermuda	Precious stones	90
Burundi	Coffee	85
Rwanda	Coffee	80
Uganda	Coffee	96
Cuba	Sugar and honey	75
Réunion	Sugar and honey	76
Dominica	Fruit and nuts	67
Guinea	Base metal ores	90
Papua New Guinea	Base metal ores	58
Malawi	Tobacco	66
New Caledonia	Pig iron	61
Zambia	Copper	82
Chad	Cotton	48
Mali	Cotton	41
French Guiana	Fish	54
Malta	Transistors	38
Nepal	Floor coverings	34
Pakistan	Textiles	54
Togo	Fertilisers	51

Source: United Nations, 1993.

Box 7.2 Main exports of selected developed countries, 1992

Main exports	% of total exports
USA	
Aircraft	6.6
Motor vehicle parts	3.7
Automated data processing equipment	3.5
Office equipment and parts	3.3
Passenger motor vehicles	2.8
Transistors/valves	2.8
Control and measuring instruments	2.3

Engines and motors	2.0
Telecommunication equipment	1.8
Maize (unprocessed)	1.8
Wheat (unprocessed)	1.5
Internal combustion engines	1.4

UK

Crude petroleum	4.6
Automatic data processing equipment	4.0
Ships and boats	2.8
Motor vehicle parts	2.8
Engines and motors	2.8
Passenger motor vehicles	2.6
Control and measuring instruments	2.4
Precious stones	2.4
Aircraft	2.4
Pharmaceuticals	2.1
Office equipment	1.9
Refined petroleum products	1.9

Japan

Passenger motor vehicles	14.3
Telecommunication equipment	5.5
Transistors/valves	4.9
Automatic data processing equipment	4.2
Motor vehicle parts	3.7
Sound recordings	3.4
Lorries	3.2
Office equipment and parts	2.9
Iron and steel plates/sheet	2.8
Electrical machinery	2.8
Internal combustion engines	2.3
Switchgear	1.9

Germany

Passenger motor vehicles	10.3
Motor vehicle parts	4.1
Polymerisation products	2.3
Non-electrical machinery parts	2.0
Specialised machinery	2.0
Aircraft	1.9
Control and measuring instruments	1.8
Switchgear	1.8
Iron and steel plates/sheet	1.7
Electrical machinery	1.5
Lorries	1.5
Internal combustion engines	1.5

Source: United Nations, 1993.

Table 7.7 Changes in the product composition of exports and imports, selected countries, 1970 and 1990, by value (%)

Countries		Exports				Imports			
		Food	Fuels	Base metals	Manu-factures	Food	Fuels	Base metals	Manu-factures
Developing									
Argentina	1970	85	0	0	14	15	5	8	73
	1990	62	3	2	33	8	8	6	78
Dominican Republic	1970	88	0	0	4	18	7	2	71
	1990	22	0	1	70	14	35	1	50
Ecuador	1970	97	0	0	2	8	6	2	83
	1990	49	48	0	3	9	2	3	84
India	1970	35	1	12	52	30	8	10	49
	1990	22	6	6	66	12	27	8	51
Kenya	1970	75	12	1	12	8	10	2	77
	1990	72	14	1	12	9	20	2	69
Malawi	1970	96	0	0	3	19	5	1	72
	1990	93	0	0	6	9	13	2	76
Mexico	1970	49	3	15	32	12	3	4	81
	1990	14	37	6	44	20	4	3	72
Nigeria	1970	31	58	4	1	9	3	2	83
	1990	2	93	1	1	17	1	2	80

Table 7.7 Continued

Countries		Exports				Imports			
		Food	Fuels	Base metals	Manu-factures	Food	Fuels	Base metals	Manu-factures
Developed									
France	1970	19	2	4	74	22	12	8	58
	1990	16	2	3	77	12	10	4	74
Germany	1970	5	3	3	88	25	9	11	52
	1990	6	1	2	89	13	8	4	72
Italy	1970	10	5	2	83	29	14	11	46
	1990	7	2	1	88	18	11	5	64
Japan	1970	5	0	1	93	33	21	21	25
	1990	1	0	1	96	21	25	9	44
UK	1970	7	3	5	80	33	10	11	44
	1990	8	8	3	79	14	6	4	75
USA	1970	21	4	5	67	21	8	8	61
	1990	16	3	3	74	8	13	3	73

Note: Figures do not add up to 100 per cent because of unallocated products.

Source: United Nations, 1992.

Table 7.8 Leading exporters and importers in world trade in commercial services, 1992

Rank 1979	Rank 1992	Country	1992 Value (US$ billions)	1992 Share (%)
Exporters				
1	1	USA	162	16.2
2	2	France	102	10.2
4	3	Italy	65	6.5
5	4	Germany	64	6.4
3	5	UK	55	5.5
6	6	Japan	50	5.0
7	7	Spain	36	3.6
8	8	Netherlands	36	3.6
9	9	Belgium and Luxembourg	35	3.5
10	10	Austria	25	2.8
12	11	Switzerland	19	1.9
17	12	Singapore	18	1.8
18	13	Hong Kong	17	1.7
14	14	Canada	16	1.6
13	15	Sweden	16	1.6
16	16	Denmark	15	1.5
11	17	Norway	13	1.3
15	18	Mexico	13	1.3
19	19	Korea, South	13	1.3
22	20	Taiwan	11	1.1
26	21	Australia	10	1.0
32	22	China	9	0.9
51	23	Thailand	9	0.9
28	24	Greece	9	0.9
20	25	Turkey	8	0.8
		Total exporters	826	82.6
		Total, world*	1001	100.0

For some developing countries the high price of oil has had a significant impact on the proportion of their exports accounted for by fuels (for example, Ecuador, Mexico, Nigeria). Exceptions to this pattern include Malawi and Kenya, where agriculture continues to dominate the economy. In the case of the leading developed countries, manufactures have long dominated their export structures; rising *per capita* incomes and trade liberalisation have, however, led to a sharp increase in the proportion of their imports accounted for by manufactures. For example, the proportion of manufactures in total German imports rose from 52 per cent in 1970 to 72 per cent in 1990, and from 44 per cent to 75 per cent of total UK imports.

Table 7.8 Continued

Rank			1992 Value	1992 Share
1979	*1992*	*Country*	*(US$ billions)*	*(%)*

Importers

1979	1992	Country	Value	Share
3	1	Germany	112	11.3
1	2	USA	108	10.9
2	3	Japan	97	9.9
4	4	France	84	8.5
7	5	Italy	67	6.8
5	6	UK	47	4.8
6	7	Netherlands	36	3.6
9	8	Belgium and Luxembourg	33	3.3
10	9	Canada	27	2.8
11	10	Spain	22	2.2
20	11	Austria	20	2.0
13	12	Taiwan	19	1.9
27	13	Sweden	19	1.9
8	14	Switzerland	17	1.7
14	15	Saudi Arabia	15	1.5
23	16	Norway	15	1.5
12	17	Korea, South	15	1.5
15	18	Australia	14	1.4
26	19	Hong Kong	12	1.2
17	20	Mexico	12	1.2
32	21	Singapore	11	1.1
19	22	Denmark	11	1.1
30	23	Thailand	10	1.0
34	24	China	9	0.9
36	25	Malaysia	8	0.8
		Total importers	840	85.0
		Total, world	988	100.0

* Discrepancy in export and import figures due to recording differences

Source: GATT, 1993.

7.1.3 International trade in commercial services

Although world trade continues to be dominated by exports and imports of merchandise, international trade in commercial services (principally transport, tourism, business and financial services) has increased in importance and in 1992 accounted for around 21 per cent of total world merchandise and commercial services trade (up from 17 per cent in 1980). In part this mirrors the structural changes that have occurred in the economies of the USA, Japan, the European Union and other leading countries (where the service sector of the economy has expanded relative to the industrial sector), but, again, it is also due to the creation of more open trading conditions between countries. Table 7.8 lists the twenty-five leading exporters and importers of commercial services in 1979 and 1992. Five countries increased their ranking substantially (Singapore, Hong Kong, Taiwan, Thailand and Turkey). Changes were even more pronounced on the import side with Nigeria, Iran, Venezuela, Brazil, South Africa and Yugoslavia, which were among the top twenty-five importers in 1979, dropping out in 1992, to be replaced by Taiwan, Hong Kong, Singapore, Thailand, Finland and Malaysia. It will be noted that the same group of leading countries (the USA, Germany, Japan, France, Italy, the UK and the Netherlands) which dominate merchandise trade are also the most prominent exporters and importers of commercial services.

Published data on the product composition of internationally traded commercial services is limited. The GATT annual survey of international trade, while comprehensive on merchandise trade, contains only one table on commercial services (reproduced above), while the International Monetary Fund publishes balance of payments data on a highly aggregated basis (Table 7.9).

Table 7.9 World trade in commercial services by main category, 1977 and 1992 (US$ billion)

Category	1977	1992
Transport	73.4	300.4
Travel	52.2	282.5
Business and financial	74.6	338.6

Source: IMF, *Balance of Payments Statistics Yearbook*, 1993.

Box 7.3 Aspects of comparative advantage

Factor input costs differ between countries, reflecting differences in relative factor endowments and the general level of economic maturity attained by different countries. Table (a) indicates, for example, labour costs in the metalworking industries in selected European countries, and Table (b) shows labour costs in the textile industry in selected Asian countries. Increasingly, German engineering companies are setting up factories in lower-wage economies – Siemens, for instance, has moved the manufacture of its car wiring systems from Germany to Turkey and Czechoslovakia. Similarly, high wage costs (around $15 per hour) in the Japanese textile industry have encouraged companies to go 'offshore' to lower-cost locations elsewhere in Asia.

However, the notion of comparative advantage is somewhat more subtle than that. Wage costs need to be looked at in the context of total factor *productivity*, which emphasises the efficiency of resource use 'in the round', including, in particular, the contribution of capital in increasing productivity, and the scope for 'absorbing' labour costs by producing higher value-added products. Thus, for example, Japan is simultaneously a major exporter of sophisticated textile products manufactured in capital-intensive plants and a leading importer of standardised, labour-intensive products from countries such as Pakistan and South Korea (see Box 7.2).

Comparative advantage is often distorted by trade restrictions (see Section 7.4). Table (c) shows the production cost of bananas in a number of supplying countries. Ironically, the largest importing area, the EU (which accounts for 40 per cent of world imports), operates both a quota system and a high tariff structure which discriminates against Latin American countries (where 75 per cent of world exports originate) in favour of EU associates. Table (d) shows aluminium production costs. The EU has imposed quota limitations on imports from the Commonwealth of Independent States (CIS) claiming that access to subsidised energy supplies gives the CIS an 'unfair' advantage over EU producers.

(a) Labour costs, metalworking industries (DM per hour, 1991)

Germany	39
UK	23
Turkey	6

Source: Financial Times,
14 January 1992

(b) Labour costs, textile industry (US$ per hour, 1992)

Japan	15.0
Taiwan	4.5
Malaysia	1.0
China	0.5
Vietnam	0.1

Source: Economist, 31 July 1993

(c) Production costs, bananas (ECU per kg, 1990)

Latin America	0.2
Surinam	0.3
Cameroon	0.4
Caribbean	0.5
Martinique	0.5
Madeira	0.6

Source: Financial Times,
8 November 1991

(d) Production costs, aluminium (US cents per lb, 1991)

CIS	25
Canada	43
France	46
UK	51
USA	56
Germany	60

Source: Financial Times,
16 August 1992

7.2 THE NATURE AND SIGNIFICANCE OF COMPARATIVE ADVANTAGE

Countries trade with one another basically for the same reasons that individuals, firms and regions engage in the exchange of goods and services – to obtain the benefits of *specialisation*. By exchanging some of its own products for those of other nations, a country can enjoy a much wider range of commodities, and obtain them more cheaply, than would otherwise be the case. International division of labour, with each country specialising in the production of only some of the commodities that it is capable of producing, enables total world output to be increased and raises countries' real standards of living.

A country's choice of which commodities to specialise in will be determined in large measure by the advantages it possesses over others in the production of those things. Such advantages can arise because the country can produce particular commodities more efficiently, at lower cost, than can others (see Box 7.3). The static, or 'pure', theory of international trade emphasises that opportunities for mutually beneficial trade occur as a result of differences in *comparative costs* or *comparative advantage*. Countries will gain from trade if each country exports those commodities in which its costs of production are lower, and imports commodities in which its costs are higher.

Differences between countries and their comparative costs reflect differences in their basic *stock of factor endowments*: land (for example, differences in size of land mass, soil and climatic conditions, nature and abundance of mineral deposits, etc.), labour (for example, the size of the labour force) and capital (for example, the amount of productive capacity built up through cumulative investment in plant and equipment); the *quality* of factor inputs (for example, high/low-grade agricultural crops and mineral deposits, the skills of the labour force, high/low-grade production technologies and R&D infrastructures); the *efficiency* of resource use (for example, exploitation of economies of large-scale manufacturing, high/low productivity levels) and, more generally, the degree of economic maturity attained by a country, as reflected in, for example, wage levels, capital sophistication and R&D competence.

7.2.1 The direction of trade

The theory of comparative costs suggests that a country will specialise in the production of commodities in which its comparative costs of production are lower than those of other countries, exporting these commodities in exchange for commodities in which its comparative production costs are higher than those of other countries. This proposition is investigated, employing, to simplify matters, a two-country (A and B) and two-commodity (bicycles and tonnes of wheat) presentation.

Table 7.10 Physical output of wheat and bicycles from given factor inputs

	Commodity			Opportunity cost ratios		
Country	Wheat (tonnes)		Bicycles	Wheat (tonnes)		Bicycles
A	200	or	200	1	–	1
B	200	or	600	1	–	3
Total	400	or	800			

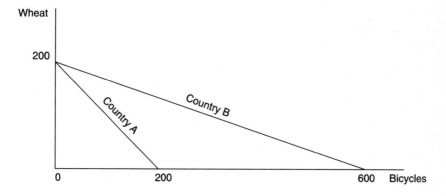

Figure 7.1 Production possibility frontiers

Let us assume that the same given resource inputs in both countries enable them to produce either the quantity of wheat or the number of bicycles shown in Table 7.10. In the absence of trade between the two countries, wheat and bicycles exchange in country A in the ratio of one tonne of wheat to one bicycle and, in country B, in the ratio of one tonne of wheat to three bicycles. These exchange ratios indicate the *marginal opportunity cost* of one commodity in terms of the other. Thus in country A the opportunity cost of producing one more tonne of wheat is one bicycle fewer, while in country B one more tonne of wheat would involve the sacrifice of three bicycles. These opportunity cost ratios are reflected in the slopes of the (pre-trade) production possibility frontiers shown in Figure 7.1.

Confronted with these opportunity cost ratios, if the two countries were both to divide their resources equally between wheat and bicycle production they could produce the (pre-trade) outputs shown in Table 7.11.

It can be seen from Table 7.10 that country B is absolutely more efficient than country A in the production of bicycles and just as efficient in the production of wheat. Superficially, this suggests that country B has

Table 7.11 Physical output of wheat and bicycles from given factor inputs, without specialisation

Country	Wheat (tonnes)		Bicycles
	Commodity		
A	100	and	100
B	100	and	300
Total	200	and	400

Table 7.12 Physical output of wheat and bicycles from given factor inputs, with specialisation

Country	Commodity		
	Wheat (tonnes)		Bicycles
A	200	and	0
B	0	and	600
Total	200	and	600

nothing to gain from trade with country A. However, it is *comparative advantage*, not absolute advantage, that determines whether specialisation and trade are advantageous or not. Country B has a comparative advantage in the production of bicycles, since the resource or opportunity cost of producing an additional bicycle is only one-third of a tonne of wheat in country B, whereas in country A it is one tonne of wheat. Country A has a comparative advantage in the production of wheat, since the resource or opportunity cost of producing an additional tonne of wheat in country A is only one bicycle, while in country B it is three bicycles. Thus in terms of real factor costs wheat can be produced more cheaply in country A, and bicycles can be produced more cheaply in country B.

Table 7.12 shows the output levels which will be achieved if country A specialises in growing wheat and country B in bicycle production. The potential gains from specialisation can be seen by comparing the totals in Table 7.12 with those in Table 7.11. Potentially an additional 200 bicycles can be produced, with wheat production unchanged.

7.2.2 Gains from trade

The combination of comparative advantages outlined above opens up the possibility of specialisation and mutually beneficial trade. Domestically, in country A, one tonne of wheat can be exchanged for one bicycle, but abroad it can be exchanged for anything up to three bicycles. Trade will be advantageous to country A if it can obtain more than one bicycle in exchange for one tonne of wheat. Domestically, in country B, one bicycle can be exchanged for one-third of a tonne of wheat, but abroad it can be exchanged for anything up to one tonne of wheat. It will be to country B's advantage if it can obtain through trade more than one-third of a tonne of wheat in exchange for one bicycle.

The limits to mutually beneficial trade are set by the opportunity cost ratios. Within these limits specialisation and trade on the basis of comparative advantage will enable both countries to attain higher consumption levels. This possibility is indicated in Table 7.13, assuming the international exchange ratio to be one tonne of wheat = two bicycles. Using its entire resources, country B can produce, say, 600 bicycles, of which it consumes 400 and exports 200 to country A. Country A can produce, say, 200 tonnes of wheat, of which it consumes 100 and exports 100 to country B. With trade the 200 bicycles can be exchanged for 100 tonnes of wheat, enabling country B to consume 400 bicycles and 100 tonnes of wheat, and country A to consume 200 bicycles and 100 tonnes of wheat.

Table 7.14 summarises the production and consumption possibilities with or without trade. *Without* specialisation and trade, country A can transform (at an internal exchange ratio of one tonne of wheat to one bicycle) 100 tonnes of wheat into only 100 bicycles, while country B can transform (at an internal exchange ratio of one tonne of wheat to three bicycles) 200 bicycles into only 66⅔ tonnes of wheat. Thus both countries gain by specialisation and trade. As Table 7.14 shows, *without* specialisation and trade, country A can produce and consume, say, 100 bicycles and 100 tonnes of wheat, while country B can produce and consume, say, 400 bicycles and 66⅔ tonnes of wheat. By contrast, *with* specialisation and trade, country A can produce up to 200 tonnes of wheat and is able to consume, say, 100 tonnes of wheat and export the other 100 tonnes of wheat to country B in exchange for 200 imported bicycles. Thus country A can,

Table 7.13 Consumption of wheat and bicycles, after trade

Country	Wheat (tonnes)		Bicycles
		Commodity	
A	100	and	200
B	100	and	400
Total	200	and	600

Note: One tonne of wheat = two bicycles.

Table 7.14 Production and consumption possibilities with and without trade

Possibility	Country A	Country B
Production and consumption without specialisation and trade	100 bicycles and 100 tonnes of wheat	400 bicycles and 66⅔ tonnes of wheat
Production (with specialisation)	200 tonnes of wheat	600 bicycles
Consumption with trade	200 bicycles and 100 tonnes of wheat	400 bicycles and 100 tonnes wheat

Note: International exchange rate: one tonne of wheat = two bicycles. Internal exchange rates: one tonne of wheat = one bicycle in country A; one tonne of wheat = three bicycles in country B.

through specialisation, consume as much wheat as before (100 tonnes) but is now able to consume an extra 100 bicycles (200 bicycles compared with only 100 bicycles). Similarly, *with* specialisation country B can produce up to 600 bicycles and is able to consume, say, 400 bicycles and export the other 200 bicycles to country A in exchange for 100 tonnes of imported wheat. Thus country B can, through specialisation, consume as many bicycles as before (400 bicycles) but is now able to consume an extra 33⅓ tonnes of wheat (100 tonnes compared with only 66⅔ tonnes).

The gains from trade are shown in Figure 7.2, where A and B represent the initial consumption possibilities of the two countries without specialisation and trade, while A_1 and B_1 show the consumption possibilities of the two countries after specialisation and trade. It can be seen that in both cases specialisation and trade have generated net gains, enabling both countries to consume more wheat and/or bicycles than their production possibility boundaries had previously allowed.

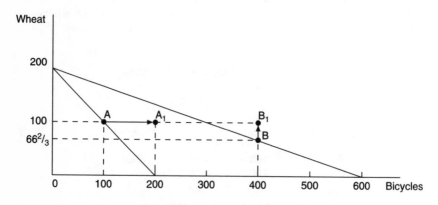

Figure 7.2 Production possibility frontiers and the gains from trade

How the gain is shared between countries A and B depends essentially upon the strength of demand in the two countries for the goods they import. If country A's demand for bicycles increases, the trading ratio of one tonne of wheat to two bicycles would be likely to move against country A. Thus it might require more wheat exports to obtain two bicycle imports (say, one tonne of wheat = one and a half bicycles), pushing country A nearer the limit of mutually beneficial trade.

7.2.3 Changes in comparative advantage

A basic assumption of this presentation is that factor endowments, and hence comparative advantages, are 'fixed'. Dynamically, however, comparative advantage may well change. It may do so in response to a number of influences, including:

1 The initiation by a country's government of structural programmes leading to resource redeployment. For example, a country which seemingly has a comparative advantage in the supply of primary products such as cotton and wheat may nevertheless abandon or de-emphasise it in favour of a drive towards industrialisation and the establishment of comparative advantage in higher value-added manufactured goods.
2 International capital movements and technology transfer, and relocation of production by multinational companies. For example, Malaysia developed a comparative advantage in the production of natural rubber only when UK entrepreneurs established and invested in rubber-tree plantations there.
3 Process and product invention and innovation over time (see below).

7.3 OTHER EXPLANATIONS OF TRADE FLOWS

In Section 7.1 it was noted that international trade flows have become increasingly based on the exchange of manufactured goods between the industrialised countries. While the traditional theory of comparative advantage provides an explanation of trade flows in dissimilar goods (for example, the exchange of agricultural goods for manufactured goods) it needs to be augmented to provide an explanation of trade in *similar* goods (for example, the UK exports cars to, and imports cars from, Germany, the USA, France, etc.). This kind of trade pattern is based on a combination of product innovation by *suppliers* and a demand for product differentiation by *consumers*. The gains from trade in this case stem from the ability of countries to consume products otherwise unobtainable from local suppliers (because of a 'technology gap') or in a form which meets local consumers' desire for value added rather than cheap products, as emphasised by the traditional theory of trade.

7.3.1 Technological gap and product life cycle explanations of trade

These two theories have so many elements in common that any exact distinction between them is arbitrary, but it is to be noted that the technological gap theory focuses primarily on production factors while the product life cycle theory emphasises marketing elements. The technological gap explanation of trade patterns is based on a dynamic sequence of innovation and imitation. Technologically advanced countries with a high propensity to innovate (such as the USA) are able to achieve trade advantages by being able to offer sophisticated new products on world markets, initially unobtainable from other sources. Over time, however, technology is diffused and other countries are able to produce the products concerned for themselves. Trade thus arises for the duration of the 'imitation lag'.

A similar process of innovation and imitation is postulated in the product life cycle model. According to this model the life cycle of products that save labour or appeal to high income consumers can be divided into four main parts.

1 Initially, as new products are introduced, the consuming country is likely to be the producing country because of the close association between innovation and demand. This original producing country – typically the USA – becomes an exporter to other high income countries.

2 In the second phase of the cycle, production begins in other major industrial countries, and the innovating country's exports to those markets are displaced.

3 As these countries' own demand for the product reaches sufficient size to enable producers to take advantage of economies of scale, they too become net exporters, thereby displacing the innovating country's exports in non-producing countries.

4 Finally, as the technology and product become very standardised, so that relatively unskilled labour can be used in the production process, semi- and less developed countries with lower costs become exporters of the product. The innovating country becomes a net importer of the old product and shifts its resources into the manufacture of new products.

This conceptualisation of the international product life cycle is, of course, a generalisation, and many variants are possible in particular cases. Thus, for example, the innovating country may not entirely lose its competitive advantage, despite imitation, because of 'cumulative experience', increasing returns to scale in production, and marketing expertise. On the other hand imitating countries may be better endowed with some factor in the production of the commodity than the innovating country, so that once the basic technology has been diffused the innovator's initial advantage is quickly lost.

Looked at broadly, empirical work to date has provided evidence consistent with the technological gap/product life cycle hypotheses: the high new product content of US, Japanese and German exports; the dominance of standardised manufactured products, originally developed elsewhere, in the exports of middle income countries such as Greece, Spain and Argentina; and in general the fact that the exports of manufactured products from the less developed countries tend to be from relatively mature industries (textiles, for example).

7.3.2 Demand aspects

No explanation of trade patterns can be complete without taking into account income and demand influences. As the above theories have indicated, new products typically appear in a high income country and then find new markets in countries where demand patterns are similar. Various models have been developed which relate product differentiation demands to countries' income levels, specifically emphasising the importance of similarity in demand preferences as a cause of trade. The 'preference similarity' theory maintains that a country will not be skilled in manufacturing and selling abroad commodities for which there is no 'representative' domestic demand. A country's exports are thus an extension of production for the home market. Such production caters for the needs of the majority of domestic buyers, and it is through producing for that market that a country acquires a comparative advantage in the product and then comes to export it. A minority of domestic buyers have slightly different demands, demands which can be satisfied by imports from countries where such tastes are those of the majority. Since the kinds of commodities demanded in a country are determined in large measure by the level of *per capita* income, most exchanges of manufactures take place between countries of a similar

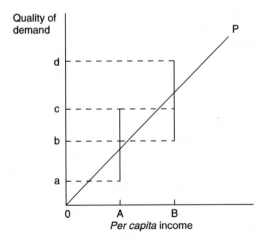

Figure 7.3 Preference similarity

industrial structure, each exporting and importing essentially similar commodities. Through trade the variety of manufactured products available to consumers is extended, and the gain from trade derives from the satisfaction of being able to consume the precise brand or variety of product demanded.

The 'preference similarity' hypothesis is illustrated in Figure 7.3 for trade between two countries, country A and country B, which have different *per capita* incomes and therefore different demand patterns. *Per capita* income is shown on the horizontal axis, and the degree of 'quality' or 'sophistication' of the demand structure on the vertical axis. The line OP is drawn on the assumption that the higher the *per capita* income the higher will be the degree of quality characterising the demand structure as a whole. The average quality of demand, however, will be composed of different qualitative degrees of the various products; therefore, a range of qualitative degrees of demand around the average degree on OP will be formed. Thus, for country A, the various products demanded will lie inside a qualitative range a–c, and for country B the range will lie within b–d. The qualitative range b–c is common to both countries and it is in such products where demand overlaps that trade may take place between the two countries.

Despite the vagueness of such terms as 'quality' and 'sophistication', this model can usefully be extended to explain the duality of some countries' export structures. Japan, for instance, exports skill-intensive products (electronic equipment) to high income European countries and labour-intensive products (textiles) to the rest of Asia. The preference similarity model is also interesting in that it can be used to reconcile the tendency on the supply side for countries to standardise production (in order to achieve scale economies) with, on the demand side, affluent consumers' demands for product variety and differentiation.

International trade offers a number of other potential benefits to participating countries. First, international trade creates larger (international) markets for products, facilitating large-scale production and lowering production costs through economies of scale. Second, free international trade opens up domestic markets to competition from abroad, reducing the monopoly power of large local suppliers. Third, international trade serves to increase consumer choice by making imported products available alongside domestic products. Finally, international trading links serve to heighten the interdependence between trading countries and so may reduce political rivalry between nations and encourage co-operation between them, increasing the stability of international relations and reducing the threat of conflict.

7.4 PROTECTIONISM

Consideration of the benefits of international trade suggests that the optimisation of such benefits is best achieved by conditions of free trade. In practice, however, the benefits of cross-border trade are often unequally divided between countries and this tends to induce countries to take protectionist measures to shelter domestic industries from competition and reduce imports and increase exports, thereby assisting the country's balance of payments. Protection, because it is motivated by and promotes national self-interest, is invariably harmful to the interests of other trading countries, with the danger of retaliatory action on their part and the escalation of trade restrictions, ultimately leading to a reduction in the growth of, or even, as in the 1930s, a fall in, international trade in general (see Box 7.4).

7.4.1 The rationale of protectionism

While there are arguments for protection especially appealing to sectional interests, protection cannot, for the most part, be vindicated as being in the best interests of the national and international community. Take, for example, the often cited contention that tariffs are needed to equalise wage rates between countries. The UK and US textile industries complain that their positions are undermined by foreign suppliers who employ 'cheap labour'. It should be noted, however, that for the economy as a whole high wage rates are the *result*, not the cause, of productive efficiency, and that other industries successfully meet foreign competition in both domestic and foreign markets despite higher wages. This is because they rank higher in the order of comparative advantage. Protection of industries which come low in the order of comparative advantage distorts the industrial ranking and leads to inefficient resource utilisation. Foreign competition would force contraction of the textile industries, and the resources released from it could then be devoted to products in which the country has a comparative advantage.

Protection may be necessary, it is suggested, in the short term to facilitate the orderly restructuring of industries (particularly where manpower resources are highly localised), but there is the danger that such protection may become permanent in the face of vested interests. Additionally, longer-term protection is often sought as a means of protecting the traditional way of life of a work group, for example, farmers on marginal agricultural land. However, such protection impedes the necessary redeployment of labour from uncompetitive industries and their retraining and redeployment to more competitive industries.

Other grounds for protection, while superficially appealing, can usually be achieved more effectively by alternative means. Thus selective tariffs and quotas may assist in restoring balance of payments equilibrium, but they

Box 7.4 Protectionism and the collapse of world trade

Countries are often tempted to raise tariffs, etc., to protect domestic industries in times of recession. Protectionist measures which lead to a 'trade war' as countries engage in widespread and escalating beggar-my-neighbour tactics are likely to prove self-defeating and, in the extreme, can result in a fall in total world output and trade volumes. The 'Great Depression' of the late 1920s and early 1930s, for example, witnessed a slump in world output of some 15 per cent and a collapse of world trade, the value of world trade falling from $3 billion a month in 1929 to around $0.5 billion a month in 1933, as the chart shows.

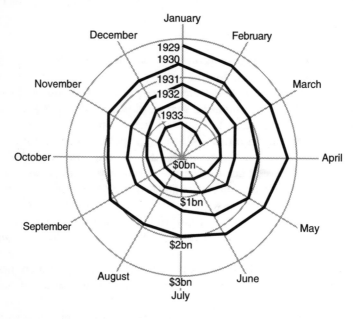

World trade, 1929–33: total imports of seventy-five countries (monthly values, US$ billions at constant prices)

Source: World Bank, *World Development Report*, 1984, cited in *Financial Times*, 9 November 1992.

distort the ordering of industries by comparative advantage. By contrast, aggregate fiscal and monetary policies and exchange-rate adjustments affect all foreign transactions.

There are, however, some seemingly respectable arguments for protection. From the viewpoint of the welfare of the world as a whole the most popular claim made for tariffs, etc., is the so-called infant industry argument. Protection can be an effective means of stimulating the development of an industry that is well suited to a country (in terms of potential comparative advantage) but which finds it impossible to get started unless it is protected from imports. Over time, suitably protected, such an industry is able to acquire internal economies of scale (i.e. lower costs through exploiting a larger domestic market) and take advantage of various external economies (a well trained labour force or the 'learning-by-doing' effect). Eventually the new industry is able to become as efficient as, or more efficient than, its older competitors. The tariff can then be removed, leaving behind a viable and competitive industry.

Such temporary protection of industries does not conflict with the goal of free-traders: maximum specialisation on the basis of comparative advantage. It is only through the temporary equalisation of competitive conditions that the industry is able to reach the stage of development which allows it to realise its full potential. There are problems, however. Industries are frequently selected for protection not on the basis of a favourable comparative advantage but for nationalistic reasons (e.g. diversification of the economy); 'infant industry' becomes a slogan to justify promiscuous protection without regard to merit. The protection afforded may be excessive and continued for longer than is strictly necessary. Furthermore, attempts to encourage industries which produce import substitutes may lead to the encouragement of industries which are not necessarily well suited to the country and have no underlying comparative advantage.

Under GATT rules tariffs can be used to counteract the 'dumping' of products in the local market by foreign suppliers. Dumping occurs when a product is exported at a price below that charged for the same product in the supplier's own domestic market. As such dumping is considered to constitute 'unfair' trade. However, in industries with high fixed costs and low variable unit costs it may be difficult to discern whether a firm is 'dumping' or merely pricing at near to variable unit cost in order to generate sales to utilise surplus production capacity and make a contribution to fixed overhead costs.

A country may also impose tariffs on imports as a means of retaliating against trade barriers erected by other countries against its exports to them. Retaliation may succeed in forcing other countries to drop their trade barriers. However, it carries the danger that retaliation may simply provoke further protectionist measures among trade partners and escalate a 'beggar my neighbour' raising of trade barriers.

A further argument presented for protectionism is the need to protect 'strategic' industries, notably defence and defence-related industries, and possibly agriculture (to ensure self-sufficiency in food). Whilst the logic of this argument is compelling there is the danger that more and more industries may be added to the protected list as their managers seek to stress their strategic importance to gain protection.

Other arguments presented for protectionism are more valid. One is the need to protect established brand names by excluding imported counter-feight products which might undermine their quality image. Another is the need to enhance the environment by protecting domestic industries that are required to meet stringent anti-pollution requirements against compe-tition from imports which are produced more cheaply because they use 'dirtier', more damaging production processes.

7.4.2 Forms of protection

Operationally, protection comes in a number of guises. The most trans-parent forms are the imposition of tariffs on imports, the use of controls to limit imports (quotas), and export restraint agreements. Less obvious, or indirect, forms of protection include government subsidies to domestic industries, government procurement policies favouring domestic suppliers, local content rules and complex import documentation requirements and procedures.

7.4.2.1 Tariffs

A tariff is a duty (tax) that is levied on imports. There are two main types of tariff: an *ad valorem* duty, which is levied as a fixed percentage of the value of the product, and a *specific* duty which is levied as a fixed sum of money per unit of the product. The economic effects of a tariff are illustrated in Figure 7.4. DD and SS are the domestic demand and supply curves of a particular product, say textiles. OP_w is the world supply

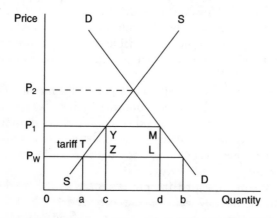

Figure 7.4 Effect of a tariff

Table 7.15 Trade-weighted average tariff rates in developed economies, 1992 (%)

Country	Tariff
Australia	14.0
Austria	10.4
Canada	6.6
EU	4.8
Japan	4.0
Sweden	3.0
USA	3.0
Switzerland	2.8

Source: World Bank, 1993.

price, and this price will prevail domestically in the absence of trade restrictions. At price OPw domestic consumption is Ob, domestic production is Oa and imports, being the difference between the two, are equal to ab.

The imposition of a specific tariff, T, will cause the domestic price of imports to rise by the full amount of the duty, to price OP_1. At price OP_1 domestic consumption falls from Ob to Od, domestic production increases from Oa to Oc and imports are reduced from ab to cd. The area YZLM (import volume cd times tariff per unit P_wP_1) represents government revenue from the tariff. A tariff which raises the domestic price to OP_2 would remove all imports.

Table 7.15 gives details of the *general* level of duties applied by a number of countries. *Selective* tariffs are often imposed on products found to have been dumped. For example, the USA imposed a countervailing duty of 109 per cent on imports of British Steel's steel plates following a ruling by the US International Trade Commission that the product had been dumped in the US market.

How effective the tariff is as a means of protecting the domestic industry will depend upon the price elasticity of demand for the imported product. If import demand is highly price-inelastic, there will be only a small reduction in the volume of imports. In that case a more effective means of protection is a quota.

7.4.2.2 Quotas

A quota is an administrative device which places a physical limit on the volume of imports allowed into the country. This may include a degree of selectivity both in terms of source countries and in the selection of particular supplying firms. By restricting supplies a quota, like a tariff, serves to raise the domestic price of the product affected.

In July 1993 the EU introduced a revised quota of 2 million tonnes a year on bananas imported from Latin America, the most cost-efficient producing region. Latin American imports are subject to a duty of £77.60 per tonne while (under the EU's Lomé Convention) banana imports from Caribbean and African suppliers have tariff-free access for the remainder of the EU's needs, around 1.5 million tonnes annually.

7.4.2.3 Subsidies

Subsidies can be used to lower the supply costs of domestic producers, thus making them fully price competitive against imports. This is illustrated in Figure 7.5. In the figure DD and SS are the domestic demand and supply curves of a particular product. OP_w is the world supply price and this price will prevail domestically in the absence of trade restrictions. At price OP_w domestic consumption is Ob, domestic production Oa and imports, being the difference between the two, are equal to ab. If a production subsidy is given to domestic producers which lowers their costs by XY per unit (making it profitable also for previously uneconomic producers to supply the product) it operates to shift the domestic supply curve of the product from SS to S_1S_1. As a result all domestic demand is met from domestic sources, thus eliminating imports.

However, countries may go beyond this by providing even bigger subsidies to domestic firms which lower their supply costs to levels below the current world price, thus giving them an 'unfair' competitive advantage in world export markets. In 1992 the USA imposed a 14.5 per cent tariff on Canadian softwood lumber imports after ruling that Canadian sawmills were subsidised by low tree-cutting fees in provincial forests which enabled

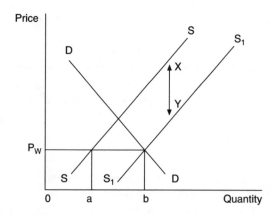

Figure 7.5 Subsidy

them to undercut the price of US lumber. Also in 1992 the USA raised tariffs on EU white wines, rapeseed oil and wheat gluten as a retaliation against EU farm subsidies, particularly in respect of oilseeds. (See Section 8.1.)

7.4.2.4 Export restraint agreements

An export restraint agreement is a voluntary arrangement between an exporting country and an importing country that limits the volume of trade in a specified product. Specifically exports/imports between the two countries are limited to an agreed number of units, or percentage share of the market for that product in the importing country. Japan, for example, has operated a voluntary export restraint agreement in motor cars with the EU for some years. A 1.09 million vehicle ceiling for 1993 had been originally agreed, but as a result of the recession in the EU car market a new ceiling of 980,000 was set in September 1993 (representing around 9 per cent of the EU car market). Sales from Japanese-owned plants in Europe are not covered by the deal. Such plants produced some 320,000 cars in 1992.

7.4.2.5 Local content rule

Stipulations on the minimum proportion of locally sourced components used in a finished product may be laid down so as to limit imported components. Such stipulations are designed primarily to discourage so-called 'screwdriver' plants which assemble final products from imported components, often in order to circumvent duties applied on the final product itself. Under the North American Free Trade Agreement between the USA and Canada cross-border car exports are tariff-free *provided* that vehicles contain a minimum of 50 per cent North American content. In 1992 the USA imposed a 2.5 per cent import duty on Honda Civic cars produced in Canada and exported to the USA, ruling that they contained less than 50 per cent local content.

7.4.2.6 Public procurement

Governments may restrict trading opportunities for foreign suppliers by favouring domestic producers and contractors when awarding public works and equipment contracts. In 1993 the EU offered to waive Article 29 of the Utilities Directive, which offers a 3 per cent price preference to European companies tendering for government supply contracts on condition that the USA was prepared to take reciprocal steps to open the US market in transport, power generation and telecommunication equipment to European countries.

7.5 CONCLUSION

International trade is going to play an increasingly important role in the economic well-being of countries. For the majority of countries international trade has led to both consumption gains (lower prices, access to new products, etc.) and production gains (improved resource allocation). However, the fact that the global gains from trade have not been equitably distributed has created tensions in trading relations and in some cases has resulted in a resurgence of protectionism.

7.6 IMPLICATIONS FOR BUSINESS

Exporting, together with strategic alliances and foreign investment, can be used by a firm to expand its international operations (see Chapter 9). The ability to trade cross-border as well as within a firm's own domestic market provides additional opportunities for sales and profit growth. Where demand for a firm's products in its domestic market is small, or where domestic demand has reached maturity/decline, exporting may represent a crucial means of ensuring viability and sustaining further expansion. For many firms export sales constitute an important means of securing low supply costs through exploiting economies of large-scale centralised production. In many cases exports account for the greater proportion of the firm's turnover: in 1993, for example, export sales accounted for 65 per cent of the turnover of the UK kitchen appliance producer Kenwood; 85 per cent of the turnover of UK aerospace group Rolls-Royce; and 72 per cent of the turnover of the UK speciality chemical firm Holliday.

Different market sizes and growth rates in overseas countries require the firm to be attentive to its geographical 'spread'. Countries with large, affluent populations and which are experiencing a rapid growth in gross national product per head generally provide good export opportunities. The attractiveness of such markets will depend upon how liberal the authorities are in encouraging trading links with other countries (see Chapter 8) and the competitive strength of the exporting firm *vis-à-vis* domestic and other foreign suppliers. However, firms should also be aware of the niche marketing opportunities for their particular products which may be available in smaller, less prosperous countries. Many developing countries can offer attractive export prospects because of the backwardness of their domestic suppliers or because of their different national tastes and demand patterns. Thus, for example, in 1994 Kia, the South Korean car producer, targeted the USA as a promising export market, launching its Sephia model to establish an initial export platform into the USA, with further models to follow. The UK group BAT Industries has diversified its product portfolio in mature markets such as the UK and the USA but has continued to expand and reorientate its core tobacco interests by meeting the growth in demand for cigarettes in the developing countries of Asia and Eastern Europe.

In seeking export opportunities firms can gain considerable market intelligence by examining international trade statistics relating to their particular industries and products. In addition, government agencies such as the export branches of the UK's Department of Trade and Industry can provide detailed information and advice on overseas technical standards, national safety laws, export documentation requirements, tariffs, etc., and, in some cases, financial assistance (for example, export credit guarantees).

QUESTIONS

1 Outline and comment on the main trends in the regional and product composition of world merchandise trade.
2 Explain what is meant by the term 'comparative advantage' and discuss its significance for the structure of international trade flows.
3 Outline and comment on the 'product life cycle' and 'preference similarity' explanations of international trade flows.
4 Examine the consumption and production gains which can arise when countries engage in international trade. Are there any disadvantages in international trade?
5 Explain what is meant by 'protectionism' and discuss the reasons why governments may choose to apply protectionist measures.
6 Discuss the main forms which 'protectionism' can take.

Chapter 8

International trade

2 Multilateral and regional trade policies

As the previous chapter has demonstrated, in principle, most countries stand to gain from the establishment of 'free trade', that is, the complete removal of all restrictions on cross-frontier trade such as tariffs, quotas and foreign exchange controls. Recognition of the benefits of free trade has been given operational validity at the policy level by the establishment of multilateral trade organisations such as the General Agreement on Tariffs and Trade (GATT) and the formation of various regional free-trade alliances such as the European Union (EU) and the North American Free Trade Agreement (NAFTA). This chapter examines the policy issues behind the growing influence of the multilateral and regional free-trade movements and considers their impact on trade flows.

To begin with, it will be useful to demonstrate the potential welfare-creating effects of free trade as illustrated in Figure 8.1, which, to simplify matters, is confined to a tariff cut by one country (A) and one product.

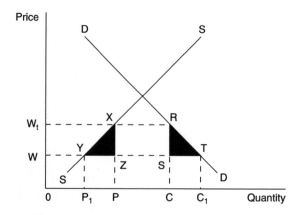

Figure 8.1 Trade and the pro-welfare economic effects of the removal of a tariff

DD and SS are the domestic demand and supply curves for the product in country A. OW is the world supply price of the product. Initially country A imposes a tariff on imports of the product, raising its price in the home market to OW_t. At price OW_t domestic production is shown by OP, domestic consumption by OC, and imports by PC.

The removal of the tariff reduces the price of the product in the home market to OW. At price OW, imports increase to P_1C_1, domestic production falls to OP_1, and domestic consumption increases to OC_1. The home market obtains an increase in economic welfare from this expansion of trade, indicated by the two triangles XYZ and RST. XYZ is the 'production gain' resulting from reallocation of factor inputs to more efficient domestic industries; RST is the 'consumption gain' resulting from lower prices to consumers.

The period since World War II has witnessed a gradual process of trade liberalisation, multilaterally through the establishment of international organisations such as the General Agreement on Tariffs and Trade and the United Nations Conference on Trade and Development, and regionally through the formation of several customs unions and free-trade areas such as the European Union (formerly the European Community) and the European Free Trade Association.

8.1 MULTILATERAL TRADE POLICY

8.1.1 The General Agreement on Tariffs and Trade

The General Agreement on Tariffs and Trade (GATT) was established in 1947 alongside the International Monetary Fund (IMF) and the World Bank to provide an international framework for promoting free trade as a means of increasing worldwide economic welfare. All the developed countries and a very large number of developing countries are contracting partners in GATT, whose total membership now exceeds over 120. GATT members meet periodically to negotiate multilateral trade concessions under the supervision of the GATT secretariat, whose headquarters are located in Geneva, Switzerland. GATT not only co-ordinates the implementation of agreed tariff reductions but also operates a number of 'arbitration' panels to settle cases of dispute. The main concern in this latter respect is to ensure that trade is conducted in a 'fair' way: GATT rules, for example, allow members to retaliate against imports which have been 'dumped' (that is, products which are sold in a foreign market at prices below their domestic prices) by subjecting them to countervailing duties to raise their prices in the local market.

GATT has two key operational principles. The first principle is that of *reciprocity*, which requires that where a member has agreed to lower its tariffs against another member's exports that other member will reciprocate by agreeing to introduce matching tariff reductions. The second principle, *non-discrimination*, prohibits members from granting preferential treatment to another country. This means that members must extend to every other member the most favourable terms negotiated with any one trading partner – the so-called 'most favoured nation' principle. In practice, this principle has been waived in the case of regional free-trade alliances with the proviso that, for example, in the case of a customs union the union's 'common external tariffs' will be no higher post-union than applied on an individual basis pre-union.

GATT has supervised eight major multilateral rounds of tariff negotiation (see Box 8.1) which, as Figure 8.2 shows, have resulted in a substantial reduction in average tariff levels in the developed countries. In the main, tariff cuts have applied only to manufactured goods. The 'Uruguay round' (1986–93) was likewise concerned with manufactures but emphasis was also placed on obtaining major tariff reductions in agricultural produce. The 'Uruguay round' was due to be completed in 1990 but encountered a number of obstacles. One main sticking point was the subsidisation of agricultural produce and limitations on market access, where the EU and USA in particular found themselves at loggerheads. This issue reached flashpoint in 1992 when the USA imposed additional tariffs on EU exports of white wine, rapeseed oil and wheat gluten in retaliation for the EU's refusal

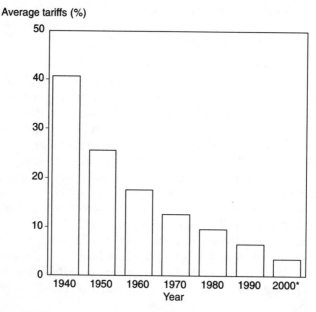

Figure 8.2 GATT rounds and the decline in industrial countries' tariffs

* Estimate
Source: GATT

Box 8.1 GATT rounds, 1947–93

Round	Main provisions
1947 Geneva (twenty-three participants)	45,000 tariff cuts agreed covering $10 billion of trade in manufactures
1949 Annecy, France (thirteen participants)	5,000 tariff cuts on manufactures
1950–1 Torquay, England (thirty-eight participants)	8,700 tariff cuts on manufactures, equivalent to a 25 per cent cut in 1948 tariff levels
1956 Geneva (twenty-six participants)	2,500 tariff cuts covering £2.5 billion of trade in manufactures
1960–2 Dillon round (twenty-six participants)	4,400 tariff cuts covering $5 billion of trade in manufactures
1964–7 Kennedy round (sixty-two participants)	Tariff cuts averaging 35 per cent, covering $40 billion of trade in manufactures
1973–9 Tokyo round (ninety-nine participants)	Tariff cuts covering $30 billion of trade in manufactures
1986–93 Uruguay Round (117 participants)	Tariffs on manufactures by the industrial economies to be lowered to an average of 3.9 per cent from 6.3 per cent, first concerted attempt to introduce major cuts in tariffs and subsidies on agricultural produce (see Table 8.1) and liberalise trade in commercial services

to remove oilseed subsidies. The US complained to GATT that the heavy subsidisation of oilseeds by the EU discriminated unfairly against cheaper US exports, costing its exporters around £650 million in 'lost' sales. Two separate GATT panels in 1988 and 1991 had adjudged that the EU's oilseed subsidies were 'illegal' and should be discontinued. An agreement was drawn up in late 1992 between the EU and the USA (the 'Blair House' pact) to reduce subsidies for oilseeds and other farm products so as not to prejudice the wider Uruguay round talks. In addition to agreeing to substantial cuts in industrial and agricultural tariffs and subsidies (see below), the Uruguay participants also agreed to various initiatives to liberalise trade in commercial services and gave a firmer commitment to enforce intellectual property rights and to open up government procurement contracts to greater international competition. Furthermore, it was decided to replace GATT itself by a new body – the World Trade Organisation (WTO). While GATT operated largely on an 'informal' basis the WTO (established in 1995) is intended to be a more powerful international trade overlord.

According to a study published in 1993 the Uruguay round programme would add around $213 billion (£138 billion) a year to world income by the year 2002 if fully implemented. The study estimates the 'global price' of distortions due to protectionism at around $477 billion (see Table 8.1). The Uruguay round proposal to cut average tariffs and subsidies for agriculture would yield a gain of $190 billion while an average 30 per cent cut in the remaining tariffs on industrial products would result in a gain of $23 billion.

In the present recessionary economic climate it is unlikely that all the Uruguay round proposals will be duly implemented in full. For example, the USA and the EU have failed to make substantial progress on cutting agricultural and steel subsidies or on the opening up of their public procurement business to international competition, while the USA and Japan remain in dispute over the further opening up of the Japanese market to US goods and services. Moreover, developing countries remain pessimistic about the

Table 8.1 Estimated average annual gains from the Uruguay round by the Year 2002

Average annual gain	$ billion
Global price of distortions due to protectionism	477
Gains of partial liberalisation as a result of Uruguay round:	
1 Remove 30 per cent of tariffs and subsidies for agriculture:	
(a) Gains for industrial countries	120
(b) Gains for developing countries and former planned economies	70
Total gains through farm trade reform	190
2 Cut tariffs on manufactured goods by 30 per cent:	
(a) Gains for industrial countries	14.7
(b) Gains for developing countries and former planned economies	8.3
Total gains through industry trade reform	23
Total gains from Uruguay round liberalisation	213
Cost of remaining distortions	264

Source: Trade Liberalisation: What's at stake?, World Bank, 1993.

removal of export subsidies for agricultural produce, by the EU in particular, which have served to depress world prices of, for example, cereals.

GATT initiatives, together with the operations of the International Monetary Fund in removing exchange controls on currencies, and sustained economic growth in the developed countries, combined to bring about a record expansion of world trade down to the early 1970s. Since the onset of recessionary conditions in 1973, however, much of the work of GATT has been undermined by the resurgence of protectionism. The 'new protectionism', as it is commonly referred to, is based not on tariffs but, as noted in Chapter 7, on devices which are much less visible and hence more difficult to detect and control, for example local content requirements, subsidisation of domestic industries, etc.

8.1.2 The United Nations Conference on Trade and Development (UNCTAD)

While the original GATT format served to advance the interests of developed countries, developing countries felt that it did little to help their cause. First, GATT tariff cuts in the 1950s and 1960s were applied almost exclusively to manufactured goods, which most developing countries did not produce to any great extent. Second, the reciprocity and non-discrimination principles were considered unfavourable to developing countries. In their case it was felt that some form of *preferential* treatment (for example, tariff-free market access for developing countries' exports) was desirable not only to assist their traditional industries, but also to help newly established manufacturing industries. The dissatisfaction of the developing countries led to the creation of the United Nations Conference on Trade and Development in 1964.

The major role of UNCTAD has been to 'lobby' on behalf of developing countries for a more favourable trading environment. As a result GATT adopted a 'special and differential treatment' provision which waived the obligation on developing countries to reciprocate liberalisation measures where they would be inconsistent with their development and trade needs. Equally important, pressure from UNCTAD led to the adoption by GATT of a 'generalised system of preferences' (GSP) which gave developing countries' exports tariff-free or tariff-reduced access to the markets of developed countries. However, this promising development has been substantially undermined by the use of non-tariff measures (quotas, in particular) to exclude developing countries' exports, particularly competing agricultural products and low-technology manufactures. The Multi-fibre Agreement, for example, uses a quota system to restrict developing countries' textile exports to developed country markets.

In addition to its work in obtaining tariff concessions, UNCTAD has promoted the extension of International Commodity Agreements aimed at increasing and stabilising the export prices of primary products as a means of raising developing countries' foreign exchange earnings and producers' incomes (see Box 10.5), and it has attempted to secure a greater volume of financial assistance and technology transfer from the developed countries.

8.2 REGIONAL TRADE INTEGRATION

The regional approach to trade liberalisation is exemplified by free-trade areas, customs unions, common markets and economic unions.

8.2.1 Regional trade integration: an overview

1 A *free trade area* is an alliance of countries where member countries eliminate trade barriers between themselves but each continues to operate its own particular barriers against non-members.
2 A *customs union* is an alliance of countries whose members eliminate trade barriers between themselves and establish uniform barriers against non-members, in particular a 'common external tariff'.
3 A *common market* is a form of customs union which also provides for the unrestricted movement of labour and capital across national boundaries.
4 An *economic union* is a form of common market which also provides for the harmonisation of national business practices and regulations, and the harmonisation and integration of monetary systems (including the establishment of a common currency), fiscal and other macro-economic policies.

The European Free Trade Association (EFTA) and the North American Free Trade Agreement (NAFTA) are examples of free-trade areas, while the European Union (EU) now embraces facets of all the other three forms of trade integration (see below).

Unlike the international approach, the regional approach may or may not lead to an improvement in world economic welfare and efficiency, for it contains an important element of discrimination against non-member countries. Such integration combines features of free trade and protection. On the one hand, the *trade-creating* effects of the removal of trade barriers between member countries will serve to increase welfare and efficiency *within* the bloc. On the other hand, the expansion of trade within the bloc may be at the expense of non-member countries, this *trade-diversionary* effect serving to lower other countries' welfare. By way of illustration of these effects, consider a three-country world in which countries A and B form a customs union to the exclusion of C. In other words, A and B abolish all trade restrictions among themselves, while their imports from C become subject to the common external tariff. The action has two effects.

With respect to products in which A and B are competitive, the elimination of tariffs between them causes the replacement of some high-cost production by imports from the partner country. This effect, known as 'trade creation', is favourable to welfare, since it rationally reorganises production within the union. An additional favourable outcome takes place on the consumption side, as consumers are able to shift to more desirable consumption mixes of the goods produced and traded within the union.

Second, for products in which country C is competitive with one of the integrating countries, A or B begins to import from the other what it earlier imported from C. If C is the most efficient producer, it will be the major supplier so long as its product receives the same tariff treatment as those of its competitors. But the tariff discrimination induces diversion of trade away from C and towards a member country. This effect, known as 'trade diversion', is unfavourable, because it reorganises world production less efficiently. Production shifts from the most efficient locations in C to less efficient ones inside the union. This shift is compounded on the demand side by a move to less desirable consumption patterns.

The two effects can be illustrated with the help of diagrams, pertaining to one type of goods imported into country A. For simplicity, we assume that A is a smallish country, facing infinitely elastic (horizontal) supply curves from countries B and C.

First let us consider the case of trade creation. In Figure 8.3, DD and SS are the demand and supply curves for an industry in country A. PP is the supply curve of country B, and FF is the supply curve of country C. Let us assume that prior to the union the home country has a uniform tariff on imports from both B and C. Owing to the tariff, the price of these imports in the home country will be equal to OP^1 and OF^1 respectively.

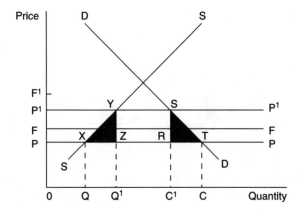

Figure 8.3 Trade creation

Note that country B is competitive; C is not. The price in the home market will thus settle at OP^1. Domestic demand is shown by OC^1, domestic production by OQ^1, and imports from B by Q^1C^1. Suppose now that A and B form a customs union. The home country must eliminate its tariffs on imports from its partner, B, while retaining its tariffs on imports from the third country. The price of the product in country A will now fall to OP, consumption will expand to OC, domestic production falls to OQ, while imports from the partner increase to QC. The home country will have obtained an increase in economic welfare, shown by the two triangles XYZ (the production gain) and RST (the consumption gain). These two types of gain constitute the trade creation effect of the union. Note too that the increase in export demand for B's product will serve to raise real incomes in country B through domestic multiplier effects (see Chapter 1).

Suppose now, however, that import prices are lower from country C (supply curve FF) than from the partner country B (supply curve PP). Initially, assuming the home country has a uniform tariff on imports from both B and C, all imports will come from country C, the most efficient supplier. The domestic price will settle at OF^1; domestic production is OQ^1, consumption is OC^1 and the country imports Q^1C^1 from country C. Post-union, as Figure 8.4 shows, with the elimination of the tariff on imports from the partner country, the price of B's imports in country A falls from OP^1 to OP. Since OP is less than OF^1 consumers will now divert their purchases from country C to the partner country. As the price in the home country falls to OP, domestic production falls to OQ, consumption rises to OC and imports from the partner become QC. The welfare-increasing trade-creation effect is shown, as before, by the triangles XYZ

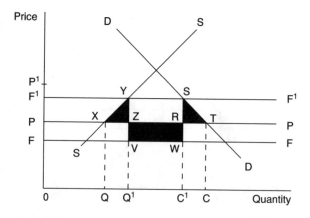

Figure 8.4 Trade creation and trade diversion

(the production gain) and RST (the consumption gain). But there is now a welfare-decreasing trade-diversion effect to consider. This is shown by VZRW. The distance VW (or ZR) is the quantity of imports obtained from the third country prior to integration, and VZ (or RW) is the extra real cost of obtaining those imports from the partner instead of from country C. VZRW therefore shows the cost of diverting purchases from a country with low costs of production to a country with high costs.

The relative magnitude of these two effects determines whether the customs union is on balance favourable to worldwide allocative efficiency. A number of factors have a bearing on the issue: the gain from trade creation will be greater, the greater the differences in real supply costs between the integrating countries; in general, the higher the pre-union tariff rates the better the chances of more trade creation as those rates are removed; the lower the common external tariff the less will be the scope for trade diversion.

In addition to trade gains, free-trade blocs and customs unions, but more especially common markets and economic unions, can be expected to promote other, longer-term, dynamic changes conducive to economic efficiency, including:

1 *Competition.* The removal of tariff and other impediments to cross-frontier trade can be expected to widen the area of effective competition; high cost producers and inefficient industries are eliminated. Efficient and progressive suppliers are able to exploit new market opportunities.
2 *Consumer choice.* Consumers are able to choose from a wider range of products offered by domestic and foreign suppliers.
3 *Economies of scale.* A larger 'home' market enables firms to take advantage of economies of large-scale production and distribution, thereby lowering supply costs and enhancing comparative advantage.
4 *Technological advance.* Wider market opportunities and dynamic competition can be expected to encourage firms to innovate new techniques and products.
5 *Investment and economic growth.* Finally, the 'virtuous circle' of rising *per capita* incomes, growing trade, increased production efficiency and investment may be expected to combine to produce higher growth rates and real standards of living.

8.2.2 Regional trade integration: the case of Europe

A number of regional trade alliances have been established, including the European Union (see below) and the European Free Trade Association (see below), the MERCOSUR customs union, the North American Free Trade Agreement, the Caribbean Union and the ASEAN Free Trade Area (see Box 8.2).

Box 8.2 Some regional alliances

Mercosur

Mercosur was established in 1995 with the objective of creating a free trade area between Argentina, Brazil, Paraguay and Uruguay. Mercosur provides for the tariff-free movement of goods between member countries and operates a common external tariff against imports from non-member countries.

North American Free Trade Agreement (NAFTA)

NAFTA was established in 1989 to create a free-trade area between Canada and the USA. NAFTA aims to remove trade barriers from most manufactured goods, raw materials and agricultural produce over a ten-year period, as well as restrictions on cross-border investment, banking and other financial services. Mexico joined NAFTA in 1994.

Caribbean Union (CARICOM)

CARICOM was established in 1973 as a mechanism for fostering greater trade integration among its thirteen members: Bahamas, Barbados, Belize, Guyana, Jamaica, Trinidad/Tobago and the islands of the Organisation of East Caribbean States (OECS) – Antigua/ Barbuda, Dominica, Grenada, Montserrat, St Kitts–Nevis, St Lucia and St Vincent/Grenadines. CARICOM's main trade orientation is with the EU (through the Lomé Convention).

ASEAN Free Trade Area (AFTA)

AFTA was established in 1992 by the six member countries of the Association of South East Asian Nations (ASEAN): Singapore, Malaysia, Thailand, Indonesia, the Philippines and Brunei. The aim is to reduce mutual tariffs (currently averaging over 20 per cent) on all goods, except agricultural produce, to between 0 per cent and 5 per cent within fifteen years.

8.2.2.1 The European Union and the European Free Trade Association: background

The roots of the European Union (EU) and the European Free Trade Association (EFTA) date back to the late 1940s and 1950s, reflecting a political desire to create a European unification movement aimed at eliminating the possibility of warfare between the European countries and a recognition that the economic prosperity of those countries could be advanced more effectively through the establishment of a regional free trade bloc. Political divisions, however, made it difficult to secure an agreement on a comprehensive pan-European alliance, and the result was the formation of two separate trading blocs. Those countries in favour of the 'common market' approach and a commitment to deeper integration of their economies over time duly formed the European Community. A number of other countries, for a variety of reasons such as colonial connections and a political preference for neutrality, chose to establish only a 'free-trade area', the European Free Trade Association.

There were six founding members of the Community, which was established by the Treaty of Rome in 1958: France, West Germany, Italy, the Netherlands, Belgium and Luxembourg. Five of these countries (the exception being the Netherlands) had previously participated in the European Coal and Steel Community, established in 1951 to promote free trade in coal and steel. The first major enlargement of the European Community occurred in 1973 when the UK, Denmark and Ireland joined. Greece was admitted in 1981 and Spain and Portugal in 1986. Austria, Sweden and Finland joined in 1995, increasing the total membership to fifteen countries. The European Community was renamed the European Union in 1993.

The European Free Trade Association was established by the Stockholm Treaty of 1959. There were seven original members of EFTA: Austria, the UK, Denmark, Norway, Portugal, Sweden and Switzerland. Finland joined in 1961, Iceland in 1970 and Liechtenstein in 1991. As noted above, six members of EFTA left to join the EU: the UK, Denmark and Portugal, Austria, Sweden and Finland. Membership of EFTA thus comprises four countries.

Although distinct alliances, the EU and EFTA have maintained close trading relations. In 1972 a number of free-trade agreements were concluded between the two blocs which provided tariff-free access to each other's markets for a wide range of manufactured goods. This has since been carried a stage further with the establishment of the European Economic Association (see below), which extends the provisions of the EU's Single European Act (see below) to the EFTA countries, eliminating the remaining tariffs on manufactured goods and establishing free trade in agricultural produce and services.

The very future of EFTA itself, however, has been put in the melting pot by the defection of Austria, Sweden and Finland to the EU in 1995.

8.2.2.2 Features of the European Union

The strategic and main operational policies of the EU are formulated by member countries' governments, acting through the Council of Ministers and the democratically elected European Parliament. The European Commission is responsible for the day-to-day administration and co-ordination of Union policy, control of the EU's general budget finance and,

Box 8.3 European Union's tariff structure

Products imported from non-EU countries are subjected to the EU's common external tariff, and in some cases to quotas (for example, textiles under the Multi-fibre Agreement) and other non-tariff restrictions (for example, imports of cars from Japan are subject to voluntary restraint agreements limiting market access in France, Italy, the UK, Spain and Portugal). The common external tariff ensures that products imported from non-EU countries are subject to the same level of duty whichever country they enter the EU through.

The tariff rates applied to imported goods vary considerably, generally being higher on agricultural products such as beef and grain which compete with EU-produced items than on manufactured goods, and lower on non-competing raw materials and semi-processed goods than on finished goods. Overall, however, tariff rates are modest. The table lists a number of tariff rates by way of example.

To qualify as authentic EU-produced goods, products must satisfy the EU's 'rules of origin' test, which specifies that the product must be produced wholly in an EU country or that the 'last substantial operation in the processing or manufacture of the product was carried out in that country'. This latter condition is open to interpretation and can cause difficulties in determining precisely what constitutes a 'substantial' operation; for example, some EU countries are not prepared to accept that Japanese cars produced in the UK, partly using imported components, should qualify as EU products.

EU tariff rates currently applied to selected products (%)

Natural rubber	None
Chemical wood pulp	None
Freezers	3.8
Vacuum cleaners	4.0
Machine tools	4.4
Lathes	5.0
Fork lift trucks	5.9
Fertilisers	8.0
Motor cars	10.0
Aluminium bars and rods	10.0
Tableware and kitchenware	13.5
Coats	14.0
Cucumbers	22.0
Peas	24.0
Beer made from malt	24.0

Source: UK Customs and Excise.

together with the various specialist agencies set up to run particular programmes, is involved in the detailed implementation of Union policies. The European Court of Justice acts as the final arbiter in cases of dispute between member countries, and between companies, etc., and the European Commission. The main economic developments within the EU to date include:

1 The formation of a *common market* providing for free trade in goods and services through the removal of tariffs, quotas and other obstacles to cross-frontier trade, and for the free movement of labour and capital across national boundaries. The EU operates a common external tariff against non-member countries (see Box 8.3) but it has been progressively reduced by cuts negotiated through GATT, while tariff-free entry to EU markets is allowed under various trade pacts with, for example, certain developing countries (the Lomé Convention – see Box 8.4) and member countries of the European Free Trade Association. A large number of internal obstacles to trade have arisen out of historical differences between countries in the application of, for example, technical standards, description of goods, documentation procedures, road and rail regulations, etc. These are being removed through 'directives' emanating from the Single European Act 1986 (popularly known as the '1992' initiative).

2 The free-trade philosophy of the EU is underpinned by the fair trade provisions of the EU's *competition policy*, which prohibit price-fixing, market-sharing cartels, etc., between rival suppliers, and the abuse of a dominant market position to reduce or eliminate intra-EU trade. The EU has introduced a merger and take-over regulation to control structural changes likely to have detrimental competitive effects.

3 A *Common Agricultural Policy* (CAP) which provides for the subsidisation and protection of the farm sector. Around 75 per cent of EU farm produce benefits directly from the operation of a price support system which maintains EU farm prices at levels usually well in excess of world market prices. Variable tariff rates on imported farm produce are used to keep out unwanted imports. The CAP is the largest single component of the EU's total budget, accounting for around 65 per cent of all EU spending in 1994. The CAP has been heavily criticised for encouraging wasteful over-production of agricultural produce within Europe while denying market access to non-member countries. As noted earlier, the CAP has been a major sticking point in the Uruguay round of GATT negotiations.

4 The establishment of a mechanism, the *European Monetary System*, for co-ordinating member countries' exchange rates to provide a greater degree of stability in external currency values as a means of promoting cross-frontier trade. Over the longer term the EU's objective is to move

Box 8.4 The Lomé Convention

The Lomé Convention is a comprehensive agreement embracing preferential trading arrangements and developmental aid. It aims to improve the economies of member countries by opening markets to their exports and by providing financial and technical assistance. There are sixty-nine members of the Lomé Convention – forty-six countries in Africa, fifteen in the Caribbean and eight in the Pacific. These African, Caribbean and Pacific (ACP) members, as they are commonly called, are mostly former colonies of the EU countries, mainly France and the UK. The first Lomé Convention was signed in 1975, for a period of five years, and there have been four subsequent agreements, including the current agreement, Lomé IV, signed in 1990.

Lomé's central trade provision is the granting of duty-free access to the EU market for most ACP exports. However, there are two main limitations on this access. First, products which compete with EU products falling within the Common Agricultural Policy (CAP) are not granted unlimited free access. ACP cane sugar, for example, is granted, under the Sugar Protocol, free access up to a specified quota, as the EU CAP is concerned to protect the local sugar-beet industry. Any sugar sold to the EU in excess of the quota is subject to variable import duties.

The second limitation is that ACP exports are subject to rules of origin criteria. Specifically, ACP products are only allowed duty-free access to the EU provided that one-third of their value originated within the ACP countries. This has caused problems for many ACP countries, since few of them have a developed industrial base and their export industries tend to be assembly operations using imported inputs.

The removal of the EU sugar preferences for ACP members, should there be a complete liberalisation of the worldwide sugar market, as mooted at the GATT Uruguay round, has been estimated by UNCTAD to be of the order of US$230 million. The loss of other preferences, particularly with the USA, pushes this figure much higher; equivalent, for example, to a loss of foreign exchange revenue of the order of 20 per cent for Guyana and 6 per cent for Barbados.

towards greater integration of the economies of member countries by harmonising economic policies and the centralisation of fiscal and monetary control, involving, for example, the replacement of individual national currencies by a single European currency (see Chapter 10).

8.2.2.3 The Single European Market

The Single European Act 1986 is concerned specifically with sweeping away a large number of less visible obstacles to trade arising from historical differences in the policies and practices of individual EU states. The general intention is to end the fragmentation of the EU into 'national' markets and to create a 'level playing field' so that businesses can produce and sell their products throughout the EU bloc of some 350 million people without discrimination.

The Single European Act committed the twelve EU states to remove various impediments to the movement of goods, services, capital and people through the progressive introduction of various practices and regulations aimed at creating a single unified market by 31 December 1992. In practice the time scale for implementing some of the more complex measures has extended beyond that date. Hitherto, trade has been obstructed and costs and prices have been increased in many ways: by different national bureaucratic requirements and technical standards, different national taxation structures, and restrictive government procurement practices and subsidies to local firms.

Under the Act a large number of 'directives' – designed to harmonise members' practices on an EU-wide basis – have been agreed. They include:

1 *Removal of frontier controls on goods.* Goods are now free to move from one EU state to another without any systematic customs intervention. This eliminates the need for elaborate documentation of goods in transit. Certain frontier checks have been retained on a discretionary basis to combat the smuggling of illicit goods such as drugs, weapons and pornography.

2 *Movement of people.* Cross-border visits by tourists have been freed from passport checks and customs limit on goods purchased for personal use. However, to safeguard against illegal entry by non-EU residents and terrorists, some formalities have been retained (e.g. screening luggage at airports). Nationals of EU states have the right to go to another member state to take up employment and enjoy the same rights as domestic workers. However, various practical barriers remain to full labour mobility, for example, qualifications obtained in one member state may not be acceptable in another, and it may not be possible to transfer pension entitlements. Harmonisation in these areas can be resolved only on a longer-term basis.

3 *Value-added tax (VAT)*. The minimum standard of VAT applicable in all member states has been set at 15 per cent. The UK, however, has been allowed for the time being to continue with its zero-rating of certain goods such as children's clothing and food. For VAT registered businesses, the 'destination system' applies to goods sold in another member state – exported goods are zero-rated, with the tax being paid in the country where the product is actually purchased.

4 *Transport services*. Liberalised transport services have a central place in the single market because the transport industry (road, rail, sea and air) plays a crucial role in moving goods between member states. In the case of road haulage, for example, all permits and quotas that had previously restricted the movement of goods by road have been abolished.

5 *Public purchasing*. The bias favouring domestic firms in the award of contracts for government projects and supplies has been attacked by the implementation of various regulations taken to promote open tendering, thereby facilitating fair competition for contracts between suppliers irrespective of their national identity.

6 *Technical standards*. National technical barriers to trade have been progressively replaced by common EU standards so that products can be freely marketed throughout the EU unimpeded by different national rules, standards or testing and certification practices.

7 *Food law harmonisation*. Common standards have been introduced with regard to the use of food additives and flavourings, food labelling and food packaging materials, to promote product safety and hygiene and to enable food products to be sold across the market without discrimination.

8 *Capital movements*. The UK abolished all foreign exchange controls on capital movements in 1979, but many other EU members continued to operate restrictions until the late 1980s. A directive removing exchange controls on capital movements within the EU was adopted in 1988.

9 *Financial services*. A bank or insurance company which has obtained a licence to operate in one member state is now able to supply its services and products across the market without restriction, either directly or by setting up a branch network in other member states.

8.2.2.4 The European Economic Area

The European Economic Area (EEA) is a free-trade alliance between the fifteen-member countries of the EU and three of the four member countries of EFTA (excluding Switzerland).

The formation of the EEA and the likelihood, as noted above, of an eventual merger of the two blocs comes at a time of growing interdependence in trade between the EU and EFTA. As Table 8.2 indicates, however, individual EFTA countries export far more to the EU than they do to

Table 8.2 EU and EFTA trade, 1993

Country	% of total exports	
	EU	EFTA
EU members		
Belgium and Luxembourg	73	6
Denmark	54	24
France	64	7
Germany	54	16
Greece	61	6
Ireland	72	6
Italy	59	9
Netherlands	67	6
Portugal	73	10
Spain	62	4
UK	53	8
EFTA members*		
Austria	65	10
Finland	47	20
Iceland	68	9
Norway	65	16
Sweden	54	19
Switzerland and Liechtenstein	58	7

Source: European Commission.
*Note: Austria, Finland and Sweden joined the EU in 1995.

other EFTA members, a development fostered by various bilateral trade preference agreements giving them tariff-free access to EU markets for a wide range of goods. By contrast, the EFTA market accounts for only a small proportion of the total exports of most EU countries.

The EEA's aim is to extend the EU's 'single market freedoms' in the movement of goods, services, capital and labour to include EFTA, creating a unified market of nearly 375 million people. EFTA countries will adopt the various harmonisation measures which have been, or are being, implemented by EU countries under the Single European Act. The EEA provides for the abolition of those remaining tariffs and quotas on goods and processed agricultural produce excluded from the 1972/3 free trade agreements, and liberalises the movement of services. Thus any business established in the EEA will be free to provide services such as banking and transport throughout the EEA under the same conditions that apply within the single market. The agreement removes restrictions on capital movements and gives all EU and EFTA citizens the right to work throughout the EEA on the same terms as local workers without discrimination. The agreement also involves the removal of an extensive range of non-tariff obstacles to trade between the two blocs, involving the adoption of common technical standards and regulations and an open public authorities' purchasing policy.

It must be emphasised that the EEA is not a fully fledged customs union. Both the EU and the individual members of EFTA will continue to set their own tariffs on goods coming from non-members; border controls between the EU and EFTA countries, and between the EFTA countries themselves, will remain. Moreover, there is no provision under the EEA for EFTA countries to join the Common Agricultural Policy, so that tariffs and quotas will remain on unprocessed agricultural produce.

8.2.2.5 Assessment of the economic impact of the EU

Since the formation of the Community in 1958 there has been a substantial increase in intra-Union trade, a development that has been given added impetus by the Single European Act. The Act was introduced at a time when intra-Union trade already accounted for over 50 per cent of members' total external trade, and it helped boost that total to over 60 per cent in the immediate run-up to '1992' (see Table 8.3). Significant increases in intra-Union trade have occurred (as expected) in the case of the EU's newest members, Greece, Spain and Portugal, but sizeable increases have also been recorded by France, Italy, Denmark and the UK. For consumers, the removal of tariffs and other obstacles to trade has resulted in lower real prices for many products (notable exceptions being farm produce), greater product sophistication and choice. For businesses, the EU has provided added opportunities to expand sales and profits.

Looked at more widely, for much of the period since 1958 the EU has acted as an 'engine' of trade expansion, creating additional trade not only

Table 8.3 Intra-Union trade as a percentage of member states' foreign trade, 1980, 1985 and 1993

Member state	1980	1985	1993
Total EU	50	52	60
Denmark	49	46	54
Belgium and Luxembourg	66	68	73
Germany	47	49	54
Greece	–	49	61
Spain	–	43	62
France	49	52	64
Ireland	74	69	72
Italy	45	46	59
Netherlands	62	64	67
Portugal	–	47	73
UK	40	45	53

Source: European Commission.

within the Union but also for non-members. In recent years, however, as Figure 8.5 shows, intra-Union trade has continued to expand strongly, while imports from, and exports to, non-member countries have slowed down.

Although trade-diversionary effects have been serious for some non-member countries (a case in point being the adverse effects felt by the Caribbean cane sugar industry following the UK's entry to the EU in 1973), overall they have been limited not only by reductions in the EU's external tariff rates (through GATT) but also by trade deals with various non-member countries. The Lomé Convention (see Box 8.4), for example, between the EU and some sixty-nine African, Caribbean and Pacific (ACP) countries provides for tariff-free entry into the EU market of a wide range of ACP primary products and manufactures. Nonetheless, it cannot be denied that the EU's Common Agricultural Policy is both unduly restrictive (limiting market access) and disruptive (in so far as subsidised EU farm exports are often off-loaded on to world markets, serving to depress international prices).

Estimates of the potential gains resulting from the completion of the internal market indicate that the total economic gain to the EU is likely to be in the range ECU 174 billion to ECU 258 billion, representing

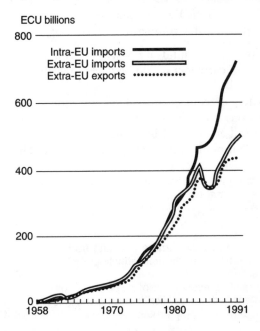

Figure 8.5 EU: internal and external trade, 1958–91

Source: Gatt Secretariat

some 4.3 per cent to 6.4 per cent of the EU's gross domestic product in 1988. A number of potential sources of efficiency gains are highlighted in Table 8.4:

1 *The removal of cross-border barriers to trade*, mainly customs formalities, and related delays.
2 *The removal of barriers to production* which not only affect intra-EU trade but also hinder foreign entrants and thus limit competition. Examples include biased government procurement, divergent national standards, regulations, testing and certification procedures, restrictions on services, in particular, banking, insurance, house finance, stock market and securities services in respect of cross-border soliciting of deposits and customers, and likewise restrictions on manufacturing, including product specifications and standards, packaging and labelling requirements, and tax rates (particularly the tax treatment of motor cars).
3 *Cost reductions through firms exploiting economies of scale more fully*, involving restructuring their operations on a pan-EU basis. This will be facilitated by the introduction of various measures noted above – harmonised technical standards and product specifications across the twelve economies.
4 *Cost reductions through the elimination of business inefficiencies* (and in some cases 'excess' profits) as national markets are opened up and local firms subjected to greater competitive pressures.

Fuller integration of the kind proposed by the Maastrich Treaty (for example, a common currency) would be likely to result in even more significant gains.

These estimates, of course, are subject to wide margins of error and may well be exaggerated, given that the directives proposed may not be implemented in full across the EU because of national tardiness and resistance. Moreover, 'harmonisation' is an elusive concept. Thus the economies

Table 8.4 Potential gains in economic welfare for the EU resulting from completion of the internal market

Gain	ECU billions	% of GDP
1 Gains from the removal of barriers affecting trade	8–9	0.2–0.3
2 Gains from the removal of barriers affecting overall production	57–71	2.0–2.4
3 Gains from exploiting economies of scale more fully	61	2.1
4 Gains from intensified competition reducing business inefficiencies and monopoly profits	46	1.6
Total for twelve member states at 1988 prices	174–258	4.3–6.4

Source: Commission of EU, 'Cecchini Report', 1988, cited in P. Cecchini, *The European Challenge, 1992*, Aldershot: Wildwood House, 1988.

of scale that can be achieved through centralised production and product standardisation may prove limited. There are significant cultural differences between EU countries, requiring firms to 'customise' their products to meet buyer requirements in particular national markets.

8.3 CONCLUSION

The growth in international trade has been greatly aided by multilateral and regional free-trade initiatives. Regional free trade has become much more prominent, particularly in the 'triad' of regions, Asia, Western Europe and North America, where reliance on trading within the region accounts for a high proportion of total trade flows. This upsurge in intra-regional trade has raised the spectre of 'inwardness' and the possibility of inter-regional trade conflicts.

8.4 IMPLICATIONS FOR BUSINESS

The removal of tariffs and other obstacles to cross-border trade provides a greater opportunity for firms to expand their sales and profits by increasing exports to foreign markets. The elimination of tariff impositions, in particular, may enable efficient, price-competitive firms to undercut the prices charged by local producers in target markets, while the dismantling of quotas can enable progressive firms to increase their penetration of hitherto protected markets.

In the case of multinational companies (MNCs) which use a combination of exporting, strategic alliances and foreign investment, the removal of impediments to exporting may lead to changes in their foreign market servicing strategies (see Chapter 9). For example, a MNC may have established a manufacturing plant in a particular country in order to overcome problems of market access because of high tariffs and quotas. With the removal or scaling down of these impositions the MNC may find it more economical to service such a market by exports, using local distributors, or through a company-owned sales subsidiary, leading to the closure of its factory in that market and concentration of production in its more efficient plants elsewhere.

The 'common market' approach to regional trade liberalisation can provide even greater opportunities for competitive firms, since the harmonisation of technical standards, labelling and packaging requirements, etc., will reduce adaptation expenses and provide greater scope for establishing pan-country brands. However, while 'supply side' harmonisation measures will undoubtedly facilitate greater exporting opportunities it must be stressed that firms will still need to be attentive to 'demand side' differences emanating from a diversity of tastes and cultural life-style factors.

QUESTIONS

1 Discuss the distinction between 'multilateral' trade liberalisation and 'regional trade integration' for international trade flows.
2 Outline the work of GATT and UNCTAD and assess their contribution to the promotion of international trade.
3 What is meant by the terms 'trade creation' and 'trade diversion'?
4 Indicate the main features of the European Union and the European Free Trade Association with regard to trade policy.
5 Outline and comment on the European Union's 'single market' initiative.

Chapter 9

International investment

International investment has long complemented international trade as a resource allocation and transfer mechanism, but in recent decades it has become significantly more important with the expansion of multinational companies (MNCs). A multinational company is a business incorporated in one country (the home or source country) which owns income-generating assets – mines, component and manufacturing plants, offices, sales subsidiaries – in some other country or countries ('host' countries). The propensity of many MNCs to use a combination of importing/exporting, strategic alliances with foreign partners and wholly-owned foreign direct investment to source inputs for their operations and to produce and market their products has led to a more complex pattern of world trade and investment flows. Thus, for example, some international trade flows involving arm's-length exporting and importing between different firms have been 'internalised' and are now conducted through intra-subsidiary transfers within a vertically integrated MNC. In some cases exporting to a particular market by a MNC has been replaced by the establishment of a local production plant to service that demand in-house; in other cases trade has been expanded by the establishment of a foreign plant which is then used primarily as an export base to supply adjacent markets. Thus trade and investment relations between countries need to be looked at as an inter-related, dynamic process rather than as an either/or situation.

The tentacular presence of the leading MNCs in a large number of countries has not only prompted a reassessment of the importance to countries of traditional international trade, based on exports and imports, but has focused attention on the MNC as an organisational 'powerhouse' having an economic capacity which transcends that of individual sovereign states. Specifically, a country is, by definition, a 'fixed' entity; the MNC, by contrast, constitutes a 'bundle' of resources which can be deployed between countries in furtherance of its corporate objectives.

This chapter discusses the growth of and reasons for international investment by MNCs. Particular attention is paid to an often overlooked issue of international investment, namely the macroeconomic implications of such flows with regard to resource transfers, domestic economy income and employment effects and balance of payments effects.

9.1 THE GROWTH OF FOREIGN DIRECT INVESTMENT

Foreign direct investment (FDI) comprises: (1) expenditure on establishing new 'greenfield' subsidiary companies; spending on setting up joint ventures; and expenditure on the aquisition of foreign companies; (2) profits of overseas subsidiaries which are reinvested abroad and (3) parent-to-subsidiary capital transfers. Economically, FDI is to be distinguished from 'portfolio investment' (investment in corporate stocks and shares, government stocks, etc., mainly by financial institutions such as pension funds and insurance companies) in so far as FDI represents the maintenance and creation of *real*, productive assets (a factory, office, etc.), whereas portfolio investment merely transfers the ownership of a *financial* asset from one individual or institution to another.

There has been a prolific growth in direct investment flows in recent years, as Table 9.1 shows. The growth in direct investment has been paralleled by a similar expansion of portfolio investment (see Box 9.1). Total FDI flows increased from US$91 billion in 1986 to over US$238 billion in 1990 before falling back to US$170 billion in 1992.

The industrialised countries accounted for 97 per cent of outward FDI over the period 1986–92. Japanese MNCs accounted for nearly one-fifth of total outward FDI over this period, followed by British and US MNCs. These three countries together accounted for some 46 per cent of total outward investment, with the top twelve countries accounting for 92 per cent of the total. Over the longer term notable developments include the fall in the share of total outward investment accounted for by the USA and an increase in the Japanese share.

A significant feature of inward FDI flows over the period 1986–92 is the dominant position occupied by the industrialised countries, which have increased their combined share of total inward FDI from an average of 72 per cent in the period 1974–80 to some 81 per cent in the period 1986–92. The table highlights the predominance of the USA as a host of FDI; the attractiveness of the USA over this period has been underpinned by the weakness of the dollar and the consequent cheapening of US-based assets, reflected in a spate of takeovers of US companies. The UK, ranked number two as a host country, has benefited particularly from its attractiveness to the Japanese as a production base from which to service the EU market. In addition to the UK, six other European Union countries are ranked in the top twelve host countries for FDI, which also include two newly industrialising countries, Singapore and China. A notable omission from the inward investment listing is Japan. In sharp contrast to its prominent

Table 9.1 World outward and inward foreign direct investment flows: total and distribution, 1986–92 (%)

Total: US$	1,212,754 million
Outward	
Industrial countries	97.0
Developing countries	3.0
of which:	
1 Japan	17.2
2 USA	15.3
3 UK	14.0
4 France	11.4
5 Germany	9.7
6 Netherlands	6.1
7 Sweden	3.9
8 Canada	3.3
9 Belgium and Luxembourg	3.2
10 Switzerland	3.1
11 Italy	2.8
12 Australia	1.7
Total	91.7
Inward	
Industrial countries	81.0
Developing countries	19.0
of which:	
1 USA	27.4
2 UK	13.5
3 France	7.3
4 Spain	5.3
5 Netherlands	4.1
6 Australia	3.8
7 Belgium and Luxembourg	3.5
8 Germany	3.5
9 Canada	3.2
10 China	2.8
11 Singapore	2.5
12 Italy	2.4
Total	79.3

Source: IMF, *Balance of Payments Statistical Yearbook* (Part 2), 1993.

position in outward investment, Japan accounted for only 0.4 per cent of total inward investment over the period 1986–92.

The upsurge in FDI flows over recent years has been largely associated with the expansion of multinational companies as they have sought to enhance their positions in the three major blocs – Western Europe, North

America and the Pacific rim. Foreign direct investment flows (and port-folio investment) have been greatly facilitated by the removal by many countries of exchange controls over capital movements and related income streams and various institutional arrangements encouraging inward invest-ment. The UK, for example, abolished all exchange controls over capital movements into and out of the country in 1979, and there are no limita-tions on the repatriation of profits. There are no restrictions on the propor-tion of local equity that can be held by foreign direct investors, nor are there any 'selective' controls on investment in particular industrial sectors.

The UK operates an 'open door' policy towards FDI, actively supporting inward investment. The Invest in Britain Bureau (IBB) was established in 1977 to act as a facilitator and conduit of foreign investment in the UK. The IBB, part of the Department of Trade and Industry, is able to offer companies practical assistance and detailed advice on all aspects of investing and locating in UK. Foreign companies are treated on an equal footing with domestic businesses with regard to, for example, financial backing if they locate in an 'assisted' region of the UK.

Similar moves to liberalise capital movements have been made by the UK's partners in the EU under the Single European Market initiative, and likewise by other major industrial countries. Developing countries have also sought to make inward investment easier and more attractive as a means of industrialising their economies. Box 9.2 gives details of FDI policies in various countries.

Box 9.1 World portfolio investment, 1986–92

Total: US$1,640,094 million			
Outward	%	Inward	%
1 Japan	32.9	1 USA	18.0
2 UK	14.5	2 Japan	13.5
3 Germany	10.0	3 Germany	11.1
4 USA	8.8	4 France	9.4
5 Belgium	9.0	5 UK	8.8
6 Italy	5.4	6 Belgium	6.1
7 France	3.9	7 Canada	5.3
8 Switzerland	3.8	8 Italy	3.4
Total of above as % world total	88.3	Total of above as % world total	75.6

Source: IMF, Balance of Payments Statistical Yearbook (Part 2), 1993.

Aggregated data on the *global* geographical and product distribution of foreign direct investment is not available from the usual sources of international financial data (the IMF and the UN). However, examination of the detailed balance of payments accounts of individual countries provides useful insights. Table 9.2, for example, shows the geographical distribution of UK and Canadian outward and inward investment. Like international trade patterns, the location of countries' investments tends to reflect traditional economic ties as well as responses to changing circumstances. Interestingly, in contrast to the situation with regard to UK merchandise exports, the proportion of UK investment accounted for by the EU has fallen slightly while investment in North America, the USA in particular, has increased markedly. In the case of inward investment, the proportion of investment accounted for by EU partners and 'other developed' countries (mainly Japan) has increased substantially, while US investment in the UK has declined in relative importance as US investment has become more diversified across the EU bloc as a whole. Canadian investment patterns, by contrast, conform to the country's merchandise trade profile, that is, notwithstanding old imperial ties with the UK, Canadian investment is still dominated by dependence on the USA, dependence which is likely to be reinforced by the conclusion of the North American Free Trade Agreement (NAFTA).

Table 9.3 presents details of the product composition of UK and Canadian outward and inward investment. Chemicals and food, drink and tobacco figure prominently in the UK manufacturing sector; wood and paper and metal products in the Canadian manufacturing sector. Financial services and the energy sector are prominent areas of investment in the non-manufacturing sector of both economies.

Table 9.2 UK and Canadian stock of outward and inward direct investment by region, 1978 and 1992 (%)

| | UK | | | | Canada | | | |
| | Outward | | Inward | | Outward | | Inward | |
Region	1978	1992	1978	1992	1978	1992	1978	1992
European Union	26	24	18	29	12	20	15	24
Other Western Europe	5	4	11	10	1	2	2	4
North America	25	44	64	45	70	61	75	64
Other developed	24	11	5	13	2	3	5	5
Rest of world	20	17	2	3	15	14	3	3
	100	100	100	100	100	100	100	100

Source: Business Monitor (UK) and Statistics Canada, 1994.

Box 9.2 Foreign direct investment policies

USA Generally, foreign investment is free of restrictions although ownership limitations exist in some sectors (communications, aviation, insurance, real estate, banking). The USA has no exchange controls and foreign investors can fully repatriate dividends, interest, etc.

Germany Generally, 100 per cent foreign ownership is permitted and there are no exchange controls or any restrictions on profit and capital repatriation. Substantial tax incentives and investment grants are available to investors in east Germany.

Hong Kong There are no limits on foreign ownership and investors have complete flexibility in the movement of capital and the repatriation of profits.

Brazil Foreign investors cannot own more than 5 per cent of the voting capital or 20 per cent of the total capital of a Brazilian company. Capital repatriation, however, is unrestricted.

Thailand Foreign shareholdings are generally limited to a maximum of 49 per cent of capital; however, foreigners may hold more than 50 per cent of the equity in export industries if exports exceed 50 per cent of total production, and 100 per cent of equity if 80 per cent of output is exported. Permission is required for repatriation of dividends and capital.

Ghana 100 per cent foreign-owned ventures are permitted, provided they meet certain requirements. The venture must be a net earner of foreign currency, wholly-owned equity investment must be greater than $100,000, while joint venture investments with Ghanian partners require a foreign equity stake of at least $60,000.

Malaysia Foreign investors in new export-oriented industries can own 100 per cent of the equity in a company if exports are more than 80 per cent of production. Projects exporting less than 20 per cent of production are limited to a maximum of 30 per cent foreign equity ownership. Full repatriation of profits is permitted.

Japan Various restrictions apply to investments in such sectors as financial services, utilities, petroleum refining and retail trades. There are no limitations on repatriation of capital or profits.

Table 9.3 Composition of stock of UK and Canadian outward and inward direct investment by industrial activity, 1992 (%)

Category	Outward	Inward
UK		
Total manufacturing of which:	*34.4*	*36.2*
Chemicals	9.4	7.7
Food, drink and tobacco	6.8	5.7
Total non-manufacturing of which:	*65.6*	*63.8*
Energy	26.0	28.9
Financial services	13.4	18.0
Canada		
Total manufacturing of which:	*44.6*	*43.9*
Wood and paper	11.7	7.4
Non-ferrous metals	10.8	4.5
Iron products	5.3	13.9
Total non-manufacturing of which:	*55.4*	*56.1*
Financial services	27.6	20.9
Petroleum and gas	7.0	17.1

Source: Business Monitor (UK) and Statistics Canada, 1994.

9.2 FDI AND MULTINATIONAL COMPANIES' GLOBAL SOURCING, PRODUCTION AND MARKETING OPERATIONS

9.2.1 *Why* FDI?

International expansion through FDI is an alternative to growth based on the firm's domestic market. Thus a firm may choose to expand horizontally on a global basis by replicating its existing business operations through direct investment in a number of countries; or through international vertical integration, backwards by establishing raw material/component sources, and forward into final production and distribution. Additionally, firms may choose product diversification as a means of developing their international business interests.

Firms may expand internationally by greenfield (new 'start-up') investments in component and manufacturing plants, etc.; by the take-over of, and merger with, established suppliers; or by the establishment of joint ventures with overseas partners. Foreign direct investment is thus one important means of sustaining the growth impetus of the firm, providing it with added opportunities for establishing cost/price and product differentiation competitive advantages over rival suppliers. (See Box 9.3.)

A firm may possess various competitive advantages over rival suppliers in the form of patented process technology, know-how and skills, or a unique branded product which it can exploit and protect better by establishing overseas production or sales subsidiaries. A production facility in an overseas market may enable a firm to reduce its distribution costs and keep in touch more closely with local market conditions – changes in customer tastes, competitors' actions, etc. Moreover, direct investment enables a firm to avoid governmental restrictions on market access such as tariffs and quotas and the problems of currency variation.

For example, the growth of protectionism by the European Union and the rising value of the yen have been important factors leading to increased Japanese investment in the EU, in particular in the UK. By the same token, firms may be able to benefit from the availability of grants and other subsidies given by 'host' governments to encourage inward investment. Again, Japanese investment such as Nissan's car manufacturing plant at Washington in northern England has been attracted into the UK by the availability of regional selective assistance (see Box 9.4).

In the case of sourcing, direct investment allows the MNC to take advantage of some countries' lower labour costs or provides them with access to superior technological know-how, thereby enhancing their international competitiveness. Moreover, direct investment, by internalising input sourcing and market servicing within the one organisation, enables the MNC to avoid various transaction costs entailed in using the market (that is, the costs of finding suppliers of inputs and distributors and negotiating contracts with them and the costs associated with imperfect market situations, for example monopoly surcharges imposed by input suppliers, unreliable sources of supply and restrictions on access to distribution channels). Direct investment also enables the MNC to take advantage of the internal transfer of resources at prices which allow the MNC to minimise its tax bill or practise price discrimination between markets.

Finally, in the case of some products (e.g. flat glass, metal cans, cement) decentralised local production rather than exporting is the only viable way a MNC can supply an overseas market because of the prohibitively high cost of transporting a bulky product or one which, for competitive reasons, has to be marketed at a low price.

MNCs in practice tend to complement direct investment in supplying global markets with exporting, strategic alliances and licensing. Each of these modes has specific attractions and drawbacks in enhancing the firms' competitiveness:

Exporting – for example, from an established 'home' production plant – is a relatively inexpensive and low-risk way of servicing a foreign market, and maximum advantage can be taken of centralised production to secure

Box 9.3 Strategic reasons for FDI

ICI (UK) In 1992 ICI opened a greenfield manufacturing plant for pure terephthalic acid in Taiwan. The £150 million facility, the biggest investment in Taiwan by a foreign group, is part of ICI's strategy of expansion in the Asia Pacific region.

Jacobs Engineering (USA) In 1993 Jacobs acquired the UK-based engineering group Humphreys & Glasgow, to provide a stronger 'springboard' into Europe. Jacobs wanted to be able to service the requirements of its US clients when they invest in Europe as well as meet the needs of European companies.

Mercedes-Benz (Germany) In 1993 the company announced that it was to build a greenfield manufacturing plant in the USA, the world's largest car market, to revive its sales against local competition. Mercedes' decision followed that of BMW, which likewise decided to shift production out of Germany to the USA in order to improve its marketing effectiveness and lower its production costs.

Coca-Cola (USA) In 1993 the company acquired a 30 per cent stake in Femsa, Mexico's leading soft drinks bottling concern, in order to exercise greater control over the distribution of its products in this rapidly expanding market.

Unilever, the Anglo-Dutch food group, and **BSN**, France's largest food company, established a joint venture to develop and market worldwide a range of new products combining ice cream and yoghurt.

Usinor Sacilor, the French steel maker, increased its penetration of the UK steel market by acquiring, in 1991, ASD, the UK's largest independent steel stockholder, creating a vertically integrated concern to rival British Steel.

Grolsch (Dutch) In 1992 Grolsch, the lager brewer, acquired the UK real ale brewer, Ruddles, having earlier bought the German brewing group, Wickuler. The acquisition was another step in the company's strategy of building a strong portfolio of premium beer brands.

economies of scale and thus lower unit costs. On the other hand, the firm could be put at a competitive disadvantage if host governments impose import restrictions, if exchange rates become unfavourable, or if the firm loses touch with changing market conditions. Moreover, in the case of firms relying on distributors to market their products there may be problems of loss of control of key marketing variables.

Strategic alliances (co-production, co-marketing) may be attractive as a means of foreign expansion if they allow partners to achieve synergistic benefits through contributing particular mixes of resources and skills to a degree unavailable to each partner separately – for example, enabling foreign firms to take advantage of host country firms' local market knowledge and distribution channels. Strategic alliances, however, need careful handling to optimise results – lack of commitment, disagreements over operational matters and strategic direction may blunt the ability to seize competitive opportunities.

Licensing involves the assignment of production and selling rights to producers located in overseas markets in return for royalty payments. Licensing may enable a firm to expand its overseas sales and profits with little additional expense, but the royalties obtained may represent a poor return for the technology transferred, and the firm runs the risk of 'losing' the technology to eventual competitors.

Thus, while wholly-owned foreign direct investment can be expensive and risky, in many cases the 'presence' effects of operating locally (familiarity with local market conditions, the cultivation of contacts with local suppliers, distributors and government agencies, the ability to supply 'just in time' from in-market plants and the provision of back-up services such as repairs and maintenance) may be critical factors in building profitable market share over the long run.

9.2.2 Some examples of FDI by UK multinationals

Glaxo is a leading global pharmaceutical producer. The company has established production and sales subsidiaries in the major markets of North America, Europe and Japan; smaller markets are serviced in the main through wholly-owned sales subsidiaries and strategic alliances with local partners. Direct investment is the company's general policy in markets where 'presence' is important in dealing with the regulatory authorities over drug approval and in developing customer contacts (especially with medical practitioners). In these cases local management is given a high degree of autonomy in running the subsidiary companies.

The company's foreign market servicing strategy in its main markets is based on a distinction between 'primary' and 'secondary' production and the advantages of 'presence' effects, especially in marketing. Primary manufacture consists of the production of patented 'active ingredients' which for competitive reasons were initially produced exclusively in the UK (they are now also produced in Singapore) and then exported to secondary manufacturing plants located around the world where they are incorporated into the final products and marketed through sales subsidiaries. Given local preferences, packaging adaptations are necessary in most markets (design, size and instructions, colours, capsules versus tablets, etc.). A comprehensive sales force 'on the ground' is also considered to be an important competitive advantage, as marketing pharmaceuticals is critically one of 'selling quality to professionals'.

Lucas Automotive is a major company supplying components to the global automobile industry. In the last decade the company has been progressively restructured to broaden its international base and to focus on growth markets and technologies. Two imperatives guide the company's strategy: one is technological leadership through continuous product innovation; two, close collaboration with major customers in vehicle design and construction, is becoming ever more important as customers' own competitive success increasingly hinges on reducing product development lead times and the introduction of reliable, high-performance vehicles. This means an international presence in customers' R&D and manufacturing locations which are centred on Europe, North America and Japan.

Lucas's policy is to have manufacturing facilities in its main customer bases – Europe (Germany, France, Belgium and the UK) and North America (the USA) and 'service' companies to support exports to other markets (e.g. Canada, Japan, Mexico, Ireland). Service companies carry stocks, and act as distributors. In the main their activities are confined to 'aftermarket' operations (i.e. the supply of replacement components and parts). In addition, sales and marketing subsidiaries operate in the company's main markets.

BT was formerly a state-owned monopoly supplier of telecommunication services to the UK market with no overseas operations. Since privatisation of the company in 1984 and the liberalisation of the telecommunications market the company has had 'to learn to compete'. Growth prospects for the company in the UK have been stunted by a combination of regulatory controls and the emergence of new competitors and this has led to an increasing emphasis on international expansion.

BT's competitive advantages lie in its telecommunications expertise, particularly in operating conventional telephone network systems and in the provision of a range of innovative telecommunication services such as cordless (that is, mobile) telephones and voicemail. Vertical (backward) integration was once seen as offering benefits through having an in-house 'captive' supply of telephone equipment, but its interests in this area have now been divested. The company's present strategy is based on the exploitation of its competitive advantages in offering differentiated packages of high value-added telecommunication services, particularly to business customers with global interests. This requires 'presence' in major user markets through the establishment of sales offices and subsidiaries to provide on-going customer contact: 'Global customers require global servicing'. In this respect, a presence in the North American market, the USA in particular, is seen as crucial, since the area is home to many of the world's largest multinational companies.

9.3 MACROECONOMIC EFFECTS OF OUTWARD DIRECT INVESTMENT

The macroeconomic effects of FDI are wide-ranging but there may be economic impacts in several particularly important areas: the balance of payments and trade, resource transfers and employment. More broadly, FDI can have a political effect via, in the case of inward investment, its impact on sovereignty and autonomy.

9.3.1 Balance of payments and trade effects

It is sometimes suggested that outward investment weakens a country's external position because it involves running down a country's foreign currency reserves and/or increasing overseas debt. However, it may well be that net capital outflows are financed out of current account surpluses so that there is no initial currency loss. The fundamental point to emphasise, however, is that outward investment, irrespective of whether it is financed by current account surpluses or by reserve drawings, adds to the country's stock of overseas assets, thereby increasing the country's external wealth and future income-earning capacity.

A number of industrial countries are net exporters of investment capital (see Table 9.4), some, such as Germany and Japan, financing overseas investment out of current account surpluses while others, such as the UK, using mainly reserves and borrowings.

Table 9.4 Net FDI flows and current account position, selected countries, 1986–92 (US$ billions)

Country		1986	1987	1988	1989	1990	1991	1992
Germany	FDI	−9.8	−7.7	−11.8	−7.7	−20.0	−14.9	−9.0
	Current account	+40.1	+46.3	+50.7	+57.7	+46.3	−19.5	−25.5
Japan	FDI	−14.2	−18.3	−34.7	−45.2	−46.3	−29.4	−14.5
	Current account	+85.8	+87.0	+79.6	+57.0	+35.9	+72.9	+117.6
UK	FDI	+10.3	−17.3	−19.0	−7.3	+14.7	+2.0	+3.4
	Current account	0	−7.6	−28.8	−35.6	−29.4	−11.4	−20.7
USA	FDI	+15.4	+27.1	+41.5	+38.9	+12.4	−5.1	−32.4
	Current account	−145.4	−160.2	−126.4	−101.2	−90.5	−8.5	−66.3
Belgium	FDI	−1.0	−0.4	+1.4	+0.2	+1.8	+3.2	−0.1
	Current account	+3.1	+2.8	+3.6	+3.2	+4.9	+4.7	+5.4

− = net outflow; + = net inflow.

Source: IMF, *Balance of Payments Statistics Yearbook* (Part 1) 1993.

Overseas investment in turn affects the current account position in two ways. On the negative side, there may be some displacement of exports of finished manufactured products as overseas markets come to be supplied from local plants. However, additional export demand may be created in the form of machinery, materials or replacement parts as a continuing back-up to the original investment. Thus the effect of foreign investment may be to change the composition of a country's exports away from some finished products to intermediate products rather than to eliminate exports altogether.

On the positive side, foreign investment enlarges the stream of interest, profits and dividend receipts available to the country. Table 9.5 shows, for the UK, what a sizeable contribution net currency earnings can make to the current account.

9.3.2 Resource and employment effects

As regards the domestic economy, outward investment could be damaging to domestic output and employment if it was associated with a significant fall in manufactured exports but, for the reasons given above, this is unlikely to be the general case. Moreover, this possibility has to be considered along-side the scope for redeploying resources to alternative domestic uses, especially those activities not directly exposed to foreign trade and investment influences.

A point not always appreciated is that foreign investment is often under-taken to protect sales in overseas markets as direct exports fall, owing to increased local competition or the erection of trade barriers, that is, a local production operation is substituted for exports as a more viable means of servicing that market. A further factor is that foreign investment often creates additional resource requirements by the home (parent) company, especially for skilled personnel in such areas as research and development, administration and finance.

A potentially more serious criticism of foreign investment centres on the possibility that it may *replace* home investment, thereby resulting in a *lower* overall level of domestic investment and consequent loss of output and

Table 9.5 UK net earnings from foreign investment, 1987–93 (£ billions)

Measure	1987	1988	1989	1990	1991	1992	1993
Net earnings from FDI	3.9	5.2	7.4	8.5	8.2	8.3	6.2
Current account position	−5.0	−16.6	−22.5	−19.0	−8.2	−9.8	−10.3

Source: UK Balance of Payments, 1994.

employment. While *portfolio* investment (that is, investment in financial securities such as stocks and shares) can readily be switched from country to country at short notice in response to interest rate differentials and currency fluctuations, direct investment in plant differs, as it involves the long-term commitment of resources in specific countries, a commitment not easily reversed once made. It could be argued, of course, that any investment abroad could have been made at home instead, but this is a superficial contention. The relevant question is: would the investment at home actually have gone ahead? The fundamental point is that FDI is usually additional to the MNC's domestic activities, representing a strategic response to an opportunity or threat in overseas markets. FDI is thus normally to be seen as complementary to, rather than as a substitute for, domestic investment.

9.4 MACROECONOMIC EFFECTS OF INWARD DIRECT INVESTMENT

Superficially, the effects of inward investment may be thought to be a mirror image of outward investment. However, there are important differences, most notably with respect to the impact on the domestic economy.

9.4.1 Balance of payments and trade effects

When the MNC establishes a foreign subsidiary, the capital account of the host country's balance of payments benefits from the initial foreign exchange inflow, although it may be a once-and-for-all effect if the subsidiary subsequently finances later expansion from local capital sources. Set against this benefit is the continuing adverse impact on the current account representing the various payments of dividends, profits, interest, royalties and administration fees to the parent company. However, it is necessary to consider the wider trade flows associated with MNC investments to obtain a more complete picture of costs and benefits.

The operation of the MNC subsidiary may be highly import-intensive, with the subsidiary importing key raw materials and components from its parent or other subsidiaries for local assembly. So-called 'screwdriver' factories fall into this category and, because they are often used as a means of circumventing tariffs and other trade restrictions imposed on imports of finished products, they may well be opposed by host country governments.

On the other hand, direct investment may involve import substitution, with inputs, or final products, now being sourced locally rather than obtained from abroad. The European Union (EU), for example, applies particular pressure on Japanese motor car manufacturers (and other MNC producers) in the EU to increase the local content of their cars to a minimum of 80 per cent. With respect to finished products, the subsidiary may be used to supply both the host country market and export markets, in which case the visible trade effects of inward investment are likely to be strongly positive. Imports of finished manufactures will be reduced as they are replaced by home production, although there will be some stimulus to imports of intermediate products.

A more significant impact, studies have shown, is on direct exports. In the case of the UK, inward investment is predominantly undertaken by US MNCs, but increasingly by the Japanese, who see the UK as a convenient and relatively cheap base from which to service European markets. In 1992 around 26 per cent of UK exports were accounted for by foreign-controlled companies.

Host country government policies can materially affect the overall trade situation; for example, the extent to which host country economic development programmes are 'inwardly' oriented (that is, focused on import substitution) or 'outwardly' oriented (that is, focused on export promotion). Most newly industrialised countries (NICs), in particular Hong Kong, Taiwan and Malaysia, have in fact favoured the latter strategy because of its greater potential for improving economic growth and have encouraged the establishment of MNC subsidiaries used primarily as export supply sources.

9.4.2 Resource transfer

Another important component of the 'package' brought by MNC investment is embodied technology. For many host countries, particularly less developed countries, domestic ability to invent and innovate is strictly limited, not only by a lack of capital but also by lack of scientists, technicians and other groups of skilled personnel. However, by adopting established technologies through the medium of MNC investment, host countries can by-pass the risky, expensive invention and innovation stages in developing commercially viable processes and products, thereby taking a significant leap forward. Moreover, although it may be reliant initially on overseas personnel to install and operate the new technologies, the host country may in time benefit considerably from the training and expertise acquired by the local labour force.

On the other hand, since know-how and technology are produced by MNCs to meet their own particular requirements, the advantages to be gained by host countries will depend on the suitability of the technology transferred and the price and method of supply. This is a particularly sensitive area of MNC operations. Technological invention is such a prized asset that it is usually patented and jealously guarded by its instigators. FDI, we have observed, is one way in which an MNC is able to recoup costly research and development as well as appropriate the monopoly revenues from new processes and products.

To this extent, inward investment to exploit firm-specific advantages may confer very little in the way of technological spin-offs on the local economy. Worse still, it is contended, is the fact that MNCs tend to centralise research and development in the parent company to protect secret know-how, so that subsidiaries become technologically dependent on their parent and are confined solely to local assembly operations.

For these reasons, many host country governments insist on joint ventures between local companies and MNCs rather than exclusive foreign owner-ship and a commitment to genuine technology transfer.

While, in theory, less developed countries stand to gain the most in terms of acquiring new technology through inward investment, developed countries, too, can benefit from the cross-fertilisation of ideas and know-how and technology transfer by MNCs. The UK, for example, has bene-fited from the rejuvenation of its motor industry deriving from the joint venture between Rover Group and Honda of Japan (ended in 1994 when Rover was acquired by BMW of Germany) and Honda's own greenfield investment in a car assembly plant at Swindon; and the greenfield invest-ments made by two other Japanese groups, Nissan, which has established a car assembly plant at Washington, Tyne and Wear, and the Toyota invest-ment in car assembly at Burnaston, near Derby (see Box 9.4).

A major benefit of the Rover–Honda relationship was a near-revolution in the quality and reliability of the supply of components with the appli-cation of Japanese production control and inventory management tech-niques. Nor is this confined to the motor industry. The Sony television plant at Bridgend in Wales is now seen as a model for subsequent invest-ment elsewhere in Europe, largely owing to the development of closer rela-tions with, and exerting commercial pressure on, both small and large-scale component suppliers. Indeed, this is an interesting case of a development from a former 'screwdriver' plant into a 'leading edge' supplier using process and product applications developed at Sony's R&D establishment at Basingstoke, England.

Other notable examples of inward investment establishing new UK manufacturing capacity include US, Japanese and European investment in computers, semiconductors (microchips), video cassette recorders and scien-tific instruments. In addition, the MNC may preserve existing capacity where the UK owner is unable or reluctant to commit further develop-ment resources, as in the case of the purchase of Inmos by the French electronics group CSF-Thomson. Finally, for many countries, managerial skills may be a scarce factor, so that an inflow of MNC investment and associated managerial resources can contribute directly to the more efficient operation of their economies. The long-term indirect effects may also be important with, again, acquisition of entrepreneurial and managerial exper-tise by local managers employed by MNCs leading on to their setting up businesses of their own or taking control of established companies.

Box 9.4 Japanese car makers' investment in the UK

Nissan
1 *Assembly and engine plant* in Washington, near Sunderland (opened 1986).
   Output: 400,000 cars a year by 1995.
   Investment: £850 million.
   Jobs: 4,600.
   European component purchases: £800 million in 1993.
2 *Car body pressings subsidiary* (80 per cent Nissan) in Washington.
   Investment: £50 million.
   Jobs: 200.
3 *R&D centre* in Cranfield.
   Investment: £31 million.
   Jobs: 250.
4 *Sales, marketing and distribution subsidiaries.*
   Investment: £40 million.
   Jobs: 400.

Toyota
1 *Assembly plant* in Burnaston, near Derby (opened 1992).
   Output: 200,000 cars a year by 1995.
   Investment: £700 million.
   Jobs: 8,000 by 1995.
   European component purchases: £750 million by 1995.
2 *Engine plant* in Deeside, North Wales.
   Investment: £140 million.
   Jobs: 300.
3 *Sales, marketing and distribution.*
   Five per cent stake in subsidiary, rising to 51 per cent in 1998 (£60 million).

Honda
1 *Assembly plant* in Swindon (opened 1992).
   Output: 100,000 cars a year by 1995.
   Investment: £300 million.
   Jobs: 2,000 by 1995.
   European component purchases: £400 million by 1995.
2 *Engine plant* in Swindon.
   Investment: £62 million.
   Jobs: 600.

Source: The company itself in each case.

9.4.3 Output and employment effects

The output and employment effect of inward investment depends partly on the initial mode of entry chosen by the MNC. The establishment of a greenfield plant leads directly to increased output and local employment, depending on the scale of the operation, while the take-over of an established firm may well reduce employment if a rationalisation programme is followed. Over the long term, however, *both* modes of entry are likely to have beneficial output and employment effects as the MNC strengthens and expands its operations. Inward investment also creates secondary jobs elsewhere in the economy by increasing the demand for locally produced component supplies, transport, financial, technical and marketing services. These effects are likely to be especially beneficial in the case of large-scale production operations which involve a high proportion of bought-in components, such as motor car assembly (see Box 9.4).

Obviously, in the case of an individual MNC, the employment it creates in a particular host country needs to be considered in terms of the permanence of the investment. To the extent that MNCs often regroup their sourcing and market servicing operations in the light of underlying world conditions and changing competitive circumstances, it may well be that new plant openings in one country are accompanied by complete or partial shutdowns elsewhere. For example, in 1990 Ford transferred production of Sierra cars from its Dagenham plant in the UK to its plant in Genk, Belgium, while Wang (US) closed its personal computer factory in Scotland, transferring production to Ireland. In 1993 CPC (UK), the subsidiary of a US group, transferred production of its Knorr brand of soups and cubes from Scotland to more modern plants in France and Italy with a loss of 350 UK jobs (see Box 9.6).

In aggregate terms, however, studies have shown the overall impact of MNC activity to be strongly output and employment-creating in most host countries. In the case of the UK, foreign-controlled enterprises, although accounting for only around 1 per cent of total UK manufacturing firms in 1993, nonetheless employed 16 per cent of the labour force and accounted for 22 per cent of total UK ouput and 27 per cent of total UK investment.

Finally, it is to be noted that, while some MNC investment is directed towards capitalising on the lower costs associated with using relatively unskilled labour, there has been a substantial amount of investment also in high-technology industries (telecommunications, consumer electronics, etc.) which has contributed towards upgrading employment skills.

9.4.4 Sovereignty and autonomy effects

The sovereignty and autonomy effects of MNCs' foreign investment are invariably viewed by host countries as a cost. Although foreign firms can

Box 9.5 Transfer pricing and unitary taxation

Multinational corporations can shift the balance of their profits between countries by charging higher or lower transfer prices for goods and service exchanged within the group. Ideally, as far as international taxation law is concerned, transfer prices should be set on the 'arm's-length' principle, as if the goods or services were sold to an unrelated company. However, transfer prices may be manipulated to under-record profits or 'remove' profits from high taxation countries to countries where tax rates are lower.

Manipulative transfer pricing: the case of Nissan (UK)
In 1993 Nissan UK, the (privately owned) former exclusive importer of Nissan cars from Japan, was found guilty of defrauding the Inland Revenue of £56 million corporation tax. Over a nine-year period between 1982 and 1991 freight charges for imported cars were artificially overstated by some 40 per cent. Nissan Japan's transport division, NMCC, had originally provided all shipping services. Nissan UK, however, renegotiated the arrangement in 1982, employing a Norwegian shipping agent who conspired to submit inflated invoices. Monies paid over were then 'laundered' into a Swiss bank account.

Unitary taxation
Countries or states therein may seek to claw back profits which they suspect have been deliberately taken out of the country to avoid tax liability. Under a unitary tax system, local taxation is based on a proportion of the *world wide* profits of a company, calculated on the size of its assets, etc., in that country instead of only on the profits actually made in that country. The figures below show a company having $1,000 million of assets both in California and in country Z and total gross profits of $200 million. Under a conventional taxation system (1) the company would pay a total of $40million in tax. Under a unitary system (2), although the company had declared no profits in California, the assets located there would be assumed to have generated half the world wide profits of the company. In this case the company's tax bill is $90 million – $50 million payable on the 'shadow' profits in California and $40 million on the actual profits declared in country Z.

	California *(50% tax rate)*	*Country Z* *(20% tax rate)*	*Tax liability*
Assets employed	$1,000m	$1,000m	
Gross profits			
1 Conventional basis	0	$200	$40m
2 Unitary basis	($100m)	+ $200m	$90m

benefit the local economy in various ways, as noted above, inevitably there is some loss of economic independence when a large segment of local industry is effectively controlled by foreign companies. Such problems arise essentially from the international nature of MNCs with policies toward any one subsidiary reflecting the pursuit of some global objective of the MNC (that is, pursuit of its 'private' interest, which may not necessarily correspond to the 'public interest' aspirations of the host country). For example, a MNC may use transfer pricing techniques to eliminate local competitors in order to monopolise the host country market, or transfer out potential value added in order to minimise its global tax bill (see Box 9.5). However, it is also the case that countries compete with each other to attract inward investment by providing investment grants and tax holidays so that in many cases MNCs are simply taking commercial advantage of situations created by governmental action (see Box 9.6)

There are equally important aspects relating to the reduced ability of the host government to pursue its desired policies. For example, host govern-

Box 9.6 'Poaching' inward investment?

Many countries use financial 'sweeteners' and other means to attract inward investment, and this often gives rise to charges of unfair 'poaching'. An example is provided by Hoover's decision in 1994 to close its vacuum cleaner plant in Longuie, France, with a loss of 650 jobs and transfer production to its Cambuslang plant in Scotland. As far as the company was concerned, the move made commercial sense, enabling it to reduce manufacturing costs by around 25 per cent through the centralisation of all production in the one plant. The French government, upset by the UK's refusal to embrace the social chapter of the Maastricht Treaty, asked the European Commission to investigate whether Hoover was unfairly or illegally 'bribed' with social and financial concessions. The UK and French authorities both offered Hoover around £5 million in plant subsidies, but the UK's opt-out of the social chapter meant that, although hourly pay rates are about the same in both countries, because social security and welfare costs are higher in France overall payroll costs are much lower in the UK. In addition, the Scottish work force made several concessions: limited-period contracts for new workers, constraints on their right to strike, cuts in overtime pay rates, flexible working hours and practices and the introduction of video cameras on the factory floor. To the French this was a clear case of the competitive undercutting of pay and conditions to attract investment, or 'social dumping' as they prefer to call it.

ment monetary policies may be circumvented by the MNC because it can draw on funds from elsewhere, although, for a developed country such as the UK, its own home-based MNCs may already pose such a threat, in the absence of exchange control. However, there has been a growing tendency on the part of MNCs to exercise a degree of 'social responsibility' in their dealings with host countries so that the interdependence that exists between the MNC and host country economies can be harnessed to their mutual benefit.

9.5 CONCLUSION

There is no doubt that the MNC has helped to promote more efficient allocation of resources world-wide and has contributed to a more integrated world economy, thereby serving to raise standards of living generally. Nonetheless such has been the global expansion of companies like ICI and Pilkington of the UK, General Motors and IBM of the USA, Hoechst and Volkswagen of Germany, etc., that their annual corporate revenues exceed those of the gross national product of many of the countries in which they have invested and have led to various questions being asked concerning the potential costs and benefits of such investment for source and host countries.

9.6 IMPLICATIONS FOR BUSINESS

International direct investment is undertaken mainly by multinational companies seeking to globalise their operations. Wholly-owned direct investment is used by MNCs alongside exporting/importing and strategic alliances to source inputs and service foreign markets. Direct investment can enable the MNC to enhance its competitive position and profitability in a number of ways. First, the MNC can take advantage of differences between countries in terms of their resource endowments and cost levels. For example, MNCs may locate their component and production plants in developing countries in order to take advantage of lower input costs, in particular the availability of cheap labour. Similarly, a MNC may locate its research and development in a more technologically advanced country to tap into that country's scientific infrastructure to develop new processes and products.

Secondly, MNCs benefit from the flexibility of being able to choose an appropriate mode of servicing a particular market as between exporting, strategic alliances or direct investment, or, in many cases, a combination of all three modes. Direct investment may be the most effective way of servicing a target market where 'presence' effects are important in building market share, or market access via exporting is limited by impositions such as tariffs. Thirdly, 'internalisation' of the MNC's operations across countries by direct investment often provides an opportunity for the firm to maximise its global profits by the use of various transfer pricing policies. Fourthly, an international network of production plants and sales subsidiaries enables a MNC to introduce a new product simultaneously in a large number of markets in order to maximise sales potential (an important consideration in the case of products having a relatively short life-cycle span). Equally important, it spreads the risk of consumer rejection across a diversified portfolio of overseas markets. Additionally, it enables the MNC to develop a 'global brand' identity (as with, for example, Unilever's new 'Ariel Power' soap powder and Foster's lager) or, alternatively, more effectively to 'customise' a product to suit local demand preferences.

QUESTIONS

1 Outline and comment on the growth and regional distribution of foreign direct investment.
2 Indicate the main reasons why firms invest in foreign operations.
3 Analyse the potential balance of payments and trade effects of outward and inward FDI.
4 Comment on some of the possible resource and employment effects of outward and inward FDI.
5 Comment on how FDI can affect (a) the relationship between host country governments and MNCs and (b) relations between the governments of different countries.

Chapter 10

Exchange rates and international monetary relations

International trade and investment flows have been discussed extensively in previous chapters. Underpinning these transactions has been a framework of international monetary mechanisms and institutional arrangements concerned with the financing of trade and investment and the adjustment and removal of payments imbalances between countries. This chapter considers three key features of an 'international monetary system', namely, the determination of exchange rates, the provision of international liquidity and international indebtedness.

International trade and investment are financed by countries exchanging their domestic currencies for the currencies of the countries they trade with and invest in. This function is undertaken by an international network of private foreign exchange dealers and by a country's monetary authorities, acting through its central bank. (See Box 10.1.) Exchange rates between currencies may be determined by the free interplay of demand for, and supply of, the currencies concerned or they may be subject to support buying and selling by countries' central banks in the foreign exchange market in order to 'fix' them at particular rates. In addition to currencies being bought and sold in order to finance trade and investment, currencies may also be bought and sold for speculative reasons, with buyers and sellers hoping to make windfall profits by anticipating currency movements.

The thousands and even millions of individual trade and investment transactions between countries will lead in aggregate terms to either a net currency inflow into a country (reflecting, as noted in Chapter 6, a balance of payments surplus with other countries) or a net currency outflow from the country (reflecting a balance of payments deficit). Such balance of payments surpluses and deficits may be only small and temporary. However, payment imbalances may be large and long-lasting, reflecting more fundamental factors – for example, a country's loss of international competitiveness. In these circumstances, balance of payments deficits and surpluses will need to be 'corrected', that is, removed or reduced to manageable proportions. In the interim, for deficit countries, the foreign exchange 'gap'

Box 10.1 The foreign exchange market

The foreign exchange market provides a conduit for exchanging or 'converting' one domestic currency into some other domestic currency, thereby enabling a cross-border (that is, 'foreign') trade or investment transaction to be completed.

The foreign exchange market by its very nature is multinational in scope. The leading centres for foreign exchange dealings are London, New York and Tokyo. In July 1993 London's average daily turnover was $200 billion, New York's $130 billion and Tokyo's $120 billion. The figure below shows the main foreign currency markets and indicates the hours on which they are open and trading.

Foreign currencies can be bought and sold on a 'spot' basis for immediate delivery or can be bought and sold for future delivery. Some two-thirds of London's foreign exchange dealings in 1993 were spot transactions.

The exchange rates quoted by dealers for pairs of currencies in each of the main centres tend to be similar as a result of 'arbitrage' using instant, computerised telecommunications systems. Arbitrage involves the buying or selling of currencies between two or more centres in order to take profitable advantage of any differences in the prices quoted in those markets. By simultaneously buying in a low-price market and selling in a high-price market a dealer can make a profit from any disparity in prices between the two, though in the process of buying and selling the dealer will add to demand in the low-price market and add to the supply in the high-price market and so help to narrow or eliminate the price disparity. International time differences between markets located in different countries mean that throughout the twenty-four-hour day currencies can be traded in one or more foreign exchange centres.

The exchange rate quoted by dealers may be stated either in terms of how many units of a foreign currency may be bought or sold per unit of the domestic currency (an 'indirect quotation'), or in terms of how many units of domestic currency may be bought or sold per unit of a particular foreign currency (a 'direct quotation'). For example, in the UK an indirect quotation of the exchange rate between the pound and the US dollar might be £1 = $2, whereas a direct quotation would be $1 = 50p.

Exchange rates are usually quoted by dealers as a 'pair' of rates, the 'offer' or sell rate and the 'bid' or buy rate, the difference between the two (the 'spread') representing the dealers' profit margin. Currencies which are traded in large volumes, such as the US dollar and German Deutschmark, usually have a narrower spread than currencies which are little used in international dealings. Similarly, the spread on current exchange rates quoted in the spot market for currencies is usually narrower than the spread on forward prices quoted in the futures market.

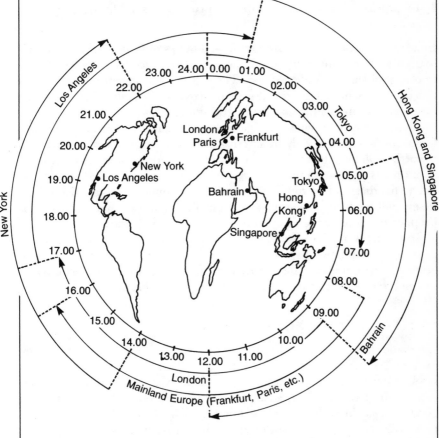

The main foreign currency markets. Opening times, shown by arrows, are expressed in Greenwich mean time, i.e. London local time. Generally they correspond with local times of 9.00 a.m. to 5.00 p.m.

arising from the failure of foreign currency receipts from exports to finance payments for imports will need to be 'plugged' by the country buying the additional currency it requires by running down its stock of international reserves or by borrowing currencies.

In sum, for international trade and investment to continue to be conducted in a mutually beneficial way there needs to exist an *international monetary system* which performs three essential functions:

1 To provide a system of exchange rates between national currencies.
2 To provide an adjustment mechanism capable of removing payments imbalances.
3 To provide a quantum of international reserves to finance payments deficits.

In addition, because of the structural weaknesses of some countries, particularly the developing countries, financial aid facilities are required to help resolve problems of indebtedness. These functions are interrelated and a crucial role is played by the degree of fixity or flexibility built into the exchange rate mechanism, as Table 10.1 indicates.

Thus, if exchange rates are rigidly fixed, balance of payments disequilibria can be removed only by internal price and income adjustments, and countries will need to hold large stocks of international reserves while these adjustments are given time to work. By contrast, where exchange rates are free to fluctuate in line with market forces, continuous external price adjustments will work to remove incipient imbalances before they reach serious proportions, thus reducing countries' reserve requirements.

The various methods which a country can use to correct balance of payments disequilibria have already been discussed in Sections 6.3 and 6.4. Some of these measures are discussed further in the following sections but in the broader context of securing international adjustment.

10.1 FLOATING EXCHANGE RATES

International trade has an impact upon countries' exchange rates. Figure 10.1 traces the monetary consequences of trade between the UK and USA. American producers exporting goods such as orange juice to Britain will require payment in dollars, whilst British customers buying American goods will pay in sterling; consequently British importers of American goods must use sterling to buy sufficient dollars to pay American exporters. At the same time British producers exporting goods such as Scotch whisky to the USA will require payment in sterling while American consumers buying the British goods will pay for them in dollars so that American importers of British goods can buy the necessary sterling using dollars. Thus there will be groups of American importers wishing to buy sterling for dollars (demanding sterling and supplying dollars) and a group of British importers who wish to buy dollars for sterling (demanding dollars and supplying sterling). These groups can acquire the foreign currency they need through organised currency markets in London, New York, Tokyo, etc.

Table 10.1 Types of international monetary system

Fixed exchange rates		Floating exchange rates	
1 Exchange rate system			
Rigidly fixed exchange rates (e.g. Gold Standard before 1914 and in 1926–33)	Exchange rates fixed but periodic re-fixing of rates permitted e.g. International Monetary Fund (1947– early 1970s) and European Monetary System (1979–)	'Managed' floating of exchange rate (as currently practised by the UK, USA)	Unregulated – exchange rates entirely market-determined (e.g. UK 1918–26 and late 1930s)
2 Adjustment mechanism			
Internal price and income adjustments	Mainly internal price and income adjustments, backed up by occasional external price adjustments	Regular external price adjustments, backed up by appropiate internal price and income adjustments	Continuous external price adjustments
3 Reserve needs			
Very substantial, as (2) tends to work slowly	Substantial	Small	Minimal

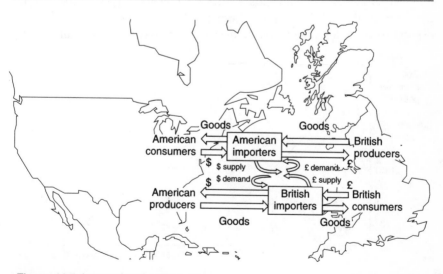

Figure 10.1 International payments

10.1.1 Market-driven exchange rates – an overview

The exchange rate between two currencies is the price of one currency expressed in terms of the other currency. Figure 10.2 shows the exchange rate of the pound sterling against the US dollar. The demand curve (DD) for pounds is downwards-sloping, reflecting the fact that if pounds become less expensive to Americans, British goods, services and assets will become cheaper to them. This causes Americans to demand greater quantities of British goods, etc., and therefore greater amounts of pounds with which to buy them. The supply curve (SS) of pounds is upwards-sloping, reflecting the fact that as the dollar price of the pounds rises American goods, services and assets become cheaper to the British. This causes the British to demand greater quantities of US goods, etc., and hence the greater the supply of pounds offered in exchange for dollars with which to purchase those items. The *equilibrium rate of exchange* between the two currencies is determined by the intersection of the demand and supply schedules, £1 = $1.60 in Figure 10.2.

Over time, exchange rates, if left unregulated by the authorities, will fluctuate according to changes in underlying market conditions, appreciating or *depreciating* depending on the strength or weakness of a country's balance of payments position and exposure to speculative activity (see Box 10.2).

In Figure 10.3(a), if UK imports from the USA rise faster than UK exports to the USA, then, in currency terms, UK demand for dollars will increase relative to US demand for pounds. This will cause the pound to fall, that is, *depreciate* against the dollar, making imports from the USA more expensive and UK exports to the USA cheaper (see Section 10.3). By contrast, if the UK's imports from the USA rise more slowly than its exports to the USA, then, in currency terms, UK demand for dollars will

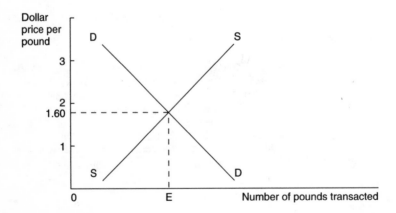

Figure 10.2 The pound–dollar exchange rate

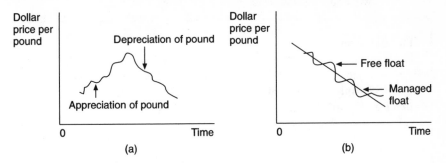

Figure 10.3 Floating exchange rates

be relatively smaller than US demand for pounds. This will cause the pound to *appreciate*, making imports from the USA cheaper and UK exports to the USA more expensive.

In theory, this should always result in an equilibrium exchange rate (that is, a rate which ensures that a country achieves balance of payments equilibrium), leaving the country more freedom to pursue desirable domestic policies without external restraints. In practice, however, external price adjustments alone are usually insufficient to restore external balance, and thus appropriate internal (domestic) measures need also to be taken (see Section 10.3). Moreover, unregulated, free-floating exchange rates tend to produce erratic and destabilising exchange rate movements, often fuelled by speculative hot money flows, which make it difficult to enter into meaningful trade (export, import contracts) and investment transactions (foreign investment deals) because of the uncertainties surrounding the profit and loss implications of such deals when exchange rates are fluctuating wildly. For this reason countries often prefer to 'manage' their exchange rates, as shown in Figure 10.3(b), with their central banks buying and selling currencies, as appropriate, in the foreign exchange markets, both to remove excessive short-run fluctuations and to smooth out the underlying long-run trend line.

Sometimes a country's intervention in currency markets goes beyond merely smoothing its exchange rate and may involve a deliberate attempt to manipulate the exchange rate so as to gain a trading advantage over other countries (a so-called 'dirty float').

10.1.2 Explanations of exchange rate movements

There are two main explanations of exchange rate movements under a floating exchange rate system:

Box 10.2 Exchange rate movements

The dollar and the yen

The Japanese yen has been appreciating against the US dollar as a result of Japan's large and continuing current account surplus with the USA, only partially offset by substantial net inflows of Japanese direct and portfolio investment into the USA.

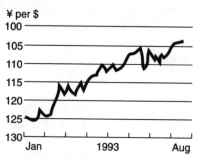

Value of the yen against the dollar, January to August 1993
Source: Datastream

Sterling and the Deutschmark

The UK pound initially floated downwards against the German Deutschmark after the UK's exit from the EU's Exchange Rate Mechanism in October 1992.

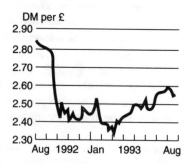

Value of the pound sterling against the Deutschmark, August 1992 to August 1993
Source: Datastream

The effective exchange rate

The term *effective exchange rate* is used to describe a given currency's value in terms of a trade-weighted average of a 'basket' of other currencies, where the weight attached to each currency in the basket depends upon its share of total international trade. The graph depicts the effective exchange rate over time of the pound against other major countries' currencies, for example the US dollar, the Japanese yen, the German Deutschmark, the French franc, etc. A fall (depreciation) in the effective (nominal) exchange rate indicates a general improvement in the price competitiveness of a country's products *vis-à-vis* its trade partners.

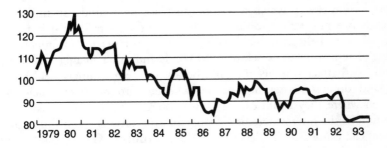

Value of the pound sterling against other major currencies, 1979–93; trade-weight average, 1985 = 100
Source: Central Statistical Office

10.1.2.1 *The purchasing-power parity theory:*

postulates that exchange rates adjust to offset differential rates of inflation between countries which are trade partners in such a way as to restore balance of payments equilibrium. Differential rates of inflation can bring about exchange rate changes in two principal ways. The first relates to the effect of changes in relative prices on import and export demand. As the prices of country A's products rise relative to those of country B, demanders of these products tend to substitute away from A and toward B, decreasing the demand for A's currency and increasing the demand for B's currency. This leads to a depreciation of the bilateral exchange rate of currency A for currency B. Thus a higher level of domestic prices in country A is offset by a fall in the external value of its currency.

A second way that exchange rates can change in response to differential rates of inflation is through speculation about future exchange rate movements. As prices rise in country A relative to country B, managers of foreign-currency portfolios and speculators anticipate an eventual lowering of the real value of the currency in terms of its purchasing power over tradeable products and tend to substitute away from it in their holdings, again causing a depreciation of currency A.

This theory therefore predicts that differential rates of inflation lead to compensating exchange rate changes. However, it is also possible that exchange rate changes themselves can lead to differential rates of inflation; if, for example, import demand is highly price-inelastic, an exchange rate depreciation may lead to an increase in domestic inflation. There is thus a problem in respect of causality (see Section 10.3).

10.1.2.2 *The interest rate parity theory:*

postulates that exchange rates adjust to offset differential interest rates between countries in which investors can place their funds. In this theory the exchange rate reflects differences in interest rates paid to investors on financial assets held in different countries and currencies. The interest rate or rate of return on the stock of bills, bonds and other financial assets of a country will affect whether the bills, bonds, etc., are willingly held by foreign and domestic asset holders or switched into other currencies and invested where they could earn a higher interest rate or return. An actual alteration in the interest rate or a change in expectations about future interest rates can cause asset holders to alter their portfolios. The resultant change in demand for holdings of foreign currency assets relative to domestic currency assets can at times produce sharp fluctuations in exchange rates.

Figure 10.4 summarises the effects of inflation rates and interest rates upon exchange rates. Current and immediate past differences in inflation rates and interest rates between countries affect the demand and supply of currencies and thus their current or spot exchange rates (that is, exchange rates of currencies for immediate delivery). In addition, expected future differences in inflation rates and interest rates will affect the future demand and supply of currencies and thus alter forward exchange rates (that is, the exchange rates of currencies for delivery at a future point in time). Forward

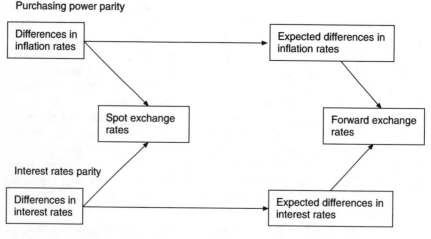

Figure 10.4 Determinants of exchange rates

exchange rates are partially based on current or spot exchange rates but also take into account trends in inflation rates and interest rates and expectations about future rates. The forward exchange rate of a country's currency will be above its spot exchange rate where investors and speculators anticipate lower inflation rates and higher interest rates in that country. Here high demand for the currency in the future will add a premium forward margin to the spot exchange rate. By contrast, the forward exchange rate of a country's currency will be below its spot exchange rate where investors and speculators anticipate higher inflation rates and lower interest rates in that country. Here low demand for the currency in the future will deduct a discount forward margin from the spot exchange rate. Foreign exchange markets trade in both spot currencies and forward currency positions.

Uncertainty about future market interest rates and likely changes in exchange rates plus the unwillingness of banks and other large financial participants in the foreign exchange markets to take substantial positions in weak currencies may diminish funds for stabilising speculation that would in turn diminish or avoid erratic exchange rate movements. If this should prove the case then financial asset-switching is likely to reinforce and *magnify* exchange rate movements initiated by current account transactions (that is, changes in imports and exports), and in consequence may produce exchange rates that are inconsistent with effective overall balance of payments equilibrium in the longer run.

10.2 FIXED EXCHANGE RATE SYSTEM

10.2.1 'Fixing' exchange rates

A fixed exchange rate system is a mutually agreed mechanism for synchronising and co-ordinating the exchange rates of participating countries' currencies. Under the system, currencies are assigned a central fixed par value in terms of the other currencies in the system which countries are then committed to maintain either irrevocably (as under the old *gold standard*) or, more realistically, to 'adjust' them periodically upwards or downwards to some new fixed/pegged value (as under former International Monetary Fund rules and the European Union's 'Exchange Rate Mechanism' – see below). A variant on the above is the so-called 'crawling peg' system in which exchange rates are changed regularly but by small amounts.

Countries are required to maintain the central par value of their currencies by 'support' buying and selling of currencies. For example, between 1949 and 1967, under the International Monetary Fund's former fixed exchange rate system, the UK maintained a rate of exchange at £1 = \$2.80 with the US dollar. If the price of the pound rose (appreciated) in the foreign exchange market the Bank of England bought dollars and sold pounds; if the

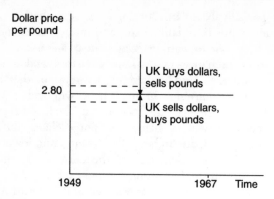

Figure 10.5 Support buying and selling

price of the pound fell (depreciated) the central bank sold dollars and bought pounds. (See Figure 10.5.) Because of the technical difficulties of hitting the central rate with complete accuracy on a day-to-day basis, most fixed exchange rate systems operate with a 'band of tolerance' around the central rate: for example, under the IMF system members' currencies could move 1 per cent either side of their central par value, while, until recently, the European Monetary System allowed members' currencies to fluctuate 2.25 per cent either side of the central par value.

Under a fixed exchange rate system member countries are expected to use appropriate domestic measures (see Section 10.3) to deal with minor balance of payments deficits and surpluses, keeping the exchange rate itself unchanged for fairly lengthy periods of time. However, countries are allowed to devalue their currencies (that is, refix the exchange rate at a new, lower value) or revalue it (that is, refix it at a new, higher value) if their balance of payments is, respectively, in chronic deficit or surplus. A devaluation is an administered reduction in the exchange rate of a currency against other currencies, for example, the lowering of the value of the UK pound against the US dollar from one fixed or 'pegged' level to a lower level, say from £1 = $3 to £1 = $2, as shown in Figure 10.6(a). Devaluations seek to remove payments deficits by making imports (in the local currency) more expensive, thereby reducing import demand, and exports (in the local currency) cheaper, thereby acting as a stimulus to export demand.

A revaluation is an administered increase in the exchange rate of a currency against other currencies, for example, as in Figure 10.6(b), an increase in the value of the UK pound against the US dollar from one fixed value to another, higher value, say from £1 = $3 to £1 = $4. A revaluation makes imports (in the local currency) cheaper and exports (in the local currency) more expensive, thereby encouraging additional imports and lowering export demand. A number of 'facilitating' conditions, however,

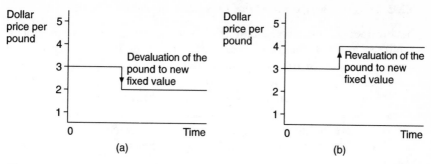

Figure 10.6 (a) Devaluation and (b) revaluation

need to be present if devaluations and revaluations are to be fully effective in removing payments imbalances (see Section 10.3).

Generally speaking, the business and financial communities prefer relatively fixed exchange rates to floating exchange rates, since they enable them to enter into trade contracts and investment and other financial transactions at known foreign exchange prices so that the profit and loss implications of the deals can be calculated in advance. The chief disadvantage of such a system is that governments often tend to delay altering the exchange rate, either because of political factors (for example, the adverse publicity surrounding devaluations) or because they may choose to deal with the balance of payments difficulties by using other measures, so that the pegged rate gets seriously out of line with underlying market tendencies. When this happens speculation against the currency tends to build up, leading to highly disruptive hot money flows, which destabilise currency markets and force the central bank to spend large amounts of its international reserves to defend the parity. If one currency is forced to devalue under such pressure, this tends to produce a domino effect as other weak currencies are likewise subjected to speculative pressure.

Proponents of fixed exchange rate systems (particularly relatively small-group blocs such as the European Monetary System) emphasise that, in order to reduce tensions between participants, economically stronger members should play their full part in the adjustment process (for example, revaluing their currencies when appropriate) rather than leaving weaker members to shoulder the entire burden; and that countries should aim for a broad measure of convergence in their economic policies with respect to both objectives (for example, low inflation rates) and instruments (for example, similar interest rate structures).

10.2.2 Fixed exchange rates: the European Monetary System

The European Monetary System (EMS) is an institutional arrangement, established in 1979, for co-ordinating and stabilising the exchange rates of member countries of the European Union (EU). The EMS is based on a fixed exchange rates mechanism and the European Currency Unit (ECU), which is used to value, on a common basis, exchange rates and which also acts as a reserve asset which members can use, alongside their other international reserve holdings, to settle payments imbalances between themselves. The EMS is managed by the European Monetary Cooperation Fund (EMCF).

Under the EMS exchange rate mechanism (ERM) each country's currency is given a fixed central par value specified in terms of the ECU and the exchange rates between currencies can move to a limited degree around these par values, being controlled by a 'parity grid' and 'divergence indicator'. The parity grid originally permitted a currency to move up to a limit of 2.25 per cent either side of its central rate (exceptionally up to 6 per cent). As a currency moves towards its outer limit the divergence indicator comes into play, requiring the country's central bank to intervene in the foreign exchange market or adopt appropriate domestic measures (for example, alter interest rates) in order to stabilise the rate. If in the view of the EMCF the central rate itself appears to be overvalued or undervalued against other currencies, a country can devalue or revalue its currency, refixing it at a new central parity rate (see Box 10.3). At the present time five of the EU's fifteen member countries, Greece, the UK, Italy, Finland and Sweden are outside the ERM arrangements.

Initially the UK declined to join the exchange rate mechanism but did so eventually in October 1990, establishing a central rate against the German Deutschmark (the leading currency in the ERM) of £1 = DM 2.95. The UK withdrew from the ERM in September 1992 after prolonged speculation against the pound had pushed it down to its 'floor' limit of DM 2.77, rejecting the devaluation option within the ERM in favour of a market-driven 'floating' of the currency. In August 1993, when the French franc came under intense speculative pressure, ERM currency bands were widened to 15 per cent either side of the central par values. These episodes illustrate one of the major drawbacks of a fixed exchange rate system, namely the tendency for 'pegged' rates to get out of line with underlying market tendencies and so fuel excessive speculation against weak currencies.

In the long term, however, it is planned that the EU will move towards eventual monetary unification. The Maastricht Treaty, 1991, proposes a three-stage plan for the irrevocable change to a single currency, the European Currency Unit. The plan (arising from the 'Delors proposals') makes participation in the exchange rate mechanism a prerequisite for all countries participating in the first stage (1991–4). In the second, transitional, stage, to start in 1994, a European Monetary Institute is to be created as the forerunner to a European central bank. In 1996 the institute and the European Commission will report on the 'fitness' of each country for inclusion in the ECU zone, based on stiff criteria of 'economic convergence', which include low inflation rates and stable exchange rates.

The third stage, locking all currencies together and placing monetary policy under the control of an independent central bank, will begin if, by 1996, a majority of seven members have met the convergence criteria and vote to decide on a starting date. Otherwise the central bank will begin work in 1998 and the third stage will start on 1 January 1999. The UK has won the right of an opt-out from commitment to the third stage, and the overall plan has been put in jeopardy by the political indecision of a number of other countries.

Box 10.3 Chronology of central rate changes within the ERM

Date		Currency	% realignment
1979	13 March	EMS launched	
	24 Sept	DM	+2
		DK	−2.9
	3 December	DK	−4.76
1981	23 March	IL	−6
	5 October	DM, DG	+5.5
		FF, IL	-3
1982	22 February	BF	−8.5
		DK	−3
	14 June	DM, DG	+4.25
		IL	−2.75
		FF	−5.75
1983	22 March	DM	+5.5
		DG	+3.5
		DK	+2.5
		BF	+1.5
		FF, IL	−2.5
		IP	−3.5
1985	22 July	BF, DK, DM, FF, IP, DG	+2
		IL	−6
1986	7 April	DM, DG	+3
		BF	+1
		DK	+1
		FF	−3
	4 August	IP	−8

1987	12 January	DM, DG	+3
		BF	+2
1989	19 June	Entry of Spanish peseta	
1990	8 January	IL	-3.7
	8 October	Entry of UK pound	
1992	6 April	Entry of Portuguese escudo	
	14 September	IL	-7
	16 September	Lira and UK pound leave ERM	
	23 November	SP, PE	-6
1993	1 February	IP	-10
	14 May	SP	-8
		PE	-6.5
	2 August	15 per cent margins introduced	
1995	9 January	Entry of Austrian Schilling	
	6 March	SP	-7
		PE	-3.5

Legend   DM = German Deutschmark   BF = Belgian franc
DK = Danish krone   IP = Irish pound
DG = Dutch guilder   IL = Italian lira
FF = French franc   SP = Spanish peseta
PE = Portuguese escudo

10.3 INTERNATIONAL ADJUSTMENT

Under a floating exchange rate regime *external* price adjustments in the form of currency depreciations and appreciations are the main mechanism for maintaining balance of payments equilibrium, while under a fixed exchange rate system a combination of *external* price adjustments and *domestic* price and income adjustments serve to restore payments balance. How do these mechanisms work and what are the problems associated with them?

10.3.1 Domestic measures

Under a fixed exchange rate system countries are expected to adopt 'appropriate' domestic policies consistent with maintaining external balance. Thus, for example, if a balance of payments deficit were to develop owing to domestic 'overheating' with a high level of domestic demand sucking in extra imports and the country's inflation rate making exports increasingly uncompetitive, then a package of deflationary measures would be in order. Demand generally, and for imports in particular, could be damped down by, for example, tax increases aimed at reducing consumers' disposable income, while a slowing down in the inflation rate would help exports. This situation could be reinforced by higher interest rates, which have the additional advantage of attracting foreign currency deposits, thus removing pressure on the exchange rate.

There are, however, limits to what can be achieved by orthodox demand management policies. For example, the balance of payments problem may be *structural* in character, reflecting supply-side deficiencies: poor productivity, lack of investment in innovation, poor product quality, etc. In this context it is interesting to note that in recent years UK imports of manufactured products have continued to increase *despite* recessionary conditions and a low inflation rate. Moreover, governments may not be prepared to adopt draconian deflationary measures to restore balance of payments equilibrium if it means sacrificing their pursuit of other macroeconomic objectives. In this case they may be tempted to use various forms of protectionism to reduce imports and expand exports (for example, import surcharges and export subsidies).

In the case of countries running balance of payments surpluses the 'rules of the game' dictate that such countries should attempt to remove the surplus by expansionary domestic measures aimed primarily at increasing import demand. Income tax cuts and low interest rates, by increasing manufacturers' demand for raw materials and components, will stimulate economic activity generally and, depending on the propensity to import, the demand for imports. Additionally, if domestic expansion serves to increase local prices, then this may encourage buyers to switch from domestic products in favour of imported items as well as making the countries' exports less price competitive.

Again, due account must be taken of the root causes of the surplus. The surplus may reflect an exceptionally strong export performance, underpinned by high productivity, investment and product sophistication as has been the case with Germany and Japan, or a country's propensity to import may be on the low side.

10.3.2 External price adjustments

Currency *devaluations/depreciations* and *revaluations/appreciations* may be used, respectively, to remove a balance of payments deficit or surplus.

10.3.2.1 Currency devaluation/depreciation

A devaluation/depreciation of a currency's value makes imports (in the local currency) more expensive and exports (in the local currency) cheaper, thereby reducing imports and increasing exports, and so assisting in the removal of a balance of payments deficit. For example, as shown in Table 10.2, if the pound–dollar exchange rate depreciates from £1 = $1.60

to £1 = $1.40, this will allow British exporters to reduce their prices by a similar amount, thus increasing their price competitiveness in the US market. By the same token, the devaluation/depreciation serves to raise the sterling price of US products imported into Britain, thereby making them less price-competitive than British products in the home market.

In order for a currency devaluation/depreciation to work, three basic conditions must be satisfied:

1 How successful the devaluation/depreciation is depends on the reaction of export and import volumes to the change in relative prices, that is, the price elasticity of demand for exports and imports. If these volumes are low, that is, demand is inelastic, trade volumes will not change much and the depreciation may in fact worsen the situation. On the other hand, if export and import demand is elastic the change in trade volume will improve the payments position. Balance of payments equilibrium will be restored if the sum of export and import elasticities is greater than unity.

2 On the supply side, resources must be available, and sufficiently mobile to be switched from other sectors of the economy into industries producing exports and products which will substitute for imports. If the economy is fully employed already, domestic demand will have to be reduced and/or switched by deflationary policies to accommodate the required resource transfer.

3 Over the longer term, offsetting domestic price rises must be contained. A devaluation/depreciation increases the cost of essential imports of raw materials and foodstuffs, which can push up domestic manufacturing costs and the cost of living. This in turn can serve to increase domestic prices and money wages, thereby necessitating further devaluations/depreciations to maintain price competitiveness.

In addition, the impact of a devaluation/depreciation may be 'damped' down by firms deciding not to reduce their export prices by the full amount of the devaluation/depreciation in order to increase unit profit margins. By the same token, foreign suppliers may choose not to increase their prices, in order to maintain key export markets.

Table 10.2 Effect of a depreciation on export and import prices

Exchange rate	UK domestic price of a product	Price of the UK product exported to to USA	US domestic price of a product	Price of the US product imported into UK
£1 = $1.60	£1	$1.60	$1	62p
£1 = $1.40	£1	$1.40	$1	71p

10.3.2.2 Currency revaluation/appreciation

A revaluation/appreciation of a currency's value makes imports (in the local currency) cheaper and exports (in the local currency) more expensive, thereby encouraging additional imports and curbing exports. How successful a revaluation/appreciation is in removing a balance of payments surplus depends, again, on the reactions of export and import volumes to the change in relative prices, that is, the price elasticity of demand for exports and imports. If demand is price-inelastic, trade volumes will not change very much and the revaluation/appreciation may in fact make the surplus larger. For example, Japan's trade surplus with the USA has continued to increase despite a massive revaluation/appreciation of the yen against the dollar. On the other hand, if export and import demand is elastic the change in trade volumes will operate to remove the surplus. Balance of payments equilibrium will be restored if the sum of export and import elasticities is greater than unity. Also, whether or not a revaluation/appreciation works in restoring balance of payments equilibrium depends on a number of factors, including the reaction of domestic firms. For example, domestic firms may cut prices to match lower import prices. While this would be good for containing inflationary pressures, it will limit import growth; by the same token, exporters may hold their prices in foreign markets, accepting lower profit margins in order to maintain market share.

10.3.3 Real and monetary adjustment

It will be apparent from the discussion above that a crucial requirement in securing the removal of balance of payments disequilibria between countries is for there to be a *real* adjustment, not merely a *monetary* adjustment. An example will reinforce this point. Let us assume that, because UK goods are more expensive, the UK imports more manufactured goods from France than it exports manufactures to France. Since each country has its own separate domestic currency, this deficit manifests itself as a monetary phenomenon – the UK runs a balance of payments deficit with France, and vice versa. Superficially, this situation can be remedied by, for example, an external price adjustment: currency devaluation/depreciation of the pound and currency revaluation/appreciation of the franc.

But price differences in the domestic prices of manufactured goods themselves reflect differences between countries in terms of their *real* economic strengths and weaknesses, that is, causality can be presumed to run from the real aggregates to the monetary aggregates and not the other way round: a country has a strong, appreciating currency because it has an efficient and innovative real economy; a weak currency reflects a weak economy. Simply devaluing the currency does not mean that there will be an improvement in *real* efficiency and competitiveness overnight. Focusing attention on the monetary aggregates tends to mask this fundamental truth. Thus, if the UK and France were to establish an economic union in which (as mooted by the Maastricht Treaty, see Chapter 8) their individual domestic currencies were replaced by a single currency, then, in conventional balance of payments terms, the UK's deficit disappears.

Or does it? It does so in monetary terms but not in real terms, that is, the disequilibrium manifests itself not in terms of cross-border (external) foreign currency flows but as an internal problem of *regional imbalance*. The 'leopard has changed its spots' – a balance of payments problem has become a regional problem, with the UK region of the customs union experiencing lower industrial activity rates, lower levels of real income and higher rates of unemployment compared with the French region. To redress this imbalance in real terms requires an improvement in the competitiveness of the UK region's existing industries and the establishment of new industries by inward investment. For example, within the UK itself the decline of iron and steel production in Wales has been partly offset by the establishment of consumer appliance and electronics industries by American and Japanese multinational companies.

10.4 INTERNATIONAL MONEY

In addition to establishing acceptable exchange rate and international adjustment mechanisms an *international monetary system* must also be capable of providing a stock of international money or reserves which can be used to finance balance of payments deficits and borrowing and aid facilities to assist countries facing acute liquidity problems.

10.4.1 Nature and purpose of international money

The main function of money in national economies is as a medium of exchange, that is, it serves as the means of financing the purchase and sale of goods and services. Other attributes of domestic money include its use as (1) a store of value, (2) a unit of account, (3) a standard for deferred payments. The assets making up the domestic money supply and their acceptability by traders and the general public for transaction purposes is determined either by their designation by the government as official *legal tender* (for example, Bank of England notes) or through customary use (for example, commercial bank deposits).

'International money' and the use to which it is put differs from domestic money in two important respects. In the first place, those monetary assets such as gold and the US dollar which have come to be recognised as 'international money' have been elevated to that position through 'customary' use rather than legal endorsement. The only general exception in this respect has been the creation of the Special Drawing Right (SDR) unit under the direct control of the International Monetary Fund (IMF). Second, the main function of international money is as an international reserve asset, to be used in the settlement of balance of payments deficits. Most countries engaged in international trade will at some time incur a deficit in their balance of payments, and it is for this reason that they accumulate a reserve, or stock, of international money. The possession of such a reserve not only ensures that a country is able to meet its financial obligations, but also gives it time to phase the removal of its payments deficit so as to cause the least disturbance both to its own economy and to world trade in general.

'International liquidity' may be said to include all those monetary assets (plus facilities for borrowing them) that are generally acceptable in the settlement of payment deficits between countries. The major components of the stock of international money in recent years have been gold, certain foreign currencies such as the US dollar, International Monetary Fund drawing rights and Special Drawing Rights and, for member countries of the European Monetary System, the European Currency Unit. Table 10.3 gives details of the relative importance of these components (excluding ECUs) in 1992 and indicates the main individual country holders of the world's stocks of international reserves.

To be effective an international monetary system must be capable of generating a total stock of international liquidity sufficient for reserve requirements. How much is sufficient? Nobody really knows. This issue cannot be divorced from that of the effectiveness of international adjustment. If balance of payments deficits are removed quickly before they reach sizeable proportions then countries' need for reserves will be limited. Thus it is argued that reserve requirements under a continuous, floating exchange rate adjustment mechanism will be very much smaller as compared with a fixed exchange rate adjustment mechanism, where countries take action to correct deficits only when they reach crisis proportions. An additional issue is the distribution of the stock of liquidity. As the table indicates, a high proportion of existing reserve assets are held by only a small number of countries. Developing countries in particular tend to have acute liquidity problems as a result of their industrialisation programmes and over-reliance on a limited number of export specialities. In their case, reserve holdings tend to be inadequate to service their payment deficits, and this can give rise to serious problems of indebtedness (see Section 10.5).

Finally, because the countries involved in international trade operate with different national currencies, an international monetary system must provide for the interchangeability of currencies and reserve assets. The link between the components of international money, their relationship with national currencies, and the relationship of the multitude of national currencies between themselves is provided by the obligation of countries (under IMF rules) to maintain *full convertibility* of their currencies at existing exchange rates, avoiding the use of exchange controls.

Table 10.3 Components of international reserves and main individual country holders, 1992

Total reserves (SDR millions)	
Countries' reserve position in IMF	33,902
SDR holdings	12,867
Total held by IMF	46,769
Foreign currency holdings (mainly countries' central banks)	646,350
Gold holdings (mainly countries' central banks)	225,472
Total	918,591
Distribution of reserves (%)	
Industrial countries	58.0
Developing countries	42.0
of which:	
Germany	9.6
Taiwan	8.3
USA	7.3
Japan	7.3
Spain	4.6
Singapore	4.0
UK	3.8
Switzerland	3.7
France	3.1
Italy	3.1
Total of above ten countries	54.8

Source: IMF, *International Financial Statistics*, 1993.

10.4.2 International trade and investment: currency and reserve implications

Before we look more closely at the components of international money it will be useful to see how international trade and investment are financed. Figure 10.7 shows by way of illustration the currency flow and reserve position consequences of trade between two countries, the UK and France. Assume that the UK is in payments deficit to France to the extent of £10 million and that the pound–franc exchange rate is fixed at £1 = 10 francs. At the *private* level, to finance the importation of French goods, UK importers must obtain 100 million francs with which to purchase such goods; this is because French exporters quite naturally wish to be paid in their own currency. Thus UK importers must apply through their banks to obtain the necessary francs from the 'working balances' held by the Bank of England. In the absence of exchange controls these will be made freely available on the in-payment of the sterling equivalent.

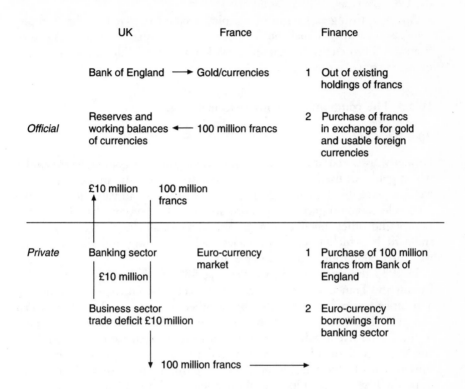

	UK	France	Finance

Bank of England ⟶ Gold/currencies   1   Out of existing
                                           holdings of francs

Official   Reserves and
             working balances ⟵ 100 million francs   2   Purchase of francs
             of currencies   in exchange for gold
                                                          and usable foreign
                                                          currencies

£10 million   100 million
   ↑   francs

Private   Banking sector   Euro-currency   1   Purchase of 100 million
                                 market   francs from Bank of
               £10 million   England

            Business sector   2   Euro-currency
            trade deficit £10 million   borrowings from
                                                      banking sector

               ↓ 100 million francs ⟶

Figure 10.7 Currency flow and reserve implications of a UK trade deficit with France; exchange rate £1 = Ffr 10

At the *official* level, the foreign currency obligation to the private sector may be met simply by running down the Bank's existing working balances of francs. However, it could be the case that these working balances are already so low that it is deemed necessary to acquire additional quantities of francs. That being so, a number of possibilities arise. The Bank of England might secure the French central banks' agreement to release francs in exchange for gold or for some particular foreign currency the French themselves are short of. In both cases the UK's official reserves are depleted. Alternatively, the Bank might approach some other central bank and obtain the necessary francs against a gold or currency transfer, or the UK could exercise its IMF drawing rights. Again, the effect is to reduce the UK's reserves. Exceptionally, because of the decline in the status of sterling as a reserve currency, the French might be prepared to accept sterling in exchange for francs. This would have a neutral effect on the reserve position in the short run, but would increase the UK's overseas sterling liabilities.

A deficit arising as a result of a capital account transaction (for example, overseas investment) may be financed by borrowing the necessary funds from the 'Euro-currency' market, a market which provides financial instruments such as Eurobonds.

10.4.3 The components of international money

10.4.3.1 Gold

Formerly, as noted above, many countries operated a gold standard under which gold was used as the basis of a country's domestic money supply, as well as being used to finance payments deficits. Gradually, however, the pure gold standard gave way to domestic monetary systems based on paper money and other metallic coins and, internationally, to the gold exchange standard in which foreign currencies such as sterling and the US dollar were used alongside gold as reserve assets.

In 1935 the price of gold was fixed at $35 per fine ounce by the USA, Britain and France as part of a monetary pact between the three countries. This price was officially adopted by member countries of the International Monetary Fund on its formation in 1947; gold was used as the numeraire of the Fund's fixed exchange rate system in setting par values for members' currencies, and members were required to pay a quarter of their quota subscriptions to the Fund in gold. Gold continued to serve as the linchpin of the IMF system, and its official price remained pegged at $35 per ounce, down to 1971, when the Fund's fixed exchange rate system gave way to floating exchange rates. Countries had, however, found it increasingly difficult to hold the price at the $35 per ounce level as world demand for gold as an industrial metal and for ornamental purposes continued to expand. In 1961 a 'gold pool' was set up to regulate dealings in the metal, but in 1968 Fund members bowed to the inevitable and a two-tier price structure was established: gold continued to be priced at $35 per ounce for official transactions between countries' central banks and the Fund, while the free market price was left to be determined by market forces.

In 1972 gold was dropped as the numeraire of the Fund and replaced by the Special Drawing Right unit; the Fund's existing gold holdings were sold off and members were required to subscribe their quotas in a non-gold form. Outside the Fund, however, gold has continued to hold on to its status as the most important component of international reserves. The attractiveness of gold as a reserve asset is underpinned by the fact that unlike national paper currencies (which are intrinsically worthless) it has a value in exchange as a commodity related to its use as an industrial metal and for ornamental purposes. Gold holdings, however, suffer from the disadvantage that compared with other assets such as stocks and shares they yield no interest return. In 1993 the market price of an ounce of gold fluctuated between $350 and $408.

10.4.3.2 Foreign currency

Interest-bearing foreign currencies now constitute the greater part of international reserves. The elevation first of the pound sterling (in the period before 1914) and the dollar (post-1945) to reserve currency status was due primarily to the dominance of the UK and the USA in international trade. In the nineteenth century the UK was the leading trading country and it became customary for her trading partners to hold substantial amounts of pounds for working balance purposes; these countries in turn found it convenient to settle imbalances between themselves by pound transfers. Similarly, the extensive use of the US dollar after 1945 owed its origins to the Marshall Aid programme, which poured dollars into war-devastated Europe, US dominance of world trade down to the late 1950s, and countries' need for additional liquidity in the face of a slow-growing gold stock.

However, although the US dollar has continued to occupy a prominent position in countries' reserve positions it has been increasingly augmented by holdings of strong currencies such as the Japanese yen, the German Deutschmark and the Swiss franc.

10.4.3.3 IMF drawing rights

Member countries of the IMF have certain drawing rights with the Fund. The Fund's resources consist primarily of a pool of currencies which are subscribed by its members in accordance with their allotted quota (the size of a member's quota reflects that country's relative importance in international trade). Each country pays 75 per cent of its quota in its own currency and 25 per cent in international reserve assets (mainly other countries' currencies). Countries are given *borrowing* or *drawing* rights with the Fund which they can use, together with their own nationally held international reserves, to finance a balance of payments deficit.

A member country exercises its drawing rights by purchasing the currencies it requires to finance a deficit; it does this by paying into the Fund an equivalent amount of its own currency up to a limit of 125 per cent of its quota. The first 25 per cent (the 'reserve tranche') may be drawn on demand; the remaining 100 per cent is divided up into four 'credit tranches' of 25 per cent each, and drawings here are conditional on members agreeing with the Fund a programme of measures (for example, deflation/ devaluation) for removing their payments deficit. Members are required to repay their drawings over a three to five-year period. In this way the provision of liquidity is linked with the 'adjustment mechanism', requiring positive action by members to restore balance of payments equilibrium.

In addition to the general borrowing facility, the IMF operates a number of other arrangements designed primarily to assist members (mainly developing countries) suffering particularly acute liquidity problems (see Box 10.4).

The resources of the Fund have increased substantially since its inception in 1947, as a result of nine increases in members' quota subscriptions. In addition, under the General Arrangement to Borrow provision, the Fund itself can borrow currencies from members.

10.4.3.4 Special Drawing Rights (SDRs)

In 1970 the IMF introduced the SDR. Unlike other reserve assets such as gold, SDRs have no tangible life of their own. They are created by the IMF itself and take the form of bookkeeping entries in a special account managed by the Fund. The initial SDR issue totalled US$ 3.4 billion and SDRs were allocated to members in accordance with their Fund quotas. There have been five subsequent issues of SDRs.

The important thing to note about the SDR scheme is that *SDRs can be transferred to another member only in exchange for usable foreign currencies*. When a country wishes to use some of its SDRs it informs the Fund, which then designates another country (normally one with a payments surplus and large reserves) as its partner in the SDR–currency exchange. The net effect is that the deficit country obtains the currency of its 'swap partner'; in exchange the swap partner's SDR account is credited with an equivalent amount of SDRs transferred (that is, debited) from the deficit country's account.

The SDR is valued in terms of a weighted basket of five currencies: the US dollar, the German Deutschmark, UK sterling, the French franc and the Japanese yen. Thus the value of the SDR itself can change if the exchange value of any of these currencies changes. The value of a SDR unit in terms of the US dollar was $0.96 in 1986 and $0.72 in 1993 and he value of an SDR unit in terms of the UK pound was £1.2 in 1986 nd £1.1 in 1993.

4.3.5 European Currency Unit (ECU)

ECU is used by member countries of the European Union to value the nge rates of members' currencies and to settle payments imbalances ·n them. Like the SDR, the ECU (currently) has no tangible life of . ECUs are 'created' by the EMS's European Monetary Cooperation exchange for the in-payment of gold and other reserve assets by and take the form of bookkeeping entries in a special account

Box 10.4 IMF special funding facilities

Extended Fund Facility (EFF)
The EFF was established in 1974 to make funds available for longer periods and in large amounts to members experiencing severe balance of payments difficulties, particularly countries whose development policies have been held back as a result.

Compensating Financing Facility (CFF)
The CFF was established in 1963 to assist members, particularly primary producing countries, experiencing balance of payments difficulties due to shortfalls in earnings from exports. The *Compensatory and Contingency Finance Facility* superseded the CFF in 1988, adding 'contingency' support for adjustment programmes approved by the Fund.

Supplementary Financing Facility (SFF)
The SFF was established in 1979 to provide assistance to members facing payments difficulties that are large in relation to their economies and their Fund quotas.

Buffer Stock Financing Facility (BSFF)
The BSFF was established in 1969 to provide assistance to members with a balance of payments need related to their participation in arrangements to finance approved international buffer stocks of primary products.

Systematic Transformation Facility (STF)
The STF was established in 1993 as a temporary facility to help member countries (such as Eastern European countries) with severe payment problems arising from a shift away from trading at non-market prices to multilateral, market-based trade.

Enhanced Structural Adjustment Facility (ESAF)
The ESAF, which was established in 1988, offers credits at concessional interest rates to developing countries that carry out Fund-supervised economic reform programmes. Some seventy-three countries are eligible for the 0.5 per cent credits, which are paid back over a period of ten years.

---

managed by the Fund. The value of the ECU is based on a weighted basket of members' national currencies. The value of the ECU per UK pound was £1.30 and the value of the pound per ECU was 77p in 1993.

At some time in the future the European Union (as envisaged by the Maastricht Treaty of 1991) hopes to secure full monetary unification on the basis of a single currency, the ECU. In that case the ECU will become a tangible currency freely circulating throughout the EU bloc as a medium of exchange and its role as a reserve asset will cease as exchange rates and conventional balance of payments accounts between members are eliminated.

10.5 INTERNATIONAL INDEBTEDNESS AND FINANCIAL AID

Many countries, mainly developing countries have experienced long-term liquidity problems and have been forced to borrow heavily to sustain their economies. In part their debt problems stem from traditional reliance on exports of a very limited range of agricultural produce or primary commodities, making them vulnerable to adverse cyclical and secular price movements. Over the long run, commodity prices have tended to decline relative to the prices of manufactured goods (see Box 10.5). In recent years attempts to diversify their economies through industrialisation programmes have necessitated heavy reliance on imported capital goods. The oil price increases of 1973 and 1979 caused a further deterioration in their external finances and for a time the debt problems of some countries reached 'crisis' proportions. Over the long-term the industrialised countries have attempted to assist developing countries in various ways, in particular by allowing tariff-free entry to developing country exports of commodities and manufactures and the provision of bilateral and multilateral economic aid packages. In addition, as noted in Chapter 9, multinational companies have been an important source of new capital and technology transfer for some developing countries.

10.5.1 The debt problem

Since the 1970s the external indebtedness of developing countries has increased substantially. Between 1984 and 1992, as shown by Table 10.4, the total external debt of the developing countries increased from US\$ 874 billion in 1984 to US\$ 1,427 billion in 1992 and total interest payments from US\$ 124 billion in 1984 to US\$ 168 billion in 1992. These absolute figures, however, need to be put into perspective. External debt as a ratio of developing countries' exports and GDP peaked in 1986 and has since fallen, as has the debt service ratio (interest payments as a percentage of exports). While this is encouraging, a more sombre picture is painted by the fact that, as general recessionary conditions persisted through the 1980s, many developing countries experienced a fall in net transfers (that is, new funds in the form of official loans and grants, private loans and foreign direct investment, less repayments of principal, interest payments and profit repatriation). Table 10.5 shows a reversal in resource transfer for

Box 10.5 Commodity prices and price support schemes

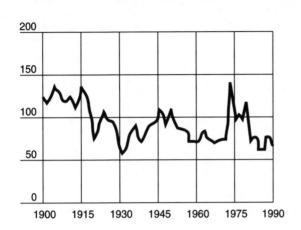

Non-fuel primary commodities *v.* manufactures: relative price index, 1900–90 (1977–9 = 100)
Source: World Bank, *World Development Report*, 1991

Developing countries have used various cartel mechanisms (in particular, International Commodity Agreements) to reduce price volatility and improve commodity terms of trade. OPEC has proved reasonably successful in raising oil prices but many others have collapsed, owing to internal disputes over production quotas and poor demand conditions. The developed countries initially participated in commodity support schemes seeing them as a means of channelling resources to the developing countries but increasingly withdrew their support in the 1980s when huge increases in output by producing countries made the schemes extremely costly to run. In 1985 the International Tin Council's support scheme, for tin prices collapsed, while in 1989 the International Coffee Organisation's price support scheme disintegrated. Those schemes that remain are in difficulties. For example, in September 1993 the International Natural Rubber Organisation made a cash call on members to finance the buying-in of rubber on an over-supplied world market in order to prop up prices. Natural rubber prices in 1993 were 30 per cent lower in real terms than six years previously.

However, even when 'successful', group and individual schemes for boosting prices can bring added problems. For example, Madagascar's export revenues from vanilla have been undermined as buyers have switched to cheaper synthetic flavourings, while the cost of stockpiling 'surplus' output has soared. In 1991 stockholding costs totalled MgFr 9 billion, compared with MgFr 10 million in 1980.

Table 10.4 Indicators of external debt for developing countries, 1984-92

Year	Total external debt (US$ billions)	Debt service payments (US$ billions)	Ratio of external debt to exports (%)	Ratio of external debt to GDP (%)	Debt service ratio* (%)
1984	874	124	136	34	19
1985	944	129	154	36	21
1986	1,039	133	178	39	23
1987	1,153	141	165	38	20
1988	1,178	151	146	36	19
1989	1,206	146	133	33	16
1990	1,281	144	126	32	14
1991	1,362	157	127	29	14
1992	1,427	168	123	27	14

Source: United Nations, World Bank, 1993.
Note: *Debt service ratio = debt payments as percentage of total external debt.

a number of developing countries, with net transfers becoming negative in many cases.

10.5.2 Official and private capital flows

Debt servicing problems became so severe for some countries that they were forced to suspend repayments (for example, Mexico in 1982). As a result official creditors (see below) have written off some debts and rescheduled others and have provided new aid packages on highly concessionary terms. Bilateral official creditors have rescheduled under the Paris Club arrangements. The 'club' was convened to devise an international response to the debt crisis. Under the arrangements, bilateral official creditors who have extended non-concessionary loans may choose between cancelling one-third of the consolidated amount, extending repayment or cutting interest rates. For commercial debt, under the 'Brady initiative' (1990), official creditors have offered to support debt and debt service reductions for countries that adopt appropriate adjustment programmes. Reductions take place through the technique of 'buy back' – the exchange of old debt for new debt at reduced interest rates.

Official development assistance (ODA), on highly concessionary terms, is the principal form of capital transfer to the poorest countries. Official aid (see Table 10.6) is extended by member governments of the Development Assistance Committee (DAC) of the OECD, on both a bilateral (country to country) and a multilateral basis (through the DAC), the World Bank (see Box 10.6), the EU European Development Fund and the European Investment Bank. In 1990 the ratio of official aid to GNP ranged from 0.15 per cent for the USA to 0.32 per cent for Japan and 0.94 per cent for Denmark. Through the 1980s some countries (France,

Table 10.5 Net transfers, selected developing countries, 1980 and 1992 (US$ millions)

Country	Total external debt		New funds		Repayments of principal		Interest payments		Net transfers	
	1980	1992	1980	1992	1980	1992	1980	1992	1980	1992
Tanzania	2,476	6,715	404	353	42	109	45	60	317	184
Pakistan	9,936	24,072	1,061	2,317	353	1,133	247	598	461	586
Philippines	17,417	32,498	1,854	5,705	541	3,261	579	1,316	734	1,128
Tunisia	3,526	8,475	611	1,401	259	884	228	411	124	106
Hungary	9,764	21,900	1,552	2,699	824	2,930	636	1,614	92	-1,845
Mexico	71,046	113,378	11,581	11,683	4,760	12,184	4,580	5,959	2,241	-6,460
India	20,611	76,983	2,180	6,388	755	2,995	532	2,846	893	547
Kenya	3,449	6,367	637	288	205	261	169	180	263	-153
Honduras	1,470	3,573	345	395	87	204	83	159	175	32
Zambia	3,261	7,279	603	338	212	248	116	236	275	-146
Morocco	9,710	21,305	1,178	1,675	590	935	618	937	-30	-197
Colombia	6,941	17,204	1,071	1,574	263	2,390	310	1,150	498	-1,966
Congo	1,526	4,751	520	32	34	94	37	25	449	-87
Nigeria	8,934	30,959	1,752	706	232	2,081	531	1,656	989	-3,031
China	4,504	69,321	2,539	15,232	613	5,204	318	2,823	1,608	7,205
Argentina	27,157	67,569	4,708	1,888	1,853	1,480	1,337	2,401	1,518	-1,993

Source: World Development Report, 1994.

Italy, Norway, Sweden) increased their aid–GNP ratio, but for others the ratio declined (UK, Germany and the USA). As a result, the overall DAC aid–GNP ratio remained constant at around 0.35 per cent.

Private capital transfers to developing countries have declined in relative importance. However, while private loans have plummeted, the share of capital flows accounted for by direct foreign investment has increased significantly.

In addition to these long-term resource flows, developing countries have benefited from the various short-term and medium-term financing facilities offered by the International Monetary Fund (see Box 10.4).

10.5.3 Trade and 'tied' aid

Ideally, from a borrowing country's perspective, financial aid should be available at low interest rates and *unconditional*, the recipient country being able to decide for itself how to spend the monies received. In many cases, however, the provision of *multilateral* financial aid (as noted above, for example in respect of IMF credit tranche borrowings) is conditional on the recipient implementing various structural reforms to strengthen its economy. A related area of concern is the provision of *bilateral* aid whereby recipients are obliged to use the funds provided to purchase goods and services from firms in the donor country. The amount of 'tied' aid has increased in recent years, and for some countries it accounts for a high proportion of the total official aid they provide. For example, around 75 per cent of the official aid provided by Spain was 'tied' aid and similarly

Table 10.6 Aggregate long-term net resource flows to developing countries, 1980, 1989 and 1995

Component	Level (US$ billions)			Share (%)		
	1980	1989	1995*	1980	1989	1995*
Net flows[†]	82.8	63.3	103.0	100.0	100.0	100.0
Official grants	2.5	18.6	25.0	15.1	29.4	24.3
Official loans (net):	20.1	18.0	31.0	24.3	28.4	30.1
Bilateral	12.2	6.1	10.0	14.7	9.6	9.7
Multilateral	7.9	11.9	21.0	9.6	18.8	20.4
Private flows	50.2	26.7	47.0	60.6	42.2	45.6
Private loans	41.1	4.3	12.0	49.6	6.8	11.6
Direct foreign investment	9.1	22.4	35.0	11.0	35.4	34.0

* Projections. [†] Excluding IMF transfers.
Source: World Bank, 1990.

Box 10.6 World Bank (International Bank for Reconstruction and Development)

The World Bank was established in 1947 to provide economic aid to member countries – mainly developing countries – to strengthen their economies. The Bank has supported a wide range of long-term investments, including infrastructure projects such as roads, telecommunications and electricity supplies; agricultural and industrial projects, including the establishment of new industries, as well as social, training and educational programmes.

The Bank's funds come largely from the developed countries, but it also raises money on international capital markets. The Bank operates according to 'business principles', lending at commercial rates of interest only to those governments it feels are capable of servicing and repaying the debt. In 1960, however, it established an affiliate agency, the *International Development Association,* to provide low interest loans to its poorer members.

Another affiliate of the World Bank is the *International Finance Corporation,* which can invest directly in companies by acquiring shares.

Cumulative Lending Operations as at 30 June 1993 (US$ million)

Activity		*Region*	
Agriculture	67,663	Africa	45,437
Development finance		East Asia and Pacific	65,579
companies	24,499	South Asia	60,837
Education	17,315	Europe and Central	
Energy	57,371	Asia	35,820
Industry	19,534	Latin America and	
		Caribbean	79,879
Non-project-based	30,965	Middle East and	
		North Africa	25,418
Transport	42,565		
Urban development	14,978		
Water supply	14,030		
Other	24,050		
	312,970		312,970

Table 10.7 Tied aid: selected countries, 1991

Country	Total official aid (US$ million)	Tied aid as % of official aid
Spain	430	75
Italy	3,352	52
Belgium	831	51
Finland	930	49
France	7,484	41
UK	3,348	40
Germany	6,890	38
Canada	2,604	23
USA	11,362	18
Sweden	2,116	11
Japan	10,952	10
Netherlands	2,517	4

Sources: World Development Report, 1994 (for total aid), Actionaid, London, 1994 (for percentages).

40 per cent of UK official aid was locked into the purchase of UK goods and services (see Table 10.7). While the provision of tied aid is seen to be good for the donor country's domestic industries and the balance of payments it is often seen to be less welcome than non-tied from the recipients' point of view because it restricts their choice of sourcing goods and services and is generally more expensive. (It has been suggested that the prices of goods and services provided under a tied aid arrangement are higher than their free market prices.)

10.6 CONCLUSION

An effective international monetary system is one which facilititates the expansion of world trade and investment. This requires a workable system of exchange rates, an adjustment mechanism capable of removing payments imbalances and the provision of a stock of international reserves (and borrowing facilities) which can be used to finance payments imbalances. As with trade and investment, to be effective an international monetary system needs co-operation between countries and the avoidance of individualistic 'beggar my neighbour' acts.

10.7 IMPLICATIONS FOR BUSINESS

Regarding exchange rates, companies which are owed money (for exports, etc.) expressed in foreign currency terms risk losses if the rate of exchange of the foreign currency falls *vis-à-vis* their own currency before the debts are paid. Similarly companies which owe money (for imports, etc.) expressed in terms of foreign currency risk losses if the exchange rate of their own currency falls *vis-à-vis* the foreign currency before the debts are paid. A company's exposure to the risk of losses from adverse exchange rate changes depends upon the magnitude of its foreign currency debts and the amount of money owed to it.

There are a number of mechanisms whereby a firm can reduce its exposure to losses resulting from exchange rate changes. First, a firm can seek to prevent an exposed position from arising by using such internal exposure management techniques as:

1 *Currency matching*, that is, matching foreign currency holdings with equal foreign currency borrowings.
2 *Leading and lagging*, which involve accelerating or delaying foreign currency payments and receipts where the exchange rate of the currency is expected to change.
3 *Netting* of currency receipts and payments between subsidiaries of a multinational company (offsetting receipts and payments against each other so as to leave only a single net intra-company balance to be settled in foreign currency).

Second, the firm can use external contractual arrangements to reduce or eliminate whatever exposure remains, hedging risks by:

1 *Forward foreign exchange contracts* with banks. These contracts involve the buying or selling of a currency in the forward market at a guaranteed forward exchange rate. The cost to the firm of providing such forward cover is the difference between the spot exchange rate at the contract date and the forward exchange rate.
2 *Forward (option date) foreign exchange contracts.* These are forward contracts which fix the exchange rate when the forward contract is made but leaves open the exact maturity date for the firm to decide as long as it falls within the option period.
3 *Financial futures contract.* This is an agreement to buy or sell standard amounts of a particular currency for delivery at one of a number of specified future dates. By taking a position in future contacts that is equal and opposite to its currency exposure a firm can minimise its exchange risk.
4 *Currency option.* This entails the right (but not the obligation) to buy or sell a standard amount of a particular currency at a particular exchange rate at any time before the specified expiry date. Buy or call options conferring the right to purchase currency and sell or put options conferring the right to sell currency can be used by a firm to protect itself against downside exchange rate risk, in return for payment of an option premium.

Financial futures and currency options in the major currencies can be bought and sold through organised futures and options markets in the main foreign currency centres such as London.

In addition to the above arrangements various trade credit facilities may be employed to reduce exchange rate exposure. For example, where an exporter is paid by means of a bill of exchange, the exporter can arrange to discount the bill for less than its face value and receive payment before the settlement date, so protecting himself against exchange rate exposure during the credit period up to the date when the bill matures. In the same manner the exporter could arrange to sell an outstanding debt to a bank or specialist factoring organisation for less than the face value of the debt, thereby avoiding the exchange rate risk on the debt. Finally, by paying an additional insurance premium, a firm could arrange insurance cover against adverse exchange rate movements as well as default by customers.

Regarding reserves and borrowings, the possession of an adequate stock of international reserves, together with the ability to access borrowing facilities, is important for countries, as it enables them to finance a balance of payments deficit and 'buy time' to introduce appropriate measures to eliminate it. Specifically, international liquidity enables countries to attend to balance of payments difficulties without having to resort to crisis measures such as the imposition of import quotas and foreign exchange controls which are highly disruptive of international trade. Thus international liquidity plays an important facilitating role in the world economy by underpinning the expansion of international trade in general and by enabling companies to export and import goods and services without undue restriction.

Multinational companies (MNCs) which are engaged in both intra- and inter-company trade in a large number of countries, will often accumulate an 'internalised' pool of foreign currencies which they can use to fund their international operations without necessarily having always to resort to the foreign exchange market. Moreover, through international trading they also tend to build up internal reserves of foreign currencies which can be used, for example, to finance the establishment of a new plant in a country which is using foreign exchange controls to prevent currency conversion.

The provision of foreign aid programmes to strengthen and develop the economies of recipient countries is also of general interest to businesses in so far as it has knock-on effects in terms of increasing the demand for imported capital equipment, etc. Tied aid programmes in particular provide additional sales opportunities for companies operating out of donor countries.

QUESTIONS

1 What are the main advantages and disadvantages of a fixed exchange rate system?
2 What are the main advantages and disadvantages of a floating exchange rate system?
3 What do you understand by the term 'international adjustment'? What measures can governments take to restore external balance?
4 Outline and comment on the main forms of international money which can be used for reserve purposes.
5 What factor can cause countries to become heavily indebted? Comment on the sources of financial aid for debtor countries.

Bibliography

Students are recommended to consult the following books for a more in-depth treatment of the subject matter:

Begg, D., Fischer, S., and Dornbusch, *Economics*, fourth edition (1994) McGraw-Hill, Maidenhead, England.

Gowland, D., *Understanding Macroeconomics* (1990), Edward Elgar, Aldershot, England.

Maunder, P., Myers, D., Wall, N. and Miller, R.L., *Economics Explained*, second edition (1991), Collins Educational, London, England.

Parkin, M., and King, D., *Economics*, second edition (1995), Addison-Wesley, Wokingham, England.

Index

accelerator 26–7
activity rate 72
actual GNP 21–2, 26–8; and demand
management 42–7; and economic
growth 126–7; *see also* potential
GNP
aggregate demand 18–26; and demand
management 42–7; and economic
growth 135–8; and fiscal policy
51–5
aggregate demand schedule 19–20
aggregate supply 18–26
aggregate supply schedule 19–20
aid 272–6
appreciation (exchange rate) 150, 152,
248–9, 261
arbitrage 244
ASEAN free-trade area 208
automatic stabilisers 56–7

balance of payments 36, 143–63;
components of 144–8; correction of
disequilibria 148–62, 258–62; and
foreign direct investment 232–3,
234–5, 243; and international trade
243
bank deposit creation 31, 60–1, 63–4
boom (business cycle) 26–8
borrowing 17, 58, 59–60
budget (government) 50–1; and fiscal
policy 51–7
budget deficit 56–7; financing of
57–60
budget surplus 56–7
business cycle 26–8; and demand
management 42–7
businesses: and circular flow of
national income model 6–8

capital account (balance of payments)
144–5
capital consumption 13
capital formation and economic
growth 132–4
capital stock 129–30, 132
Caribbean Union (CARICOM) 208
circular flow of national income
model 6–8
classical economics 19, 82–8, 102–3
Common Agricultural Policy 211,
212, 217
common external tariff 204, 208,
210–11
common market 204–7; and
European Union 208–14
comparative advantage (international
trade) 164–5, 178–85
consumption expenditure 8–11; and
circular flow of income model 6–7
consumption schedule 9,11
convertibility: and exchange controls
157–8, 214, 224, 226, 263
corporation tax 52
cost-push inflation 96–101, 103–5,
111–14
credit creation 31, 60–1, 63–4
customs union 204–7

deflation 42–7; and balance of
payments correction 153–6, 258–9;
and control of inflation 111
deindustrialisation 73
demand-deficient unemployment
82–3
demand management 42–7; and
balance of payments 153, 156,
158–9, 161–2; and economic

growth 135–8; and fiscal policy
47–60; and inflation 105–7, 111;
and monetary policy 60–7; and
unemployment 82, 89–90
demand-pull inflation 96–103, 111
depreciation (exchange rate) 150–3,
154–5, 248–9, 259–60
depression (business cycle) 26–8
devaluation (exchange rate) 150–3,
154–5, 254–62
direct controls 39
directive 63
direct taxes 52–3
disguised unemployment 76
disposable income 9, 11, 12, 52–3
dissaving 9, 11, 12
distribution of income 121, 123
distribution of wealth 123
dumping (protectionism) 191

economic growth 36, 118–42; and
aggregate demand 135–8; and
capital investment 132–4; determinants of 124–6; and environment
118–19; and indicative planning
139–40; and labour 126–32;
measurement of 120–1; and
supply–side measures 140–1; and
technology 134–5
economic growth rates 121–2, 124,
133
economic policy: see macroeconomic
policy
economic union 204–7
ECU: see European Currency Unit
effective exchange rate 250–1
EFTA see European Free Trade
Association
employment 21–2; and unemployment
71–7
environment: and economic growth
118–19
ERM: see Exchange Rate Mechanism
EU see European Union
Euro-currency market 265–6
European Currency Unit (ECU)
256–7, 268–70
European Economic Area 214–16
European Free Trade Association
(EFTA) 204, 208–9, 214–16
European Monetary System 211, 213,
254, 256–8, 268–9; and UK

monetary policy 68
European Union 204, 208–19
exchange controls 157–8, 214, 224,
226, 263
exchange rate mechanism (ERM)
256–8
exchange rates 149–50, 243–58; and
European Monetary System 256–8;
and firms' foreign exchange
exposure 276–8; fixed exchange
rate systems 150–3, 253–5; floating
exchange rate systems 150–3,
246–53; and inflation 98, 152,
154–5, 260; and interest rates
252–3
excise duty 53
expectations: and exchange rates
251–3; and inflation 98–9, 107–11,
112, 114
expectations-augmented Phillips curve
107–11; see also Phillips curve
expenditure measure of national
income 5–6
export restraint agreements 195, 210
exports 10, 18; and balance of
payments 143–8; and circular flow
of national income model 7–8; and
trade dependency 158, 160; and
world trade 165–78

factor inputs: and circular flow of
national income model 6–8
financial policy 40, 60–7, 68–9
fiscal policy 39–40, 47–60; budget
(government) 50–1; and crowding-
out 59–60; and demand management 51–5; financing budget
deficits 57–8; and national debt
57–8; types of tax 52–3
fixed exchange rate system 152–3,
253–5; 259–62; and balance of
payments correction 150–3; and
European Monetary System 256–8
floating exchange rate system 152–3,
246–53, 259–60; and balance of
payments correction 150–3
foreign currency/exchange 243–5,
264–6; and international reserves
263–6, 267
foreign direct investment 222–7;
balance of payments and trade
effects 232–3; resource and

employment effects 233–4, 235–8; sovereignty and autonomy effects 238–41
foreign exchange market 244–5
free trade 165, 198–9; and General Agreement on Tariffs and Trade 199–203; and regional trade integration 204–19; and United Nations Conference on Trade and Development 203–4
free trade area 204–7
frictional unemployment 82
full employment 21–2, 36, 71–92
futures market 244–5, 252–3, 277–8

GATT: see General Agreement on Tariffs and Trade
GDP: see gross domestic product
GDP deflator 93–4, 120
General Agreement on Tariffs and Trade 199–203; and dumping 191
GNP: see gross national product
GNP deflator 6, 120; see also GDP deflator
gold 263, 264, 266–7
gold standard 247, 253, 266
government expenditure 10, 16–17; and circular flow of national income model 7–8; and fiscal policy 51–2, 54–5
gross domestic product (GDP) 4; components of 9–18; and economic growth 120–1; measurement of 4–6, 121; sector shares in 73
gross national product (GNP) 4; and circular flow of national income model 6–8; and economic growth 120–1; measurement of 4–6, 121

hedging 277
households: and circular flow of national income model 6–8

import penetration 75
imports 10, 17–18; and balance of payments 143–8; and circular flow of national income model 7–8; and international trade dependence 158, 160; and world trade 166–7, 169, 170–1, 174–8
import schedule 17
income 9, 11–18; see also national

income
income adjustment (balance of payments) 153
income measure of national income 5
income per head 6–7, 124; and trade 187–8
incomes policy 39, 106–7, 112–14
income tax 52
indexation (inflation) 114, 116
indicative planning 139–40
indirect taxes 53
infant industry: and protectionism 191
inflation 36, 93–117; and balance of payments/exchange rate 98, 153–6, 158–9, 160–2, 251–2; cost-push inflation 96–8, 103–5; demand-pull inflation 96–9, 101–3; and demand management 105–7, 111; and indexation 114; and inflationary expectations 107–11; inflation rates 95–6; measurement of 93–4; and monetarism 102–3, 107–11; and prices and incomes policy 112–14; and unemployment 36–9, 105–10
inflation rates 95–6, 112–13
inflationary expectations 98–9, 107–11, 114
inflationary gap 21–2, 99, 101, 111
injections: and circular flow of national income model 6–8
instalment credit 63–4
interest 32; see also rate of interest
interest rate: see rate of interest
interest rate parity theory 252–3
internal–external balance model 158–9, 160–2
international adjustment 258–62
international commodity agreement 271
international debt 270–8
International Monetary Fund (IMF): and exchange rates 247, 253–4; and international money 263–9
international monetary system 246–7
international money 262–70
international reserves 262–70
international trade 164–5; commercial services 177–8; merchandise trade 165–6; regional distribution 166–70; product composition 167–75; trade policies 198–219; trade theories 180–8

international trade dependence 158, 160

investment expenditure 10, 13–15; and business cycle 26–8; and circular flow of national income model 7–8; and economic growth 132–4

investment schedule 15

invisible trade 144–5

involuntary unemployment 86–90

J-curve effect 153

Keynesian economics 19, 32–4, 39–40, 54, 64–5, 82, 88–9, 103, 105–7

labour force 72–8; and economic growth 126, 128

labour market 83–9

labour productivity 128–31

labour quality 131–2

liquidity preference 29–30

local content rule: and protectionism 195

Lomé Convention 211–12

Maastricht Treaty 218, 240, 256–7, 269–70

macroeconomic forecasting 45–6

macroeconomic objectives 36–9

macroeconomic policy 35–70; and internal–external balance model 158–9, 160–2

macroeconomics 1–3

marginal efficiency of capital/investment 13–15, 32–3

marginal propensity to consume 9, 11, 12; and the 'multiplier' 23–6

marginal propensity to import 18; and the 'multiplier' 24–6

marginal propensity to save 12; and the 'multiplier' 23–6

marginal propensity to tax 16; and the 'multiplier' 24–6

'market failure' in labour markets 86–9

Medium Term Financial Strategy (MTFS) 47–8, 66–7

MERCOSUR customs union 208

minimum wage rate 85

monetarist economics 34, 40, 47, 60, 64–7, 101–3, 105, 107–11

monetary policy 32–4, 40, 7–8, 60–7, 68–9

money 28–34; see also international money 262–4

money demand schedule 29–30

money multiplier 31, 60–1, 63–4

money supply 60–3; and monetary policy 63–7; and quantity theory of money 102–3

money supply schedule 30

multinational companies 221, 227–31

multiplier 22–6, 32–3; and the business cycle 26–8; and fiscal policy 51–5

NAFTA: see also North American Free Trade Agreement

NAIRU 36–7, 107–8

national debt 57–8

national income 4; changes in 22–6; and the business cycle 26–8; circular flow of national income model 6–8; components of 9–18; equilibrium level of 18–21; and price level 100–1

national insurance contribution 52–3

natural rate of unemployment 86–9; and the Phillips curve 108–10

newly industrialising country 197, 222, 235

non–accelerating inflation rate of unemployment (NAIRU) 36–7, 107–10

North American Free Trade Agreement (NAFTA) 204, 208

OECD 91, 272

OPEC 42; and oil prices 79, 96, 104, 122, 166, 270

open market operation 63

options 277–8

output: and circular flow of national income and model 6–8

output gap 21–2, 82–3

output measure of national income 4–5; and circular flow of national income model 6–8

participation rate 72, 78

per capita income 6–7, 124; and trade 187–8

personal disposable income 9, 11

Phillips curve 36–9, 105–8, 110–11
population: and the labour force 72
potential GNP 21–2, 26–8; and
    demand management 42–7; and
    economic growth 126–7; and
    supply-side policies 67, 69–70; see
    also actual GNP
preference-similarity: and international
    trade 187–9
price adjustment (balance of
    payments) 150–6
price index 94
prices 21–2; and inflation 93–115;
    and national income 100–1
prices and incomes policy 112–14
price stability 36; see also inflation
productivity: and economic growth
    128–31; and inflation 97
product life cycle: and international
    trade 185–7
protectionism 165, 189–95
public procurement: and protectionism
    195
public sector borrowing requirement
    58, 59–60
purchasing power parity theory 251–2

quantity theory of money 102–3
quotas: and protectionism 193–4, 210

rate of exchange 149–50; and balance
    of payments correction 150–3; see
    also exchange rates
rate of interest 32, 66; and exchange
    rate 252–3; and demand for, and
    supply of money 29–30; and
    investment 13–15, 32–4; and
    monetary policy 64–5
recession (business cycle) 26–8
recovery (business cycle) 26–8
reflation: and balance of payments
    correction 153, 259; and demand
    management 42–7
regional unemployment 83
research and development: and
    economic growth 134–5
retail price index 94; and indexation
    114
retaliation: and protectionism 191
revaluation (exchange rate) 150, 152,
    254–61
rule of origin 210, 212

sales tax 53
savings 9, 11, 12–13; and circular
    flow of national income model 7–8;
    and economic growth 133–4
seasonal unemployment 83
single currency 256–7, 269–70
Single European Act 1986 213–14
Special Drawing Rights (SDR) 263,
    264, 268
special deposit 63
specialisation: and trade 180–5
speculation: and exchange rates 243,
    251–3, 255–6
spot market 244–5, 252–3
stabilisation policy 42–7
stagflation 107
standard of living 6
strategic industries: and protectionism
    191–2
structural unemployment 83
subsidies: and protectionism 194–5
supply–side policies 67–70; and
    economic growth 140–1; and
    unemployment 89, 91

tariffs: and balance of payments
    correction 156–7; and economic
    welfare 198–9; and General
    Agreement on Tariffs and Trade
    199–203; and protectionism 192–3;
    tariff structure – European Union
    210; and United Nations
    Conference on Trade and
    Development 203–4
taxation 16, 17; and circular flow of
    national income model 7–8; and
    fiscal policy 52–5
taxation schedule 16
technical knowledge: and economic
    growth 134–5
technological unemployment 83
technology gaps: and international
    trade 185–7
terms of trade 144, 146
trade balance 144–5
trade creation 204–7; and the
    European Union 216–19
trade diversion 204–7; and the
    European Union 217
trade integration (regional) 204–19
transfer payments 16–17, 50–1,
    79

UNCTAD see United Nations
   Conference and Trade and
   Development
unemployment 21–2, 36, 71–92; and
   import penetration 73, 75; and
   inflation 36–9, 105–10; and
   internal–external balance 158–9,
   160–2; involuntary unemployment
   88–9; natural rate of 85–9; types of
   81–3; voluntary unemployment
   87–8; wages and unemployment
   85–8
unemployment rate 76–9

vacancy rate 77
value added measure of national

income 4–5
value added tax 53, 214
velocity of circulation (of money)
   102–3
visible trade (balance of payments)
   144–5
voluntary unemployment 86–9

wage differentials 83–4
wage rates 83–4; and inflation 97,
   104–5; and unemployment 85–9
wealth tax 53
withdrawals: and circular flow of
   national income model 6–8
World Bank 272, 275
World Trade Organisation 202